Dear Barefoot ...

Barefoot Doctor has been a Taoist healer and self-development guide for more than twenty years. He has written several bestselling books, including *Twisted Fables for Twisted Minds*, *Liberation* and *Handbook for the Urban Warrior*. His column has appeared in the *Observer* magazine for three years and is one of the newspaper's most popular pages.

www.barefootdoctorworld.co.uk

Dear Barefoot ...

Taoist wisdom for everyday living

BAREFOOT DOCTOR

The Observer

Atlantic Books
London

First published in Great Britain in 2004 by Atlantic Books,
on behalf of Guardian Newspapers Ltd.
Atlantic Books is an imprint of Grove Atlantic Ltd.

The Observer is a registered trademark of
Guardian Newspapers Ltd.
Observer Books is an imprint of
Guardian Newspapers Ltd.

10 9 8 7 6 5 4 3 2 1

A CIP record for this book is available from the British Library

ISBN 1 84354 252 8

Printed in Great Britain by Creative Print and Design Wales

Grove Atlantic Ltd
Ormond House
26–27 Boswell Street
London WC1N 3JZ

Contents

Introduction

When I sit to write my columns, I rarely have an idea what I'm going to talk about. I look at the screen – all pristine and white – and wait, fingers poised expectantly over the keys. I then ask the being who seems to reside in the uppermost reaches of my brain (or up in the ether above me, as you might say if you were more romantically inclined), 'What have you got for me today, then?' Then, before you know it, my fingers are darting hither and thither all over the keyboard as if possessed and I'm writing a piece. I've trained myself to override my inner critic and always desist from judging what I'm writing till I've written it. I don't even read back from the top until the final full stop has been triumphantly banged on to the screen. Then I check the word count and only then do I read back and begin chopping all the inevitable gratuitous nonsense away until what's left is hopefully ready for public consumption.

The process rarely takes more than an hour or two at the most, though there was one piece about the perfect moment which I therefore felt also needed to be the perfect piece; and that actually required a trip through the night all the way to Pembrokeshire in the winter rain and no less than twelve hours writing and honing until satisfied.

But my experience of writing the columns is not really the point. It's your experience of reading them that's the point, and more precisely your receiving something of lasting and profound value.

To this end, embedded amongst all the barefoot entertainment is information based on the failsafe template provided by Oriental medicine in which every possible condition, whether physical, spiritual, mental, emotional, social or even financial, has a resonance or correspondence in one of the five vital organs and for which there is always a simple way to instigate a process of rebalancing and healing, however long or complex that might eventually turn out to be. But as Lao Tzu, the godfather of Taoism, always used to say, 'A journey of a thousand miles begins with a single step'. In other words, you've got to start somewhere, and that's what I offer in these pieces – a start point to the greater adventure of simply being who you really are (behind all the necessary artifice and protective layers of self) – for it's these very moments of reaching your innermost whence your healing springs.

While the Oriental model I use originates in Taoism, I'm no puritan – am indeed a spiritual libertine if ever there was one – and thus find myself liberally borrowing from Buddhism, Hinduism, Animism, Humanism, Existentialism and any other -ism I've spent time studying. Western medicine still has among its adherents those who would tend to poo-poo these concepts, which is why much of the advice is prefaced with such sentiments as, 'according to Oriental medicine' – slightly tiresome, I know, as it makes me feel like I'm hiding behind the t'ai chi robes of the ancient Chinese. It also explains why I am obliged to advise you now that none of the advice is intended to replace the advice of your GP – always consult your GP if in doubt over your health.

I'm not on a crusade – after all, this is merely a service I'm humbly offering, not a political cause to be championed or even debated, at least not by me.

No, I say, horses for courses. I have absolute respect and admiration for the magnificent advances in Western medical science and hope, perhaps naively, hopefully not, that those magnificent men (and women) in their flying white coats will afford the wisdom of the ancient Oriental schema I present, a similar measure of respect – even when presented by such a maverick (and general scallywag) as I.

Mostly, though, I hope you gain immense enjoyment and edification from reading this book; that you find yourself often laughing out loud; and above all, that you feel the warmth of my love for you, which informs, not just each and every word, but each and every letter.

Barefoot Doctor
London, 1 November 2003

Bliss, Healing and Spirituality

The benefits of discovering spirituality

What is spirituality and why would you want it in your life?

There is an underlying pattern to all things, an innate consciousness that informs both the 'natural' world and the complex array of intertwining events of human society. It is discernible in the memory patterns of species. Witness the way a rose always grows like a rose. Whether this intelligence is thought of as a deity, a spirit, a set of mechanical reactions or an accident, its existence is irrefutable, whatever your inherited or adopted belief system. For the sake of argument, allow me to call it 'presence'. Perhaps too romantic for the hardened pragmatist or confirmed atheist to swallow, perhaps too vague for others who would prefer God, the Tao, Buddha, Christ or Great Spirit, but bear with me.

All spiritual paths (disciplines, religions and practices) are designed to raise and perpetuate awareness of this underlying pattern. Methods vary – praying, meditating, dancing, whirling, fasting, vision questing, etc – but the desired goal is the same: consistent awareness of spirit, both within and around you.

Sounds plausible enough, but what does it do for you and how do you get some?

Adopting a spiritual discipline, whatever its flavour, requires you to be willing to trust in the essential benevolence of this 'presence'. Once this suspension of normal belief systems, tantamount to a leap of faith, has been achieved (simply by choosing it), one sets about locating the nearest access point. For some, this is found in a church, for others it may be in a beautiful view, a sunset over the mountains, perhaps, for others, especially for followers of Oriental ways, it's through the temple of your physical body.

Metaphysically speaking, located within your body are access points along the spinal column, known to yogis as chakras (literally wheels which spin your consciousness to higher levels). Proper instruction in yoga or its equivalent is necessary in the long term, but the following is offered as a taster.

Imagine a line connecting the point between your eyebrows with the point at the centre of the base of your skull. Imagine a second line connecting one ear to the other. Where these two imaginary lines intersect is the approximate region of your pineal gland, commonly known as your 'third eye' or 'original cavity of spirit'.

(After reading this) close your eyes for a moment, concentrate and gather your awareness into this point. Simply gaze from here into the mysterious darkness between and behind your eyes. Relax your body, especially your breathing, and allow yourself a few moments of undisturbed awareness of 'presence' within and all around you stretching out in all directions into infinity. This momentary experience of the unity of mind, body and spirit, if repeated daily, will, within a short while, afford you direct easy access to the so-called spiritual realms. This you can carry with you during work, rest and play. A technique common to all spiritual paths, it will in no way put you in conflict with any religious practices you already follow, whether it be praying, t'ai chi, yoga or tango dancing.

The real advantage becomes apparent when you find yourself able to remain fully aware of 'presence' while simultaneously engaged in the thick of worldly pursuits. With it, you will soon acquire a grand enough perspective of existence to be able both to cope with the disappointments and pain of life with equanimity and to optimise your appreciation of the gift in each passing moment. And pass they do. Don't waste any time. Try it now.

Healing thyself

We've all read stories of celebrities visiting healers of one sort or another, but healing as an art (and potentially lucrative occupation) is now very much established within the intrinsic fabric of 21st-century society.

There is a moment, probably just after having survived the first trimester in utero, when awareness of your surroundings has begun to dawn, but you're not yet big enough to feel claustrophobic. Provided you've been blessed with an adequately strong constitution, you are likely to have experienced a state of absolute wholeness and utter harmony with both yourself and your environment, in which your blood and energy are flowing, your thought-tone is blissful and your entire being feels weightless. Let's, for the sake of argument, call this the state of healedness (or wholeness, in correct English). We then spend our entire lives searching for this apparently lost nirvana – through love, success, possessions, friendship, travel, adventure, extreme sports, partying, spirituality, alcohol and/or drugs. The truth is, this state of wholeness was never lost. That pure foetal consciousness that once was you, still is, but has merely been buried under layer upon layer of conditioned thought and behaviour patterns.

The aim of any healing, therefore, is to facilitate a moment – because that's all it takes – of consciously accessing that original foetal state of being, wherein the body-mind complex defaults automatically to 'perfect-flow' mode. If, while in this mode, the body receives clear 'instructions', whether by needle insertion (acupuncture), touch (cranio-sacral manipulation), 'hands-on' (shiatsu or reiki, for example), substance ingestion (herbal remedies or homeopathy), or mental suggestion (hypnotherapy, meditation or psychotherapy), it will respond by mobilising its innate intelligence and set about the process of mending itself from the inside out. This self-mending process, though now fully documented and recognised by modern science, remains nonetheless inexplicable and ultimately (as with the intelligence that informs, say, jasmine to smell the way it does) ineffable.

No matter which kind of healing you go in for and no matter how great, accomplished or famous the healer, it is fundamentally you who heal yourself by momentarily accessing that underlying state of perfect 'uterine' wholeness within and issuing the appropriate internal command. Neither you nor the healer can force your body to accept the healing. You can only set up the most favourable conditions possible for its facilitation. The rest must be left up to your body's intelligence: nature, in other words.

As with every other vocation, of those members of the healing profession (ie medical doctors, psychiatrists and nurses as well as homeopaths, acupuncturists, herbalists, aromatherapists and other alternative practitioners), only a small proportion will be authentic healers, able to facilitate true healing, no matter what the discipline. The rest will be mere 'technicians'.

It's not the discipline that's important, it's the practitioner. I know many people suffering from IBS (irritable bowel syndrome), for instance, who have been helped immeasurably – in many cases 'cured' – by a consultant, not through surgical intervention, but by his gentle laying on of hands and his empathetic demeanour. For empathy is the key. The true healer is able to empathise fully with the patient's condition and, more importantly, with their experience of that condition. Simultaneously, he (or she) is able to access that 'perfect-flow' mode and thus transmit at that frequency to the patient – which is similar to the way the Dalai Lama is able to transmit his spiritual frequency to anyone gathered before him, regardless of their spiritual awareness. In fact, the mode employed is merely a dance, a ritual that guides the mind and energy of healer and patient.

While it is obviously helpful to have been thoroughly schooled in a compatible discipline, healing ability often arises in people with no training: they possess a 'gift', just as Mozart possessed the gift of music. This doesn't mean that you must be in any way special to be a healer. Anyone can be taught, but naturally some will take to it more readily than others.

Of course, if your intention is focused enough, you can heal yourself without help. For instance, place a hand lightly on each side of your head. Do nothing but relax completely. Soon you will feel a subtle expanding and contracting rhythm in your skull. Simply follow that with your palms, exaggerating the motion slightly to cause a 'pumping' effect. After a few minutes, stop and enjoy the sensation of inner peace and wholeness that spontaneously arises. Though this is unlikely to clear up all your aches and pains, it may afford you a taste of the healing flavour, and who knows, you could turn out to be the next barefoot doctor.

Defending the alternative option

In the light of recent overwhelming evidence that we may be on the brink of one of the most cataclysmic crises ever to challenge humankind – ecologically, biologically, psychologically, sociologically and geologically – you might expect the elder statespeople of the land to be focusing their years of presumably superior experience and wisdom on the problem of how to avoid extinction of the human race. That they are, in the midst of all this, in fact turning their attention to the apparent global threat posed by alternative medicine, ancient Ayurvedic and Chinese in particular, seems worthy of mention here.

As something of an alternative elder, I would like to add my own modest voice to the discussion, not to defend alternative or complementary healing methods – they don't need defending or even championing, having been around in one form or another gathering agreement for a few thousand years – but to help dispel any confusion that could arise and dissuade patients from seeking useful alternative help in the future.

What the House of Lords declares is true, of course: alternative medicine can be dangerous, and in certain cases can kill you. Sometimes, perhaps often, even the most highly trained practitioner may fail to diagnose a fatal disease. Occasionally, herbs prescribed may react adversely with allopathic medication and cause grave trouble. And there are bound to be cases of people being misled by charismatic healers and ending up broke, ill or even dead as a result. But the same rules apply to conventional Western medicine. You cannot remove human fallibility from the equation whichever way you swing.

Unfortunately, as alternative therapies grew exponentially and rapidly more popular over the past three decades, our general mindset didn't alter. We are still only just learning what it means to take responsibility for our own health and wellbeing. Many still believe doctors are responsible for keeping us alive. But the shambles of the nonetheless valiant public health service, the side effects of many prescribed drugs and their ineffectiveness to do anything more than mask a disease, and the high rate of misdiagnoses and of surgical error are enough to tell us this is not necessarily the wisest approach.

My urge to pipe up on the topic was triggered by a recent conversation with a patient I was treating with acupressure to sort out a twitch in her left eye that had been troubling her for a week or more. There's a meridian, an overflow channel that conducts protective energy up the sides of the body which becomes blocked for a variety of reasons, the most common being hormonal imbalance, digestive troubles or sometimes an excess of adrenalin from too many late nights, early mornings or both. One symptom that often arises is this troublesome twitch in the eye, as the outer corner of the eye lies directly on the meridian's flight path. There is a point at the other end of the meridian, down behind the outside ankle in the dent formed between the ankle bone and the achilles tendon, that, if stimulated, can often clear a blockage and stop the twitch within seconds. You might like to locate and massage the point now in case you ever develop such a twitch.

She pointed out that normally she would have gone to her GP about it but doubted that would have been of much use, for short of toxic muscle relaxants, she wondered what a GP would be able to recommend. The same would go for many cases of IBS, headaches, back pain, almost all stress-related diseases, and in fact all the myriad conditions that alternative medicine has already proven beyond doubt to be able to help, if not altogether cure.

I'm not resorting to grandiose claims such as that alternative medicine can in theory be used to treat the most devastating disease – if the patient is willing to use the healing process, take it by the horns and with the help of grace, destiny, nature or whatever you'd prefer to call it, actually heal themselves. For as even Hippocrates, the father of modern medicine, himself understood it, nature heals, the physician merely nurses. I'm only asserting modestly that alternative medicine – self-healing in other words – practised by someone with adequate training, experience and talent, can alleviate many of life's irksome aches and pains, and can even help you die more peacefully when the time eventually comes (if not actually prevent illness altogether and prolong life considerably), and must retain its place alongside (not in opposition to) conventional medicine.

Native American warnings

Science fiction has morphed into science fact so smoothly we've hardly noticed. We adapt to new technology more and more quickly, almost in pace with the market's roll-out rate of new products. We are blasé to the point of absurdity. We politely overlook the human fallibility factor inherent in all technology, and not so much bumble as hurtle around in a numbed state of semi-enlighten-ment, our twisted buddha minds hardly arrested by newspaper headlines such as 'Danger Junkie to return to the UK!' Imagine a Victorian trying to make sense of that. (I remember Danger Man – I remember Danger Mouse – but now we have Danger Junkie.)

Because it seems, in this sci-fact morphed sci-fi world, we have become a society of committed junkies. Whether for information, gossip, drugs, alcohol, food, excitement, sex, travel, good looks, or the plethora of assorted fashion items we simply must have, we are almost all of us junkies of at least one sort or another. Our science, in the sense of our collective gnosis, is so huge in its implications and far reaching in its sophistication it defies description, let alone assessment. No need to bore you with yet another résumé of the technological wonders on offer – most of us have gone into overload, induced inurement to it all already. In short, we have entered, perhaps illegally, into what appears to be the intelligence of the divine realm itself. Splitting the atom initiated an irrevo-cable process of splitting the very fabric of reality as we perceive it, in our quest to know more, be more and have more (and of everything).

We have earnestly attempted to eradicate all diseases, insulate ourselves fully from the elements, whether indoors or on the road, and bring the wild animals who would normally be eating us for breakfast under our dominion. And we have been successful. We have managed disease well and instead now face a series of global plague epidemics. We have insulated ourselves so effectively using fossil fuel as the glue, that we've created an unpredictable weather monster capable of wiping out entire cities with a gust of wind and a touch of tidal action. Moreover, we've done such a good job with the lions, tigers and all other species of the wild, we shall soon have none left.

As we sail forth into the sunset of the next global recession and whatever social or geopolitical chaos that may unleash, our faces will be handsome and taut with botox and face lifts. As we wander the streets full of knife wielders and gun toters, we will do so WAP-phones in hand, with boldness and aplomb. In the midst of a world order crumbling before our eyes, we will display equipoise and courage.

And why? Because we have finally discovered our spirituality. Perhaps a little late in the day to prevent disaster on a scale hardly imagined, but certainly not too late to help us all find inner peace and enjoy the show to the max, online or off, until the lights finally go out.

Two thousand years ago, the Hopis, the revered spiritual fathers of all Native Americans, made a prophecy that at precisely this time in history we would cede the dominion game to rodents and insects and proceed to destroy our world, unless we made a rapid reversal in our consumeristic tendencies. This message was elucidated with understated elegance almost 20 years ago in the film, *Koyaanisqatsi*, Hopi for 'Dire warning – world out of balance!' Twenty years have passed. Two thousand years have passed and we still really haven't listened much. Now I'm a healer, not a prophet of doom, and have personally witnessed many miracles of healing in the course of treating supposedly terminal cases. I have also witnessed things go the other way. I have learned not to make rash prognoses. No one alive has access to enough of the relevant data to be able to make a truly informed prognosis. So rather than give way to pessimism, we would be better advised to continue to explore the mysteries of healing and spirituality: in other words, those methods that will enhance our innate enjoyment of life. Because only from the state of joy will come the inspiration that could guide us, and specifically our scientists in all their many guises, to find the miraculous solutions we so crucially and urgently require to facilitate our very survival as a species at this time.

One thing's for certain. Whichever way destiny's pendulum swings, and you can be sure there will be a lot of swinging action forthcoming, we'll all enjoy it a lot more if we learn to breathe and relax. It is also true to say that the world we have created has, in all its myriad forms, been instigated by people's ideas. Architects, designers, philosophers and their like, have through the ages helped mould the sculpture we call civilisation. It follows then that if we wish to engineer a subtle change of course in order to avert global disaster, we must, like them, start with the idea or vision. To this end, you may feel occasionally moved to visualise our globe spinning majestically, enveloped in a sheath of other-worldly healing 'light', as if after having eaten Readybrek, and imagine that light bringing common sense, balance and uncommon wisdom to the minds and actions of us all. Fairies at the bottom of the garden stuff, perhaps, but if enough of us share the vision, while it may not move many mountains, it might prevent the oceans moving us from our homes. So do be optimistic, for as any healer will tell you, while there's still life there's still hope.

The enchantment of chanting

Driving to the park the other morning to take Walter (the spiritually enlightened dog) for his morning air, I found myself caught in unexpected gridlock. In every direction, as far as the eye could see, were four-wheeled people carriers.

Walter, who is no small beast, getting restless in the back, jumped into the front passenger seat. He looked at me pragmatically for a moment as if to suggest I let him out for a pee in light of our obstructed position. 'No, dude, you know you went nuts last time I did that and ran amok among the traffic, peeing on the wheel of that Mercedes. You'll just have to hold it. Won't be long now.'

But he wasn't having any. He started that whining, whimpering sound he makes which, coming from such a large and magnificent animal, is guaranteed to melt your resolve every time. I held firm. 'Walter,' I commenced negotiations. 'We're going to chant to calm ourselves down.' Now, Walter is no stranger to the exotic vocal traditions of the east. Heaven knows, there are many who swear he's the reincarnation of an ancient Hindu sage. In fact, if I hit a low F#, he will invariably join me in a duet, howling along in tune.

So I took a deep breath in, letting my ribcage expand laterally, and chanted 'Namu Amida Bhutsu!' ('Hello and welcome, Buddha of Compassion!'), repeatedly until I hit that F# and Walter kicked in with his holy howling. After some moments of this extraordinary behaviour from the two of us, causing people to peer curiously through windscreens – and I can't talk for Walter on this, but it felt like we were sharing the experience – I found myself having somehow transcended the realms of relativity. Right or wrong, good driving or bad, I was now enjoying the perspective of none other than the Compassionate Buddha him (or her) self.

In that moment, everything was perfect exactly as it was. Everyone was simply doing the very best they could at this moment in the world's evolution. We were all just children in the playground playing traffic jams.

And this was exactly where Walter and I were meant to be. Walter howled along without a whimper till our compassion caused the gridlock to clear and we made it to the park in time for him to explode out of the door and disappear into the distance at 80mph in a frenzied dash for relief.

In fact, the sensation of compassion for humankind lasted throughout the day – so much so, I felt I would risk ridicule by disclosing these rather personal details about my relationship with Walter and the spiritual moments we often enjoy together and share with you a little of the wonders of chanting. Chanting has been used as a self-entrancing device by Eastern and Western spiritual paths for as long as any Bodhisattva round here can remember. From repeating Hail Marys to hailing Ganesh the Hindu elephant god, we have always used vocal sound to instigate an altered state of mind, one that transcends local concerns and sees beyond the world of distinctions to the perfection within (it and oneself).

In a way, it wouldn't matter what sound you repeated: the actual vibrations would engender physical comfort and relaxation from within, like an internally applied sonic massage. However, I must report from personal experience that there is an essence carried in these sacred chants of East and West, passed down by disciples and holy ones through the ages, which seems to affect you more profoundly than would, say, chanting, 'Roll me out into the marketplace' or other such nonsense.

But more importantly, and this is the deep purpose of all the 'om' ch
there is an a priori sound – the very sound of creation. It's the one referred
the opening lines of the Bible: 'God spoke, and said let there be light' (excuse m
waxing so, but it is Sunday). The yogis refer to this sound as 'shabd', which, if one
trains oneself to listen out for it in deepest meditation, will confer on one a profound sense of peace and wellbeing. All the omming and ahhing is just an
attempt to mimic that original sound in order to set up a field of resonance. Try
it now, if it doesn't feel too exotic for comfort. Take a full inbreath, allowing your
ribcage to expand laterally and gently allow to escape from deep within your
belly the sound 'AUM!', stretching out the 'AU' as long as possible before closing
your lips for the final 'M'. If you find that vaguely relaxing, try repeating it for up
to nine breaths' worth. Then rest for a moment or two in the inner silence and
see if you can hear (or hear if you can see) the original sound of creation for
yourself.

Mastering the art of spacing out

A Japanese friend of mine – transatlantic, transpacific entrepreneur and pro-moter in the fashion and music business, and partner to a magazine publisher and mother, who does, it must be said, bear a striking resemblance to Yoko Ono both in looks and demeanour, and who is one of the hardest-working people on the planet – somehow never manages to lose her composure.

Stoical and unfussily serene, she takes whatever life throws her way with the apparent equipoise and containment of a Zen master.

Treating her over the years, I have been struck by her absolute humility in being able to accept and respect the irony of a comparatively clumsy Westerner practising Oriental medicine and teaching Oriental life strategies. But more, I was surprised by how she readily admitted to feeling extraordinarily stressed and internally quite out of kilter, when all along I'd assumed her to be a re-incarnation of the Buddha herself.

What was really remarkable, though, was how quickly during treatment she would sink into what can only be described as 'Zen mode'. With only the slight-est prompting, she became empty. Empty of self and therefore entirely available and receptive to treatment almost instantly, as if she'd been trained to do so as a child. There were fewer layers of social defences to dissolve before we got down to that necessary place of stillness where the healing takes place.

I've found it the same with all the Japanese people I've had the pleasure to work with – including even the nervous teenage student with mobile phone, minidisc, dyed-tangerine hair, exotic skateboardwear and IBS who mixed up 'r's and 'l's and giggled almost continually in between, or the overstressed banker

with a propensity for bowing endlessly, attending wild, drunken karaoke
maintaining underage schoolgirl 'mistresses' and stomach ulcers. It se
easier for them to get to that 'Zen space' than for us internally baggage-laden
Westerners.

I first encountered the 'Zen space' in Tia Honsai, my Aikido master when I was
just a lad. He was also a healer who had learned to channel 'ki', the Japanese
version of 'chi', or life force. He called it 'super ki' and claimed it had the power to
stop a locomotive as well as heal the gravest disease, but to access it, one had to
learn to completely still one's thoughts and fine-focus the now empty mind on
the area to be healed. Then one had to merge one's consciousness with the 'pure
consciousness' of the universe, thus overriding the local mind, and think about
'one point', the tantien, 2in below the navel, the acupuncture point that controls
the 'sea of breath', or 'hara', where 'ki' is generated.

In fact, to develop 'hara' is considered crucial to being a fully rounded person.
In the practice of Zen archery, for instance, the master observes the student's
tantien, ignoring the target board altogether, yet can predict a bullseye accurately every time according to the archer's visible degree of hara-centredness or
'one-pointedness'.

In this empty minded, hara-centred mode, Tia Honsai believed us to be inde-
structible. If there was 'no-mind', as the Zen Buddhists call it, what or who could
there be to destroy?

To help the Zen student achieve this imperturbable no-mind state, the
master or 'roshi' asks a non-linear question – a koan – designed to make the
mind momentarily crash. Something like: 'When a tree falls in the forest and
there is no one there to hear it, does it make a noise?' or that old favourite:
'What is the sound of one hand clapping?' The student would be sent away to

contemplate the koan and expected to come back with an answer. If a logical, linear response was attempted, the student would be sent away again to reconsider, perhaps with an admonishing tap on the forehead from the roshi's stick. If, on the other hand, the student returned with a non-rational, lateral response, showing an appreciation for the innate 'isness' or 'suchness' of a tree falling silently or the improbable thwack of a hand clapping the air – perhaps playfully tweaking the roshi's nose as his answer – the student would be considered to have 'got it'.

Zen aficionados also talk of developing 'beginner's mind', that ability to remain fresh in every new moment, uncluttered by prejudices gathered from past experiences. Every experience is new, no matter how many times you've been there before. Like a baby, you absorb without judgement and never allow yourself to be deluded into becoming jaded.

Look at a Zen garden or the interior of a traditional Japanese home – the inspiration behind our own Western ideas of minimalist design. The spacious unclutteredness is meant to represent the serenity of an empty and therefore tranquil beginner's mind.

But it would be misguided to believe that all Japanese people are potential Zen adepts, just as it would be to believe all Westerners are potentially great footballers. Indeed, the Japanese are the most prolific inventors and consumers of gadgetry designed to distract from inner silence of any nation on earth. But beneath the face of pocket robots, micro cameras, drunken karaoke sessions and instant noodles, the potential for reaching the 'Zen space' seems culturally programmed from birth into every individual.

We, though blessed with many other fine attributes (our quirky sense of humour, for one), are, however, not so well-endowed in the Zen sense. We find it hard to be empty of self. If you don't believe me, try now sitting 'sazen', meditation-style, preferably with back straight but relaxed (on the floor with knees bent and buttocks perched on heels is best but in an armchair will do), and eyes three-quarters open. Allow your breathing to settle down and deepen, then quite purposefully proceed to think about absolutely nothing for 20 minutes.

If you find that level of inner stillness hard to achieve, don't commit hari kari over it. Instead, consider a visit to a practitioner of shiatsu, and have your Zen done for you while you lie there and relax.

This is a mildly rambling (like the streets of Tokyo) Barefoot Doctorsan bidding you a fond sayonara till next week.

Living in the here and now

Imagine being isolated from all human and animal contact, from nature, or from beauty of any kind, for the rest of your life, thereafter to be isolated in perpetuity. There, we've faced it – the unthinkable horror that lurks not far beneath the surface of every mind. Indeed, the dread of isolation provides a common theme informing most cases of depression. This dread is not logical or rational but is perhaps a major motivational force behind the human survival instinct. It arises from the depths of your existential inner soup and is only temporarily allayed by contact with other people.

The only true antidote is to remove all inner blocks that are otherwise isolating you from yourself. Because once the connection is remade with your true (underlying) self (as opposed to the self you present to the world), the theory, according to the Taoists, is that you will instantaneously feel reconnected to the rest of creation, and thus all sense of isolation be dissolved.

If you look down at your body, you may ask incredulously: 'Isolated from myself? How can that be – I'm all here, aren't I?' Well, are you? When was the last time you stopped to feel what's going on in your pelvic region, belly, or chest? When was the last time you weren't pondering the past or attempting to outguess the future? When, in other words, were you fully present, with all parts of your mind as one, in the here and now, simply being in a state of pure existence?

The fact is that, other than at moments of extreme challenge or during meditative activities of any kind, most of us spend our days (and nights) more or less one removed from the reality of the moment. That's why there's such an uptake of alcohol and mind-altering substances these days. It's because we're desperate to find the switch that will turn off the local (chattering) mind with all its judgements and criticisms, to let go of the control and release ourselves into the deeper life current that flows beneath the surface. For when you are flowing at this depth, you are swimming in the current that carries all life and can't help but feel connected (and unisolated).

Now, although it's not for me to judge or criticise the use, misuse or abuse of substances of any kind, it's fair to say there are healthier, more life-enhancing ways to disinhibit oneself enough to enter the deeper stream. What alcohol and the other 'social substances' – the personality lubricants, in other words – have in common is the sensation of warmth in the chest and relaxation in the belly they seem to trigger, which in turn allow you to override the (over)critical faculties in the head. It is this warmth – the heart energy, in Taoist terminology – that gives you the courage to interact.

So rather than having you ingest something to ward off isolation, the Oriental approach is to mechanically and systematically release those tensions in the head, chest and belly that prevent you from being in your natural state of connectedness. There are many ways to skin this cat, but the following are universally applicable, effective and easy to operate. Start by placing your forefinger in the notch at the base of your throat at the top of your breastbone (the clavicular fossa), and subtly press the breastbone downwards towards your pubic bone. Hold for a few moments and release. You may notice your head clearing and your energy settling a bit in the belly. Activating this point also helps stimulate throat energy, which governs communication skills in general.

Now place the fingers of your dominant hand on the dead centre of your breastbone and press gently back towards the spine. Slowly describe a 3cm diameter clockwise circle, moving flesh against bone, roughly 18 times and release. This, you may notice, warms the thoracic (chest and upper back) region by stimulating heart energy or 'fire'. Courage literally translates as 'heart essence' from the French (coeur = heart), hence according to both Western and Eastern models, this movement can be said to promote courage.

Now place your index finger approximately 9cm directly below your navel and press in till you feel a pleasant ache, and describe a clockwise circle of similar dimensions 18 times.

This point is the 'sea of energy', stimulation of which will help you feel substantial, as if you truly belong on the planet, which is requisite for balanced, healthy dialogue with the world.

Finally, place your forefinger in the centre of your forehead, 3 or 4cm above the eyebrow line. Press in until you feel a mildly tingling, pleasant sensation and describe 18 clockwise circles of 2cm diameter, maintaining constant pressure of about 110g, and release. This is known as the 'happy point', as it stimulates the pineal gland, allegedly triggers the release of serotonin, and gives you 'third eye' vision, or telepathic awareness.

Practise this short routine daily for a week and if you don't feel noticeably more connected, relaxed and in touch with this miracle we call the world, I'll eat my socks.

Saving the world with self-healing

Well, my oh my, what a mess we're in. Formerly it was considered bad manners, even eccentric, to admit it, but it's become so glaring now, I really feel I'm not making an awful social faux pas mentioning that, on every level, we as a species face an awesome challenge here on the planet. The good news is that for cockroaches, spiders and other hardier insects, rats and some of the more gruesome-looking creatures of the deep, prospects are healthy.

For all the rest, and that includes us, prospects are slightly more iffy. Whether you look at the economic picture, social behavioural trends, the ecology, uncontaminated food and potable water supply, or climatic patterns, we're up against a crisis unprecedented in living history, and to cap it all, we're losing the so-called battle against infectious disease.

Not being alarmist – being an eternal optimist, in fact – I wonder if there might still be time before hurtling into a state of abject collective chaos to somehow reverse or transform things enough to keep this magnificent show on the road a few centuries longer. As I am not writing as some crazed survivalist in a concrete bunker somewhere out in Texas, eagerly awaiting the 'end times', but as a merely semi-crazed 21st-century urban follower of Taoism, I thought I might share their ancient (as well as semi-crazed 21st-century urban) take on dealing successfully with surviving 'interesting' epochs of human history.

This is based on the Taoist idea that each of us is a microcosmic version of the whole, a homunculus of the environment that supports us.

Deep in your lower abdomen is the original fire of life (the earth's core). This is your 'kidney fire' – that which sparks you up in the first place and gives you the impetus to create, procreate and recreate. Above that, a thin crust, and then the water of life. This is the 'water of your kidneys', that which gives you the strength and will to stay alive. Sitting on top of and mixing with that, a little higher in your abdomen, is the soil which brings forth the plants and trees. This relates to your spleen, responsible according to the Orientals, for transforming food and fluids into useful nutrients. The power that makes trees grow and live relates to your liver, hence its name. These plants and trees (in your chest, as it were) relate to your lungs, transforming gases essential to your survival, just like the rainforests. And bang in the middle of your chest is the immense heat generated by the 'fire of your heart', which shines down upon your inner planet from your solar plexus (nerve centre 'of the sun') in your upper abdomen.

Nice metaphorical image, but even if you go in for this kind of Oriental fairy tale, how does it help save the human race from impending disaster? It's a long shot, but according to those Taoists – who, though famed as great metaphysicians, were only human after all, so take it with a pinch of salt – what occurs within the microcosm will follow in the macrocosm and vice versa. Hence if just one person can achieve a state of perfect inner balance, the entire ecosphere, global economy, infectious-disease scenario and social equation will proceed to reflect that. In other words, if just one person is fully healed, the whole will be, too. So as a worthy homunculus yourself, you may, in the name of global salvation, want to consider giving some time and attention now to your own healing.

Of course there are 1,000 ways to skin this cat, but they all originate with a picture in the mind of wholeness. Begin now, perhaps, by visualising the fire of the earth's core burning pleasantly in your genital region, above which the clear, unpolluted water of life flows in your lower abdomen, slowly seeping up through the rich, fertile soil above it, bringing forth magnificently healthy trees (and all manner of living things, but easy on the roaches etc), their branches reaching up into a brightly lit, ozone-repaired sky (within your chest), gaily transforming poisoned air into fresh.

It's quite potty, I know, but visualising this harmonious inner ecosphere regularly will, over the course of but a few days, begin to work great beneficial change in the way you treat yourself. Your body will begin to tell you what foods, exercise and even social milieu it needs to enable you to flourish with such strong promptings you won't be able to resist. And then, whether you do it through t'ai chi, acupuncture, colour therapy or whatever grabs your fancy, if you can follow the path the whole way to total self-healing, it could be you who saves the world. Good luck, we're counting on you.

The healing power of thought

Here's a nice little story. I get a call from Carlos Fandango: 'Johnny Toobad's in hospital. He's got a brain tumour the size of a kiwi fruit and they're operating tomorrow. He'd be very happy if you'd phone him to arrange to send him energy during the op.'

This comes out of the blue. Johnny – a highly talented 'cutting edge' sort of playwright and generally erudite scribe – is usually the epitome of vitality and health. But, it turns out, his left side has been growing progressively numb for weeks and he's been suffering severe dizzy spells. Two different GPs assure him it's a virus – where have you heard that before? – but luckily he's had the sense to call in at A&E. They've fortunately recognised the signs. I ask him if he's scared of the op. 'No,' he replies in a startlingly (authentic) positive tone. 'I've been worried for months not knowing what was wrong and now I know I can get this operation out of the way and get on with my life – I've got a lot to do, Doc!'

So, the next morning at the appointed hour, after a spot of deep t'ai chi in the garden, I sit on the ground and, dropping into a meditative state, begin tuning into Johnny's brain. I am not alone – there are a good 20 others dotted around town doing likewise. When my astral self arrives on the scene, so to speak, it's as if entering a holy place and I am clearly aware of a presence above him – to describe it as an angel, though rather a romantic notion, would be the most apt. In my perception, it's like a huge being of light, pushing more light at high velocity in a fat column through the top of Johnny's head. And though these kind of beings don't generally speak in words – words being a human concept – the message I get is, 'Thank you for lending your energy here, we're doing a miracle.' After a few minutes, I feel it right to withdraw and return to my normal waking state. That evening the news comes that the operation has gone surprisingly well – it's the first time it's been performed on screen without even looking at the patient and is such an all-round success it even makes the next day's newspaper. (That's how PR friendly this man is!) The usual recovery time after such a procedure is 10 days to two weeks minimum, and the doctors are astounded that Johnny is fully recovered and ready to go home two days later. They discharge him calling it a miracle.

And why do I tell you this story? Because it brings up a few pertinent points. One: don't believe everything anyone tells you. Two, though it could be random coincidence, it would seem that actively sending good wishes to someone from your heart does actually lend strength on an astral level to the recipient which augments recovery. Furthermore, when many band together in the same pursuit, the effect is exponentially multiplied. Three (and this carries on from 'two'), it pays in this respect, as well as every other, to be popular. The reason Johnny is so popular is probably because as well as being a sound geezer, he's also one of the most genuinely positive people on the planet. Finally, and even the doctors agreed with this, this same positivity was a major contributing factor in his rapid recovery. He didn't get sucked into the drama of being ill, in other words, and instead identified only with being well again.

I predict you'll be hearing a lot more of Johnny Toobad in the near future, if only because the sheer volume and velocity of light being pumped into him that day is bound to seek expression through his already brilliant writing. But in the meantime, you might like to think of someone you love who may be in need of a bit of help, not just with severe stuff like brain tumours – any kind of suffering will do – and selflessly send them a blast of healing energy in the following way. Sit with your spine quite straight, relax your muscles and let your breathing settle down and deepen. As if viewing from an eye in the dead centre of your brain, picture your subject in front of you with a huge angelic-looking being of light above pushing more light down through the top of your subject's head. Let your vision be impassioned by the vital force in your chest and supported from beneath by the raw energy in your pelvic region. Continue until you grow restless, then carry on as you were. And though the very idea of this procedure may run counter to any pragmatic views of reality you hold dear, the whole thing costs less than a local call, and who knows, it might just do the trick. On top of which it will fill you with a healthy sense of righteousness that'll fuel you for the day. And according to the immutable law that what goes around comes around, you should be veritably showered with blessings within four days of reading this. Pass it on!

Feeling exhilarated for ever

If I said it's perfectly OK for you to feel exhilarated and wonderful all the time from now on, would you baulk at the idea and call me an idealist? If I said it will be perfectly possible for you to hold to that state constantly from now on, even in the midst of painful or difficult circumstances, would you harrumph and say I was a dreamer?

Well, baulk or harrumph as you will, but hear me out. It's all a question of mindset. A Taoist would tell you that suffering, no matter the severity of external physical conditions, is merely a choice you make in reaction to pain, and that it's just as easy to choose the opposite response instead. The difficulty in doing so arises from the fact that having chosen the suffering response (probably as a newborn) and having adopted it (unconsciously) as a pattern, it requires disciplined persistence in accessing and retraining that original 'layer' of mind where the choice was initially made.

For many years, I treated a young woman who, because of a sudden rapid degeneration of the joints in her teen years, had had both feet amputated. However, in spite of this, as well as having a successful career in local government, a happy relationship and a strong social network, she was also, without doubt, one of the most exhilarated and wonder-filled people I've ever met. And she wasn't faking it with bravado. Never once did she reveal an ounce of self-pity. Nor did she make a point of how much courage must have been required not to default to suffering mode. She simply made the choice to feel exhilarated and wonderful all the time, and stuck to it, no matter what.

All right, so this is probably just another 'get positive' exhortation. And, yes,

I've broken the golden rule and am writing in the first person, but I have to tell you, speaking as the guy who chills the world out for a living, I got into all this self-help malarkey in the first place 30 years ago because I was so firmly entrenched in suffering mode it was killing me. My soul eventually wouldn't take that much constriction, and in its cry for release led me to RD Laing, the study of psychotherapy and a subsequent odyssey with the Hopi Indians, during which I learned the discipline of choosing exhilaration and wonder instead.

I'm only telling you this because if someone as compulsively entrenched in what felt like all the suffering of humanity as I was can turn it around enough to be the guy who gets paid to remind you to be positive, so can anyone.

But it doesn't happen overnight – or it does, but the process is subtle, so you may not notice it at first. Full-on exhilaration and wonder unfolds in a series of quantum increments as soon as you say the following magic words (like you mean them): 'It's perfectly OK for me to feel exhilarated and wonderful all the time, no matter what!'

'Selfish bugger!' says the cynic. 'What about all the suffering in the world? How can you feel exhilarated and wonderful in the face of that?' Of course, you have absolute compassion for the pain of others – and yourself. This is not about denial, but even while in the midst of the greatest pain, existence still remains exhilarating and full of wonder, if you can overcome the tendency towards self-pity. You can feel the pain and be with the pain, but still feel exhilarated and wonderful – if you choose it. After all, you won't help the suffering of others by adding to it with your own.

The most effective way to alleviate the world's suffering, including your own, is by injecting your exhilaration and wonder into the mix as an antidote. In fact, exhilaration and wonder is the natural state, and it's almost a duty to access it now for everyone's sake. Relax your body, relax your mind and gently repeat over and over, 'It's perfectly OK for me to feel exhilarated and wonderful all the time!' until it becomes the prominent pattern on the wallpaper in your mind – you will start to notice subtle yet discernible changes in your relationship with the world within 24 hours, or you get your money back.

Meantime, it really helps to support your mind in this by strengthening the physical frame that houses it and, with winter coming, what better time to pick up an exercise habit? Some Pilates to strengthen your lower back, a drop of yoga to loosen your joints, a touch of cardio-vascular to gladden your heart and lungs, and a bit of t'ai chi to make it all sit properly – but truly, any exercise that takes your fancy is better than none.

So I'm telling you, it's perfectly OK to feel exhilarated and wonderful all the time, and it is moreover perfectly possible for you to hold to that state constantly from now on, even in the midst of painful or difficult circumstances. Any takers?

Spreading human kindness

Walking down the street early the other morning, I was arrested by the sight of an elderly Indian man standing practising pranayama (yogic breath 'technology') facing the sun as it rose over the football field.

Without getting too barefooted about it, in the clean-aired foothills of the Himalayas or even on the dusty streets of Delhi, to see someone standing meditatively with one hand gracefully raised to close the right nostril while breathing deeply through the left like this would be totally unremarkable. But seeing it practised publicly in morning rush-hour in north London filled me with appreciation for the remarkable fusion of cultures occurring in our midst.

In these turbulent days, culture fusion is being increasingly seen in a negative light. But while the process of fusing two or more cultures with widely varying ideologies will necessarily cause friction at certain stages in the process, the venerable pranayama man reminded me that we all have an untold amount to share with each other. And if the thought of pranayama or other forms of yoga doesn't blow your hair back, think of the profusion of Oriental martial arts and healing techniques available on almost every high street: Latin dance classes or African drumming sessions, for example. Personally, I'd love to see a more widespread profusion of Sufism (the user-friendly, Whirling Dervish mystical aspect of Islam), as I think it would help bridge more than a few divides on a local level.

But no matter which face of the divine you choose to gaze upon, there is always more short-, mid- and long-term value in sharing with the aim of mutual cultural enrichment than in destroying or preventing cross-cultural relations for the sake of fear and ignorance.

There's little most of us can do as individuals to directly influence those on either 'side' who press the buttons, and this tends to spread a pall of impotence and insecurity over our thoughts and throw our 'life-plans' into sometimes uncomfortably unprecedented perspective, but there is a lot we can do on a personal level.

If you feel strongly about re-establishing peace in the world, start by re-establishing it in your immediate vicinity by building, rather than burning, as many bridges as you can in all directions. Because the more bridges available for you to walk across, the more choices and opportunities are open to you. The first bridge that needs rebuilding at least once a day, is the one that leads you inside to make contact with your own essential nature. It's all too easy to be distracted by events in the world or even events in your local shopping centre and lose touch with your core whence springs your personal sense of inner peace.

At some point during the day, place your palms on your belly to remind it to relax and let your breathing slow down and deepen. Imagine yourself as a hollow bamboo beneath a high-mountain waterfall. The cool, clear water cascading down through your crown dislodges all negative, festering or stagnant thoughts from your head, all self-inflated sense of self from your chest, along with all fear and angst from your belly, and washes it all away. As none of us exists in isolation (however hard we may try sometimes) spare a thought to visualise all your 'brothers and sisters', people of every creed and nationality on the planet, especially those currently with violence in their hearts, sitting shining likewise as hollow bamboos, each beneath their own waterfall, cleansed of all negativity.

While so poised, check your body for all places where any unconscious fear (of other people) has lodged itself in your musculature. This often shows up most in your chest, belly and buttocks as unnecessary physical tension and must be 'smoked out' of its hiding places immediately. This can be done simply by locating it with your thoughts and issuing the mental command to let go.

The opposite and antidote to fear of others is, as any new-age bod will tell you, love of others. Love in this context means the willingness to share human kindness with everyone, however different they are. In fact, the more different, the more important it is.

To open the energy flow required to practise what is, to all intents and purposes, minor saintliness, the Taoists of the ancient Orient suggested taking hold of one hand in the other and pressing with thumb firmly into the stigmata point in the centre of your palm for 30 seconds, one hand at a time. This activates the energy in the centre of your chest, which governs your ability to love, and, after a few days of practising it four or five times a day, you will feel human kindness (for humankind) flowing through you like a river after the rains.

As Lao Tsu, the accredited grandfather of Taoist philosophy would say, a journey of a thousand miles starts with a single step. Create an atmosphere of bridge-building and peace in your immediate local vicinity, in other words, and let that radiate in ever growing circles, and if enough of us do it, we can actually save the world. And if I'm wrong, there won't be anyone to call me a dreamer – may peace and good sense prevail!

Harnessing your inner tug and letting your spirit soar

Do you ever have those moments when a feeling comes on out of nowhere – an inner tugging in the belly that makes you want to connect with something deeper, a kind of mystical draw to an invisible realm you half remember but don't quite know how to define?

I'm asking because as I sat down to write this I suddenly found myself coming over a bit mystical. It's a feeling I sometimes used to get at school as a small boy when, for whatever reason, I found myself alone in the sports changing rooms having had to leave the others playing rugby in the mud. It was the thrill of unexpected solitude rather than the ambience or smell of the changing rooms, by the way, in case you were getting any funny ideas. Bear with me, though – this isn't a therapy session I'm having here at your expense.

The various yoga systems of India, Tibet and China teach that these onsets of the internal tug are invitations from the unseen realms to enter a state of 'enlarged' or altered awareness.

Conducting an informal survey in the mid-80s when 'spirituality' and general inward-gazing had not yet become a legitimate (or fashionable) pastime, I asked everyone I treated in my healing practice over the course of one year whether they had ever felt a similar undefined tug. Providing I could convey clearly to each what I meant by the tug, it turned out that everyone had, without exception, felt it, and that on further questioning, the natural inclination at such times for most would be to do (or want to do) something compulsive like drinking, drugs, sex, shopping, overwork, food-bingeing or what have you. However, I discovered that if I taught those who were interested to respond instead to the tug by practising any one of a plethora of psychospiritual 'techniques' culled from the above systems, this impulse could be harnessed and would confer on the practitioner a key to the spiritual zone, the unlocking of which would help them stop perpetuating the same old behavioural patterns that had previously been holding them back in life.

Entering this zone need not distract you from whatever you're doing 'down' here on earth. On the contrary, by enlarging your spectrum of awareness, you actually increase your effectiveness on the local plane through enhanced clarity, perspective, focus and energy.

Entering the zone is like taking a spiritual bubble bath, and just a few nanoseconds spent soaking in it will refresh you for hours. A Taoist would call it floating in the Tao, the great undifferentiated absolute, and consider it a great luxury to spend hours engaged in mind-altering activities to achieve it (meditation, t'ai chi, chi-gung, pa kua, hsing i, etc), bathing until pruny-skinned. A yogi would call it resting in nirvana, a Ten-Tai Buddhist reaching the pure land, a Christian mystic being one with the Godhead, and so on. But what the techniques of all disciplines share is the emphasis on keeping your feet on the ground while your spirit soars in the heavens.

This enables you to straddle two worlds at once, to be in the world but not of it, actioning your wishes on the local plane with true grace while remaining internally identified with the universal. To be enlightened, in other words.

For example, right now, if you fancy, sit comfortably in your favourite chair, with spine lengthened from coccyx to skull, sitting bones making firm contact with the seat and feet planted solidly on the floor in front of you with toes optimally spread. Take a moment to relax all your muscles, visualising them sinking towards the floor, trusting just your spine to keep you upright. Breathe in deeply and, focusing awareness on a point 7cm above the crown of your head while imagining a small ball of white light there, chant in as deep and resonant a tone as you can manage, what the yogis describe as the sound of the engine that drives the universe, 'Om'.

Let the sound originate from the seat of your pants, from way down deep in your pelvic bowl and travel slowly up your spine through the crown and 'into' the ball of light above. Start the sound, lips parted with an open 'au' or 'ow' vowel sound as it travels up your spine, filling your torso and skull with vibrations, only closing your lips towards the end of the breath as the sound reaches that point above your crown.

Repeat this at least three times, extending the note a little more each time.

When you've finished, sit luxuriating in the silence for a few minutes and then carry on as you were.

I could sell you a list of far-reaching positive effects that will result from continuing this practice daily (for the rest of your life), but it would be a lot more rewarding for you to suck it and see for yourself. Email or write in with your findings.

And now I must fly. I hear the shrill sound of a whistle and a nasty-voiced teacher shouting, 'Barefoot, stop malingering in the changing rooms – get back out here on the playing field at once!'

Finding perfect harmony with your surroundings

Standing at the foot of the Mediterranean end of the Pyrenees the other day, as you do (or should seriously consider doing some time), I was taken as if by a bolt out of the blue by one of those 'Zen moments'. By a Zen moment I mean a sudden involuntary cut-off of the usual internal chitchat that fills your consciousness along with a spontaneous shift of awareness, causing a foreclosing of the view before you, as if the camera's lens has just been defocused. And for one blissful moment, with absolute forgetfulness of self, you existentially merge with your surroundings. No longer are you looking at the tree (or lamppost) in front of you – you are that tree (or lamppost, but a tree is better if you have one to hand). No longer observing but melding, the illusion of a separate self momentarily suspended, you are now simply yet mysteriously part of the universal thrust of creation.

But as I said, it's a moment. And before you know it, the internal chitchat has started up again, like an old 'washerperson' going, 'Ooh, just look at me having one of those Zen moments (isn't it grand and how can I hang on to it?)' And as soon as you do, poof! and the moment's gone, dissipated by the cacophony of a thousand thoughts.

In fact, it is not unknown for dedicated followers of Zen to sit in sazen (sitting to meditate) for more than two hours a day, completely devoid of thought, even including being devoid of awareness of having no thought, for many such moments at a time over the course of a single session.

Taoism and Zen share a common root and are in many senses just different screen settings, so to speak, by which to view the same picture. Both philosophical 'systems' address themselves to your ability to notice the moment when it spontaneously arises, recognising the shift of awareness and sustaining it or allowing it to be sustained for as long as possible without interference from the chattering-monkey mind. Because it is as a result of such events that one is thrust through to the dimension of the gods (if you'll excuse the incongruity of cultural reference) – that dimension of existence the Hindus call nirvana, and which you or I would just call being so damn enlightened you could eat yourself. Anyway, the Taoists developed an entire shedload of techniques by which to achieve this and even to trigger its onset, not least of which is the following.

This works best when looking at a natural view, but, if none is readily available, the view directly before you will do. Press your thumb into the point at the base of your skull in the centre where your spine meets your cranium, with enough gentle pressure to produce a pleasant ache throughout the back of your head. Surrender your neck to the sensation, mentally relaxing all the soft tissue, and imagine you have an eye here. Now as if looking from this eye, soften your gaze and instead of focusing on any particular object, focus on the peripheral view, trying to see more around the edges than you normally would.

After a few seconds, everything in view begins to shift and blur, as described above. Now the trick is to attempt to refrain from passing commentary on the experience, as this will curtail it, but rather release yourself into it like a drunkard surrendering to being on the piss. If you've ever found yourself looking at one of those computer pictures and shifting focus till they change to reveal an entirely new 3-D scene, you'll be familiar with the thrill that ensues.

And, hopefully, that thrill will induce you to revisit the experience once a day, for within just three weeks of such practice you'll begin to notice a positive upsurge of the enlightenment factor for yourself.

If you are more aurally inclined, you can do the same with sound by imagining the point at the base of your skull to be an ear and listening to the ambient sound around you instead of listening to any one sound in particular.

The key is not to identify objects, but to let them remain without label and simply form part of the visual or sonic field. And I'd tell you more but I'm finding it hard to see the keys in front of me. Beam me down, Scotty, I've had liftoff – what did you slip in that Pyrenean mountain drink you gave me?

All that's important is healing – regardless of footwear

I once had the pleasure of addressing a group of distinguished NHS doctors in Runcorn. The subject of my talk: the healer's experience. I began by explaining I was not there to crusade for alternative medicine, as firstly, crusading was never my thing and, secondly, I've never regarded what I do as a viable alternative to traditional Western medicine. Instead, it's something with which to supplement the latter – useful for problems the Western docs are at a loss dealing with: stiff necks, lower back trouble, emotional distress, depression, insomnia, IBS, general stress and all kinds of things for which pharmaceuticals or surgery are ineffective or inappropriate, or are appropriate but work better if blended with holistic medicine, too.

I didn't want to set up a polarity – as I saw it, we were all physicians of one kind or another, whether barefoot or shod. Not that I've had the same kind of training as a Western doc, having never cut up a cadaver, nor spent interminable nights as a hospital intern. But then they probably haven't sat up all night playing music with RD Laing (and all the other nuts), watching him dribble down the front of his cardigan, sat holding a dying woman for two hours as she screamed in pain and terror, telling her about the Taoist approach to handling the 'crossover', or spent the night at a peyote ceremony in New Mexico to get in contact with the healing spirit. We each have a lot to bring to the treatment couch in other words, and can benefit our patients greatly by joining hands now to work together.

Interestingly, in contrast to the last time I gave such a talk to the NHS five years ago, or the classic night when I addressed the Royal Society of Medicine 20 years ago (and was thanked for providing them with a 'hugely entertaining evening'), all the docs were with me this time. Not a single one baulked at the idea of energy making things happen. (Twenty years ago, the mere mention of energy almost got me lynched.)

One particularly erudite and suave gentleman, who was wearing extremely smart shoes, incidentally, did point out that it might be better if I used different nomenclature, because it weakened my case in the eyes of those with scientifically trained minds. For example, when I am talking of 'kidney energy', if what I really mean is energy produced in that region of the body which happens to house the kidneys, and that if I am saying that kidney energy is akin to the body's battery, then I should call it battery energy. And while I agree wholeheartedly with him in principle, battery energy reminds me too much of maltreated hens, so I hope he'll understand if I stick with the old-fashioned names instead.

They didn't even baulk at the audience-participation stuff I had them do, designed to bring out the inner child, and guaranteed to make you feel like a bit of a charlie. In fact it was one of the best crowds I've worked in months and ended with everyone laughing, clapping and feeling extremely relaxed and positive about healing the world each in their own way, despite the state it's in.

What seemed to make the biggest impact was my pointing out that the efficacy of any treatment, whether traditional or holistic, depended entirely on how the physician (literally) treats the patient. If you treat someone with respect, give them the 100 per cent attention they deserve during the time you're with them, whether that's two hours or two minutes, if you truly listen to them and let them know you care, that will produce a strong healing effect in itself and they'll probably sort out the rest themselves. It's about one human being giving unconditional love to another, and the docs resonated with that deeply, bless them.

In fact, I'd like to take this opportunity to big up the docs loudly for the incredible work they do in the face of a deeply under-resourced health system. Three cheers and more power to your elbows – we'd be in a right old mess without you! Imagine only having left-fielders like me to take care of the population – if a trend like that caught on it could put the nation's shoe shops clean out of business.

Meantime, take a moment to be your own physician now. Close your eyes (when you've read this), imagine you're the doctor and ask yourself what's troubling you right now. Then listen deeply to the answer. Often, as any physician will tell you, the simple fact of being heard triggers a profound healing in itself. And that's my wish for you now. Did you get the healing?

Even dog dirt is a reminder of the greatness of life

I confess that the following is not an entirely original concept. It's already an infamous notion, due to its inclusion in my *Handbook for the Urban Warrior* as the 'I love doggy-do on my shoe contemplation'. But though I wrote it five years ago, the idea is still fresh in my nose, hence I thought I'd waft it your way today.

The basic premise is that you continually block your own enjoyment of the moment by unconsciously running your immediate experience through a series of filters, in an attempt to make order of 'reality'. These filters consist of a complex of learnt or inherited prejudices, which make you turn your nose up at almost everything that comes your way, even though at the deepest level you're actually revelling in the pure delight of being alive.

I noticed this myself – call me slightly quirky if you will – when, performing at an outdoor festival, barefoot, naturally, I wandered off into the bushes for a pee. The sun was shining, I'd just done a great gig, the audience was happy, the crew were congratulating each other, and now with bladder emptied, I hadn't a care in the world.

Then it happened – with a cold squelch and a slight skid. At first, I went into denial: that didn't happen; it did happen but it was just mud. But slowly as that all-too-familiar smell started pinging the olfactory centre in my brain, I had to admit to myself that this was pure, unadulterated festival doggy-do in all its tart and vulgar glory.

'Shit!' I muttered, with my usual penchant for overstating the obvious, imagining my social-pariah status for the rest of the day and making for the nearest stream. Clean-up is far easier on the naked foot than the usual messy malarkey you have to undergo with similarly besmirched shoes, not that I advocate actively seeking out the experience. The enlightening part was in the olfactory echoes that assailed me afterwards. Each time the smell re-registered, I realised profoundly that, just as when passing downwind of a manured field and every-one in the car's obliged to say 'Pooh!' but really, secretly, even to themselves, they all quite like it, I actually found the tartness, the pong, quite fascinating – disgusting yet fascinating. Secretly, even to myself, I realised it was only the filter I was running the experience through that was making me pre-judge this natural smell as bad.

Indeed, when composing a perfectly rounded perfume, you have to include ingredients every bit as pongy as doggy-dos, otherwise the smell floats too much and doesn't 'sit' well. Yet if you isolated those earthy ingredients, you would immediately shout 'Pooh!' I then extended the theory to include the people shouting pointlessly and drunkenly in the street outside my bedroom window at 4am, and realised it was only my filters that prevented my sheer exuberance at just being part of the general sway of humanity on a planet in space, no matter the noise.

You can extend the theory into any area of sensory input, and if you're honest with yourself, you'll find you actually love every smelly, disgusting, awful, tawdry aspect of life, simply because being alive in all its ramifications is a thrill. And that all that stops you relaxing into enjoying it fully is your complex of preconceptions.

This is no exhortation to seek pain and discomfort. This is an exhortation to allow yourself full enjoyment of the moment – because it's your moment and must not be wasted, even if that moment smells a bit tart.

Like a well-rounded fragrance, allow your experience to include all necessary ingredients, not just the sweet and soapy, but always tread carefully when stepping abroad unshod (it was actually pretty rank), filters or no filters.

Healing hands

There are a fair few people I love deeply on this planet, but perhaps none quite so deeply as my great-auntie Rae. She was the one who used to stroke my back for hours and hours in front of the fire on winter nights as a boy when we'd visit her in Manchester, and tell me wonderful stories in her exquisitely calm and soothing voice. An incredibly beautiful woman through and through. I'm convinced it was she who passed down the healing gene to me, not that I'm saying I'm such a beautiful guy, but I'm not that bad either. So it was a shock when my mum rang to tell me Rae was dying and we had to go and see her before she did.

I'm telling you this because it was one of those bizarre scenarios everyone has to go through from time to time. She's somewhere in her mid-90s, no one knows exactly how old because she hasn't let her age be known for at least the past 50 years – she's old-school like that – and the docs had decided that the diverticulitis she was apparently suffering from was going to carry her off any moment. She wasn't eating or drinking, she was in excruciating pain, she wasn't going to the loo and they surmised she wouldn't be able to last long like that. Thankfully, she was at home rather than in hospital and she was on a morphine drip, which would be gradually increased in dosage to keep the pain at bay, and this would weaken her further. So everyone was standing around waiting for her to die when I arrived with my mum, dad and sister (just like in the old days – it was nice in a funny kind of way).

She looked awfully thin and pale and was trembling at the lower lip in pain. I knelt down by the side of the bed and put my hand lightly on her forehead, tears streaming down my cheeks already and choking back sobs. She never noticed and I'm glad, as the last thing I wanted was to instigate a melodrama. I gently massaged her forehead and she seemed to calm down a bit.

'Stephen's fingers, that's all I need to make me better, Stephen's fingers,' she said a few times very quietly. I asked if she wanted me to put my hand on the pain and maybe try and ease it. She said yes, so I slid it under the covers and on to her belly. She guided it on to the epicentre of the pain. I stayed like that for about 40 minutes while everyone came and went out of the room, just allowing the heat to penetrate and talking to her intestines through my palms. I wasn't making a big deal about it, wasn't trying to heal her or make any miracles happen. It was just the only thing I could do. Making small talk or even discussing death would have been inappropriate. We both needed real contact here.

Every now and then I'd find the tears streaming again as the memories flooded back. I'll be honest with you, I'm crying as I write this, but this wasn't and isn't about me and my drama.

Eventually, it was time to leave, to drive back to London and my insane non-stop schedule (life goes on). It was weird saying goodbye, each of us knowing the next time we met it would most likely not be on earth, and off I went with my mum, dad and sister.

Anyway, the amazing thing is – and now I'm laughing aloud as I write – that night, Rae apparently got out of bed unaided and went to the loo. She started eating and drinking and the next morning asked to have her hair done. The pain subsided without an increase in the morphine and now the docs have put her on a much weaker painkiller which can be taken orally and they have all agreed she's no longer dying, just yet.

Which just goes to show you what a simple palm and a bit of love can do, and also how you should never jump to conclusions. I'm not saying it's a miracle, but I could.

However well things are going, we're never satisfied

I'm walking down a winding path through firs interspersed by the odd palm, under a Kodachrome blue sky, downhill towards the sparkling Mediterranean. This could be a perfect moment where I want for nothing. In fact, it couldn't be more perfect. So why could it not, I wonder, be a lot more perfect?

My mind just won't allow a moment of perfection to last more than three seconds before muscling in on the act and trying to find ways to improve things. It is this discontent and subsequent compulsion to reinvent and improve reality that fuels our progress as a species. It would be foolish to fight against it, so deeply embedded is it in our nature.

However, suffering arises to the extent that you identify with that within which feels the discontent and is compelled to change things. As the Buddha might have said, attachment to the process (of discontent and the subsequent need to meddle) causes the very pain which originally instigated and now perpetuates the process.

How do you know when you've become attached like this? When whatever's occurring in your mind is causing you to feel agitated, your belly (and bowels) to subtly tighten, your breathing to become shallow and irregular.

And how do you know when you're in the superhuman, Buddhalike mode? When you merely notice the discontent and accompanying physical state, but instead of feeling compelled to do or change something, you mentally release the constriction in your body, regulate and deepen your breathing, and allow yourself to relax and be happy.

This is not to advocate never trying to change things or being in denial about what ails you. On the contrary, this is about being fully aware of what's troubling you. But instead of rushing around trying to change the external conditions which are out of your control, you begin by changing the internal condition which is under your control and waiting graciously for the externals to change themselves. Perfection of the moment, in other words, doesn't arise from how blue the sky is but from how relaxed and willing to enjoy it you are.

The Taoists see it as sitting comfortably within your skin all the time no matter what the external conditions, an ability thought to be governed by your spleen. When spleen energy is weak, you tend to look more to the externals of life to induce comfort, which only ever provides momentary relief. Once the energy is adjusted, you find yourself feeling more fed from within by each moment, more content and satisfied no matter how seemingly imperfect your mind may be finding things.

You can help support your spleen energy by following a schedule for a few moments each day. First, stop holding yourself up and let yourself slump a bit. Feel the weight of your bones and settle into your skin. Stop holding your breath and let it flow freely. Relax your eyeballs and let them sink into their sockets so they're not busy constantly swivelling.

Press your fingers gently in and under your leftside front ribs to produce a noticeable sensation radiating across your belly, hold for a few moments and release slowly. Now rub your palms together briskly till they get hot and place them over the area, allowing the heat to penetrate deep inside. As you do, visualise your spleen suffused with bright yellow light and repeat words such as, 'I am willing to thrive in this moment on whatever I'm feeling, without feeling I have to change things!'

Good, I thought. Now that's written I can lie back and enjoy the beach. Mind you, I bet it would be a lot nicer to be on the deck of that cute little 35-footer out in the bay.

The healing art of... well, standing around

I'll be honest with you – and don't be envious, be inspired – I'm writing this from a subtropical island off the coast of Brazil, which my friend Mad J Riley, a retired film producer, shares with an army of monkeys, parrots, mammoth turquoise butterflies, iguanas, a mountain's worth of jungle, and pretty much no one and nothing else. He flew me out here for a week to fix his chronic back problem and talk about the possibility of us running little Barefoot healing retreats here on his island idyll, but we decided that, this being the real deal as opposed to the Club Med rehearsal scenario, with poisonous snakes and running water only after it rains, only the hardiest would even contemplate a visit, and that it might just be easier to keep it a secret.

Nonetheless, as I did my t'ai chi practice with the fragrance of frangipani flooding my olfactory nerve centre with almost too much information to handle, having slept out under the stars regrouping after a soul-stirring bumpy transatlantic night flight, I felt compelled to convey the sense of wellbeing overwhelming me now, that you may imbibe the vibe and inform your Sunday with a touch of raw paradise where quartz crystal sparkles in profusion underfoot.

But then breakfasting on the veranda on the best bananas ever tasted fresh off the tree, it suddenly felt unfair. I mean, how many of us can get jobs like this?

So to keep things fair as well as practical for general northern hemisphere usage, I analysed the rapid unwinding process I'd just engaged with and discerned the crucial technique that prevented me tipping into sensory overloadosis.

It turns out to be what those wily Taoists have set great store by for many thousands of years, claiming it rebalances even those with the greatest physical, mental, emotional or spiritual distortions – indeed, it's still used in hospitals in China – and it is ... simply standing about. Yes, simply standing can work wonders for mind, body and soul if practised correctly and daily over a long enough time frame. But you can also use it as an occasional treat to yourself, causing your blood and energy to flow more vigorously, your mind to work more clearly and your relationship with the world to take on a more colourful hue and tone.

To do it like the Taoists, stand with feet as if placed on parallel train tracks, knees slightly bent over the feet (not caving inwards), pelvis tucked under lightly, shoulders broad, back of neck relaxed and spine elongated. Breathing freely and fluidly, imagining yourself an angel with a 30ft wingspan, slowly raise your wings (arms) out in front of you as if pushing your wingtips against an invisible wall (30ft away). Keep your shoulders and face relaxed, touch your tongue to the roof of your mouth and feel yourself sinking through your soles into the centre of the earth. With every inbreath, imagine sucking life force up through your soles from the ground into your lower belly.

With every outbreath imagine it shooting up your spine, across your shoulder blades, down the outside of your arms, and out through your palms in two projectile streams aimed at the invisible wall.

Not only will just six minutes' practice make your arms fill with life force and calm pervade your mind, and make you feel more balanced than a pair of scales, it'll also make you the most magnetic girl or boy angel on the block.

A benefit I've just experienced for myself, having just magnetised old Riley up here from the beach where he was momentarily living the life of (Riley), into the kitchen to make me another of his absolutely killer cups of black coffee.

We are like a maze and our goal is to reach the centre

My life seems to have been transformed into a non-stop journey round and round the UK with an occasional stretch of the orbit to farther flung places, affording me only the occasional stop-off at HQ to repack my bag and use my own land line, which once you get used to it, as any common housefly will tell you, becomes extremely addictive, but more usefully provides time while on trains, planes and in automobiles to ponder the big wander down the 'great thoroughfare' of life.

I'm privileged in this respect because, left to my own devices, I'd just stay at home writing, being quiet and disappearing up my own large intestine and would never get to know, and hence discreetly claim as 'my own', these remarkable little islands we inhabit, meet and befriend their truly wonderful inhabitants, nor have a moment to contemplate the great mysteries – and seeing as I make my living from such contemplation would therefore soon be in the doghouse.

But perhaps the little island of the group that's impacted on my psyche most is the mysterious and immensely beautiful Isle of Man, where I've just been to give a workshop on 'The Tao of Being Amazing in Every Way!', an ambitious title and one I was only able to do justice to by the skin of my teeth. The premise being that you, in all your complex splendour, are like a maze, the goal (if there is one) being to reach the centre. When you do, all you find there, as with a real maze, is absolutely nothing – nothing that is, other than knowing you've triumphed in reaching the centre. However, if you gently train yourself to remain there, serenely observing the theatre of your life as you go about your everyday business, you become progressively more identified with your innermost spirit, itself akin to the Tao, the source of all existence and non-existence. Thus identified, life starts surprising you in the most pleasant way. No longer are you driven by the raging desires, fearful thoughts, misconceptions or other forms of delusion and disturbance of the forebrain. Suddenly, as if someone's lifted a 10-tonne weight from your shoulders, you feel spiritually light and nimble and able to accomplish whatever you choose in the manner of a small child innocently playing.

Now the Tao, if you were going to personify it for the sake of explanation, loves the sight of small children innocently playing. It naturally wants to join in – certainly much more than when it sees you playing the stultifying games of grown-ups. The Tao loves innocence, and being generous by nature will shower you with opportunities to manifest the life story you want – the more colourful, the better.

Chuang Tzu, ancient Taoist sage, said that once you've found stillness at the centre and can maintain awareness of its splendid silence as you operate on this noisy planet, even gods will flock to you, let alone mere mortals – the significance being that pretty much every opportunity comes to you through other people, hence the importance of being magnetic enough to draw others willingly into your orbit.

But how to reach this centre? Well, just as with a maze, you follow your nose. Literally, follow the line of your nose, allowing your attention to skateboard off the end and drop down into your belly. So as you sit here now, rather than being all concentrated in your brain, allow yourself the luxury of spreading out to all corners of the empire within. Your being literally fills your body from the belly outwards until you're consciously laying claim to every toe and finger, every bone, sinew, muscle, organ, blood vessel and nerve pathway – it's all yours. Obviously you don't own it, just as I don't own the British Isles, though if I did I'd adopt a low tax policy as in the Isle of Man, because I believe it generates a better economy than when everyone's being squeezed half to death as we're being on the so-called mainland – you don't own it, but you belong.

You may only achieve a momentary glimpse of the visceral sensation of being in the centre from time to time, but even a glimpse sets the magic working, and in time, with regular skateboarding off your nose, your awareness will grow until even gods will come flocking, let alone mere mortals.

Having faith in something – anything – keeps you going

I got an email from a guy asking about an *Observer Magazine* piece I once wrote in which I mentioned the Taoist myth of the 'sons of reflected light'. He asked if I knew of a web-link – www.takeallmythwithapinchofsalt.org, perhaps?

But it triggered me thinking (as these things do occasionally) about how we all – consciously or not – honour myths of one sort or another to lend authority to what we believe, think, say and do.

Take the God myth – not that I'm saying there's no God; to the contrary – but there's a distinct difference between the myth of God and God itself. Young Georgie Boy, for instance, invokes the authority of 'God' and so feels justified lowering the nuclear threshold and getting up to all kinds of world-threatening, naughty-boy war games. Or take a creationist – not that I mind what people choose to believe as long as they don't forcefully inflict it on others, and especially me. A creationist draws on the authority of the Old Testament to rationalise the world being only 6,000 years old. Without the authority of the book, most people would just laugh at them. As it is, most people just – well, they just laugh at them.

Even I myself, talking of laughter and fun – follower of the irreverent, make-up-your-own-reality-as-you-see-fit, formless Tao – could call upon the authority of those sons of reflected light of yore who were said to be 7ft tall, wear strange clothes, live in the high places, have come from goodness knows where, know everything about life, death, energy, consciousness and the Tao and who kindly passed on that information to the locals who became known as Taoists, and then vanished without trace. But, I wouldn't dream of doing so. Not because I don't think it's a quaint idea, nor without its romance. Indeed, it's an altogether scintillating notion. But as far as we know it's only that – a notion – just like all the other great myths that hold us in thrall.

So why bother? Surely the idea is to become less confused rather than more. I wouldn't want you to deprive yourself of myth, however – there's nothing like a good myth on a cold day with a bowl of hot tomato soup. Let people believe the myths they want to believe and feel free to change their beliefs as often as they choose – after all, they're only beliefs.

What's important and of real value, as opposed to relative, is not the myth you may feel tempted to use to justify yourself, but your own authority in terms of you being the one and only author of your own life story. You don't need to draw on any higher authority to justify the story you're creating – your very presence here is justification in itself.

It's a simple matter of recognising your own authority in generating your own life story. Obviously the way the story pans out is controlled entirely by the natural flow of events – the Tao – and how in accord you are with it. When you let go and flow with the way of things, always following the path of least resistance, like water, everything you've always wanted comes to you in its own time, fashion and form. How wonderful to dance with your Tao like that!

But to be in that flow you'll need to be grounded, relaxed and balanced. So here's a little Taoist exercise which, if adopted into your daily routine will, within but a few days, not only loosen and strengthen your hips and lower back, relax your shoulders and strengthen your arms, but also balance the two hemispheres of your brain and, above all, make you far more grounded – literally –

and it's called 'arse-walking', as practised by no-good, low-down Taoist bums like me for millennia.

Sit on the floor with legs out straight. Walk forward on your buttocks, first one, then the other, while softly throwing punches with the arm opposite the forward-most buttock. Do nine left and right 'steps' forward, then nine backwards. Then lie down for a moment to savour the feeling in your hips, contemplate the story you want, and say: 'It ain't nobody's business but my own!' or simply, 'I can do this!'

Creativity

Cultivating your creativity

When you hear mention of creativity, do you automatically think of some new marketing fad or team-building concept? Or do you see struggling artists in frayed knitwear on the Cornish coast? Perhaps it conjures images of art-therapy sessions or amateur photography classes. In short, does the idea of creativity elicit a response of, 'Oh, creativity, that's something for other people who haven't got more important things to do'? In fact, everyone is an artist or potential artist of some kind. The artistic or creative faculty is built into the circuitry as a preset in your DNA. That you may not yet have found the relevant command to activate it, or perhaps found it only to lose it again, is probably down to faulty conditioning by those in charge of your education.

The expression of the creative urge as some form of artistic offering to be enjoyed by others was considered by the ancient Orientals to be vital to one's wellbeing, not just emotionally, spiritually and psychologically, but also physically and energetically. They adhered to a concept known as mastering the 'five excellences', which comprised the arts of meditation, self-defence, healing, composition and presentation skills. A well-rounded, masterful individual was seen as one who was conversant in all five. The benefits of the first three are self-evident, but how, you'd probably wonder, would composition and presentation skills be beneficial to your health?

During the act of composing a piece of art, whether visual, filmic, sonic, literary, performance-oriented or indeed any other creativity-carrier of your choice, you ideally enter a quasi-meditative or contemplative state. When composing a painting, for instance, you gaze at the blank canvas until it reveals a subliminal shape, then, with mind emptied of preconceptions and with your energy extending through to the tip of the brush, you simply interpret the given shape, allowing yourself to get in the way as little as possible. If, say, you are approaching the composition of a piece of music, let the instrument or recording studio reveal the piece to you and proceed to interpret the information revealed according to your taste, allowing the music to play itself. You could call this the Tao or Sen of composition.

The necessary ego-voiding process involved allows your local mind precious moments of repose from the pressures of daily responsibilities, which helps slow your pulse and is generally good for energy flow and, by extension, immune response.

This process also implies a certain degree of conscious union with the a priori creative force, which tends to deepen your moment-by-moment experience of life in much the same way as does meditation, yoga or t'ai chi.

In the execution or presentation of the piece, you take a risk that others may deride you or your work. It requires courage to risk rejection and humiliation, making the act of carrying something through to this stage subtly exhilarating and self-esteem-building. It implies that you love or at least like yourself enough to spend time nurturing yourself. Moreover, it is at these times during which your overworked mind takes a brief holiday that some of your most original, important and life-changing ideas will emerge.

To enhance the creative flow, the ancient Taoists, who first developed the 'five excellences' concept, also devised certain meditative exercises, which, if practised on a daily basis for 30 days or so, will yield positive results.

Visualise a clear tube or channel of approximately 1in diameter beginning in the centre of the forehead between your eyebrows, running back along the midline of your skull, over the top of your brain to the medulla oblongata at the base of the skull where it meets the back of your neck.

As you breathe in, imagine you can feel the breath enter the channel through your forehead and travel backwards over the brain to the back of your head. As you breathe out, feel the breath return through the tube to the forehead. You can augment the exercise by mentally imbuing the breath with bright, clarifying light.

Repeat this cycle up to nine times each sitting. Don't make a big deal over it. Do it while watching TV or sitting on the train. As well as stimulating and enhancing creativity, this exercise brings great mental clarity, increases your ability to focus and tends to make you feel cheerful.

If you're of the persuasion that creativity is visited upon you by your muse or from the divine or heavenly realms, it also helps to visualise the top of your head opening up to receive or download information as if from above.

The biggest block to healthy and healing creative expression is the belief in an imaginary internal critic, who sits poised like a monkey on your shoulder ready at all times to tell you what you're doing is worthless and wrong. There's no point trying to argue with the critic. The best approach is either to use a stun gun or simply to ignore whatever negative messages you receive. Either way, overriding the critic is essential not only for bringing works of art to completion, but also for ensuring peace of mind in general.

The other block you'll have to surmount is impatience. It takes a long time and consistent application to develop a reliable creative channel and the skill to interpret and shape the information coming through into a form worthy of sharing.

Finally, remember creativity can be applied to every aspect of your life including the way you relate to yourself and others, the way you organise your timetable and the places you choose to spend your time in. However, pay attention lest the creative urge runs away with you and you end up a compulsive content-spewer like this barefoot doctor.

If finding your direction in life is driving you crazy, stimulate your lobes

A significant proportion of correspondence coming my way is taken up by people of all ages and circumstances attempting to find clarity and direction in life. When you're plotting your own course, you often haven't a clue what you're doing. You know you want to contribute something significant and feel fulfilled, whether in your career or personal life, but you're stumbling half-blind in the dark grasping for clues. At first you're running on raw faith alone, but your confidence grows as the path opens up before you. The more you risk stepping boldly forth, the brighter the light shines to show you the way. Like those escalators that only start once you step on them, you have to make the first move before the Tao (the mysterious process of destiny) takes you seriously and starts to deliver proof positive in the material world that you're going in the right direction.

Following the clues is like driving along in a strange town keeping an eye on the road signs, wondering whether the guys at the town hall have a perverted sense of humour – the way the signs suddenly stop at crucial points, and no matter how assiduously you've been watching out, you turn left at the T-junction instead of right and end up 20 miles in the wrong direction. Or maybe I'm just an idiot. Either way it provides a neat analogy for finding your direction in life.

Plotting your course along the 'great thoroughfare', it helps to know where you're headed, though it's not necessary to know precise details – just the vague essence will do. You don't need to specify the furniture and wall colours, in other words, just know you want to live in a suitable house that meets your requirements. You don't have to specify Brad Pitt or Penelope Cruz, it's enough to know you want a compatible, fulfilling, exciting relationship. You don't need to fantasise the job package, details, bonuses and health-care policy, you just need to know you want to be engaged in the appropriate work to satisfy you on every level.

The actual directions of how to get there, turning by turning, A road to B road and so on, come to you just like road signs as long as you're awake, alert and responsive. You'll see something, hear something, even smell something as you go about your daily business: a sign on the side of a passing truck, the smell of fresh mountain spruce (air-freshener) or the snatch of a song in the corner of your ear – and it triggers an urge to make this move or that.

And while on the subject of ears and their corners, sailors from ancient Egypt actually took to wearing earrings, having learnt from the Chinese with whom they traded that regular tugging on the ring stimulates an acupuncture point in the dead centre of the ear lobe, which boosts your intuitive faculties by energising the 'third eye' in the centre of your brain. If you don't sport a tuggable earring, support either ear lobe now with your thumb and use the corner of the nail on your forefinger to press into the lobe's centre in a brisk on-off motion, 18 times, then repeat on the other side immediately to begin stimulating your own psychic faculties. Continue to do so daily for at least three weeks and you'll see for yourself how it used to help them navigate when the stars were obscured by clouds.

Indeed, diligent regular application could have you opening your own beach-front stall in Brighton in no time, knocking Madam Rosa clean out of a job, becoming a Russian spy or indeed finding an entirely original direction you'd never previously considered. At any rate, you'll be doing better than me – now sitting here stimulating my own lobes – evidently in need of a good squeeze: you see, I've snapped off this entire piece on my travelling gizmo while utterly stuck in a monster jam heading into Manchester, when I should actually be in deepest Cheshire by now, having turned left at the junction instead of right.

Listen to your inner demons and you'll block your creativity

I was talking to a writer friend of mine, a successful novelist complaining of crippling writer's block and thinking how fortunate I am not to suffer likewise. I then sat down inspired to write a piece and fell to wondering what to write about. Is it catching? I worried for a moment.

I go through quite a process before sitting at the keyboard to write. I talk the piece through in my head while doing t'ai chi or taking a shower – sometimes for days – and then suddenly, without warning, I'm writing it and out it comes in one long uninterrupted stream – hopefully in a fashion that will add something to your life in a sensible way. I care deeply about you the individual (even though I don't even know what you look like), about humankind in general, and about the editorial staff at the *Observer Magazine* to whom I'm grateful for lending me this platform – what a privilege.

Yet like my friend, who worries so much now about his next book being thought inferior to his last that his fingers have spasmed above the keys, I too worry about what you think (about me). Even though I agonise about it sometimes, I do have a way of overriding such considerations – otherwise this page would be blank – and believe it to be a way worth sharing, as it applies to any endeavour you may be undertaking in your own life.

We all suffer from the internal critic, the one who keeps saying, 'No, that's rubbish – no one will fall for it – they'll think you're this, they'll think you're that...', and this holds true whether it's writing a piece, speaking out at a meeting, or even asking for a drink at a crowded bar. It all requires the confidence – literally, the faith in your own naked self, to bypass the negative and do, say or write what you feel in your gut to be right – even at the risk of making an utter fool of yourself.

The way I do it – it's very childish – is to picture the critic sitting in that great cinema within, watching (critically) the movie of my life story as it unfolds in my forebrain. I then approach him authoritatively and escort him round the back of the house, and there, standing against the wall, give him a slap in the style of a pre-revolution French aristocrat provoking a duel and firmly tell him to shut up. He can come back in and enjoy the movie, but he has to keep his thoughts to himself. Not particularly democratic, but it works. He comes back in, sits down, watches the movie and keeps his thoughts to himself, leaving me free to write, or in your case free to accomplish whichever task you were holding back from for fear of the opprobrium of others.

Challenging yourself physically on a daily basis also helps in this respect. For example, if you can't do three press-ups, make it your business to do three press-ups. If you can do three, make it your business to do nine and so on. Obviously, substitute press-ups for any exercise of your choice. But the point is, if you can push past the resistance in your mind enough to meet the physical challenge, you can push past resistance to accomplishing anything.

These days, anything you think of to discuss other than the headlines seems trivial. By the same token, it's hard to get anything done when your head's full of the headlines. But there's no point allowing the news to stop you being the most creative you can be. In fact, I'd say it was a duty to be as creative in your own way as you can every moment of the day for ever more – otherwise what's the point of being here?

So ask your critic to kindly step outside, give them a respectful slap, tell them to shut up, come back in, do a few more press-ups – more than you thought you could – and create something stupendous.

We know the answer already, we just have to learn to ask the question

As things get more fraught and frantic with more and more on your mind, and decisions are needed fast for all kinds of issues from the smallest detail of, say, which shirt to wear, to the biggest dilemma about what to do with your life, for instance, it becomes increasingly crucial to be able to access the intuitive part of your mind. Of course this begs the question, can you really trust your intuition? Shouldn't you use rational, logical processes to arrive at your decisions?

Not according to Einstein, who arrived at his biggest contribution through intuition, nor the ancient Taoists, who taught that the creative spark – that which gives you the answers – which originates from goodness knows where, but let's call it for the sake of argument the Tao, is accessed from that layer of self which is merged with the Tao, deep within the chest in fact – the so-called heart centre – but is only available to you if you step back from the machinations of the calculating intellect or rational mind. However, once the answer-carrying creative spark is through, you then bring your intellect to bear on how best to execute the appropriate plan of action.

I've spoken about the importance of intuition before in sourcing the correct data for decision making, but then it's an important topic, though truthfully, what inspired me today was a phone call from my beloved agent, the Silver Shadow, to say her car had just been stolen and to ask me where it was. This not because she suspected me of thieving it, but because she trusts my intuition, it having been methodically trained while studying Taoist medicine up in the mountains many years ago.

So I let my mind go blank, relaxed my chest and before I could say Christopher Robbins, up popped the answer, or rather picture in my brain. 'It's to the southwest of your house, in a road beginning with "D".' And would you know it, she went out immediately, walked in a southwesterly direction and found it two streets away in a road beginning with 'D' without a scratch or broken lock in sight. My thanks for that was being told I scared her, but nonetheless, it reignited my enthusiasm for the whole idea of developing your intuition. It takes practice – it's a natural faculty we all have, but learn to recognise the intuitive information as it arises and to trust yourself to go with it.

I've noticed it also works well for figures. When negotiating a deal with someone, for example, ask yourself what percentage they're after, drag your thoughts into the trash, clear the desktop of your mind and see the amount flash up in your forebrain, then ask them, but interject with the amount just before they say it, and more often than not you'll be right. These things are given – they already exist in the unformed universe, the latent realm – and just need discovering, but the ability to allow that process takes practice.

So next time your mobile rings, quieten your thoughts momentarily, relax your chest and see if a face or name appears in your mind. Then look at the screen to check your accuracy. And don't be disheartened if you get it wrong the first few times – like a muscle, your intuition needs exercise to come fully alive.

You can help it energetically by rubbing briskly and firmly on your upper arms, one arm at a time, approximately at that dimple where your shoulder-cap muscle meets your biceps, in an up and down motion long enough to generate palpable heat, then press firmly into the dimple with your thumb and hold for a few seconds. This point, known in acupuncture circles as l.i.14, is famous for its efficacy in promoting intuition, but also be sure to help your chest relax by placing your palm over your breastbone and rubbing slowly in clockwise circles till you feel the tension begin to drain away. Finally, practise emptying your mind – close your eyes and focus on nothing from time to time. Now tell me where I left my keys – first one with the answer gets a treatment!

How life can be like a feel-good movie

When you watch a movie, you're actually watching a succession of still frames moving along seamlessly to create the illusion of unbroken action, at a rate of 24 frames per second – just fast enough to trick the eye (and brain). If you stopped to ask one, a Taoist would suggest that this so-called real life we're all so busy living and defending, if seen from an enlightened perspective, is itself of no more solidity or validity than a movie. It is, they would say, a mere trick of the light – a series of still frames or momentary mindsets, running past you fast enough to trick the eye (and brain) into a sense of real-time continuity.

If you bothered to engage in the necessary rudimentary calculations (I used my mobile phone till it ran out of memory), to multiply 24 frames per second by the average lifespan of say 70 years, it comes out to 53bn frames. Roll that around your brain for a moment – 53bn still frames give or take a few billion. Imagine it in pounds, euros even. Doesn't it fill you with an overwhelming sense of abundance?

Even assuming you've been riveted by 20 to 30bn of the little monkeys already, you still have an enormous amount of wealth left – certainly enough to see you through to old age. I say wealth because ultimately you can only measure true wealth by the amount and quality of frames at your disposal.

So now you know, what are you going to do with it all? What kind of movie do you want from here on in? Think about tone, texture, coloration, plot and storyline, dynamics, style of co-star and supporting actors, locations, lighting, angles, philosophy, tension levels, type of ending, comedy, suspense, mysticism and violence-factor levels, shoes, clothes, hairstyles and that sort of thing.

This is because, as any budding Bodhisattva will tell you, it's entirely up to you what kind of reality you inhabit. You as an individual create your reality according to the beliefs you choose to follow. When you can vision it strongly enough it will manifest. That's the basic tenet of every religion, occult system and spiritual path since time began. The world around you will in time reflect the vision you hold to in full 'sensaround' with Dolby and the whole works.

This even includes whether the world is at peace or at war. The awful destruction we've seen in recent years is Hollywood's worst vision made manifest. So how about a vision of the entire human race finally transcending the cycle of violence and retribution, evolving beyond this infantile need to always be and, more importantly, always be seen to be, right.

And yes, I know Bertrand Russell assured us we never would achieve such a state, but maybe he was really just a negative old sod and his thinking a product of a negative time. So let's drop all limitations on our collective imagination now and envision a world where everyone from every culture, nation and creed has evolved beyond the deranged ape stage. Maybe it will require that every person learn t'ai chi or another non-aggressive martial art from childhood onwards. Maybe we'll need to spray super-concentrate MDMA powder over everyone so they all give each other a hug and go home to chill (the hippie version of chemical warfare). But maybe, just maybe, if enough of us can regularly and steadfastly hold to a vision of an entire race not governed by the constant need to be seen to be right, a race more concerned with kindness than violence and greed, and a race liable to discuss, negotiate and above all have the maturity to agree to disagree with those holding opposing views, maybe the vision will materialise out here on the planet just in time to prevent the current wave of twisted darkness taking hold of and putting a premature end to our collective destiny.

This is an amazing planet. Our existence here is an utter miracle. To waste it and to waste the lives of others in the name of a mere ideology represents the most stupid move the human race has made since agreeing to believe in religions in the first place. Let's leave the past and reverence for it where it belongs now – in the past. Let's drop this absurd reverence for the words of men long dead, however inspired they were 800 or 2,000 years ago. There've been a lot of frames under the bridge since then. Let's drop the past now and start afresh with a new storyline based on ideas we make up ourselves. And let those ideas include tolerance, wisdom, kindness and global consciousness.

Here, pass the popcorn.

Mind Power and Affirmations

Looking on the bright side

There is no such thing as a neutral thought. In any one moment, this one, for instance, you have the choice – and the right to exercise that choice – between responding negatively or positively to any new influx of information, in what-ever format it may appear (this piece, for example).

As infants, we internalise both negative and positive aspects of our impres-sions received from parents, peers and teachers; in other words, we create (imaginary) characters based on them, with whom we people the internal world of our psyches. Without realising, we tend to delude ourselves into believ-ing our thoughts are under their command. This works in our favour where the internalised qualities are positive and to our detriment where negative. Very few of us have or have had 'perfect' childhoods, so if unchecked, our minds gen-erally tend to react negatively when faced with new information. Indeed, if you've been habitually responding negatively for years, suddenly telling your-self to think positively instead feels like a con trick to train yourself to respond positively to whatever life throws up.

And that's because it is – a trick you play on yourself, requiring for its suc-cessful operation your exercise of self-confidence: as I believe, so shall it be.

It's a trick that's been used effectively for aeons. It is taught as fundamental self-preservative knowledge by every spiritual path from Buddhism to New-Ageism, including Christianity. Jesus purportedly used positive-thinking power to heal as in, 'Pick up your bed and walk!' and the patient, momentarily infused with the healer's positivity, was so convinced by it that he picked up his bed and walked (if you go with the Chinese whispers as to the way it all happened).

You choose the way your mind responds to reality, and reality in turn tends to respond to the way your mind responds to it – 'when you're smiling, the whole world smiles with you', etc.

When 'things' appear to be going against you, and you discipline yourself to focus on the benefits of the situation, however tenuous, your willingness to be positive not only makes you more pleasant to be around for yourself and others, but tends to encourage events to turn more swiftly in your favour.

Obviously, however highly disciplined, no one can remain exclusively in the positive state – it would defy the laws of physics. Even the Buddha had his bad-hair days (or at least bad-pate days). According to the fundamental principle of yin and yang – what goes up must come down – you can't know positivity without knowing its opposite. The idea is to strike a balance between them tilted at least 51 per cent into the positive most of the time. This is best achieved not by focusing on eliminating the negative – what you focus on tends to expand in influence – but on increasing input and development of the positive. The negative will then naturally fall away by itself.

The quickest way to reprogramme is through giving commands to yourself, commonly known as 'doing affirmations', in the form of writing each command at least six times. (It has been found to require a minimum of six repetitions to penetrate the unconscious fully.) Obviously, it also helps to have them scrolling across your computer screen or fixed with a magnet to your fridge door, to repeat them in your mind or out loud while stuck in traffic, and even to shout them from the rooftops, if you think you've got what it takes. The point is to inculcate positive thoughts in your circuitry to override the negative ones, by repetition.

You can use any words you like, as long as you keep it positive. The unconscious mind recognises only the positive part of any given command. If I said, 'Don't be happy now', your mind would only register, 'Be happy now.'

Imagine you've got deadlines to meet. You're talking on one phone, the other one's ringing, and the 80 emails you've just replied to have just replied back, along with 69 new ones. If you take a moment out to write down six times, 'By relaxing my mind and body, breathing and staying focused on one thing at a time, I am able to achieve superhuman amounts easily, effortlessly (even miraculously)', you may be surprised at how easily the work gets done.

Self-help bookshelves are crammed full of books on the topic, so let me not bore you now with more detailed explanations except to say that the most powerful and straightforward affirmation is to say 'yes'. Say 'yes' to life and whatever it throws in your path. Say 'yes' to optimising your experience of life, whatever the circumstances. As an exercise, try it now: when I ask, 'Don't you feel a little more uplifted after reading this?', you reply...

Think positive

It is widely accepted that positive thinking is not only good for your health and state of mind, but also helps you achieve your goals more easily. However, being the grumpy, destructive bunch we are, thinking positively is a habit we have to teach ourselves, and there is no better way than using what became widely known in the mostly California-centred 'human potential movement' of the 70s as 'doing positive affirmations'.

The way affirmation works is similar to the effect of writing 100 lines in school detention: 'I will not talk in class!', for instance. The drawback there is the unconscious mind registers only the positive section of any command and would, in the above example, register 'talk in class!' – line-writing thus only ensuring a steady flow of further detention-room traffic.

Doing positive affirmations means you have to phrase the command only in the positive. (I say 'command' because affirmations are nothing more than auto-suggestion – giving your unconscious mind a positive command.) It doesn't matter how you frame the command, as long as the crucial, active part is positive.

But there's no point kidding yourself. If you've been suffering from chronic depression, there's no way your mind will react cooperatively with such sentiments as: 'I now feel happy all the time!', no matter how many times you repeat it. This is not about brainwashing yourself. It's about accepting where you are and remembering you have the choice to change it. Your mind would be much more likely to accept, 'Through this depression, I learn to face the dark side of myself. Through facing and accepting the darkness, I grow, and in my growth process I find my peace of mind.' Or more simply put: 'Out of this darkness will come great light!'

It is not about denial. If you're struggling with your cashflow – broke, in other words – you won't fool your mind by repeating, 'I am rich, I am rich!' Instead affirm: 'Having no money is teaching me I can survive on very little. Knowing this helps me be more comfortable with the whole material-survival issue. The more comfortable I am with the material plane, the more able I am to operate effectively on it.' This commands your mind to see the positive in your present situation and to open itself to the possibility of an improvement in circumstances.

If, however, you veer more towards the magical view of life, you could affirm: 'Money is now coming to me in huge bundles from every direction at once!' (This one generally works, by the way, and I take only 10 per cent commission.)

More important, though, are affirmations designed to produce change in the way you respond to life by developing your positive qualities. If you have tried the money affirmation for three weeks and 100 grand still hasn't landed in your lap, you may wish to affirm an increase in patience and trust levels. You could repeat: 'I am capable of exercising infinite patience and trust in life's benevolence now' or simply: 'I have infinite patience and trust when I feel like accessing it.'

The most effective way to get these affirmations to lodge in your unconscious mind and thus enable you to override the negative is to write each one down at least six times each (the six or more repetitions it takes to infiltrate the brain's circuitry). Writing things down is the simplest way to fix the idea. But this is not to say that repeating affirmations out loud or even singing them to yourself isn't also highly effective.

The best time to 'do' your affirmations is when you'd be otherwise wasting time and energy sitting around worrying or getting gloomy. Instead, use your time and energy to do some positivity training. Other useful times are while sitting in trains, buses, boats and planes, or instead of doodling, sending silly emails or playing computer games while at work – procrastinating, in other words.

It generally takes about three weeks of daily affirmation-doing before you begin to see results. But natural serendipity aside, the bigger the thing you're affirming for, the longer it usually takes. Though you could always affirm: 'The bigger the thing I affirm, the more quickly it manifests for me!'

You can, in fact, completely and radically alter the entire structure of reality over time, doing affirmations (so be careful what you affirm). Although, according to that old Scottish 'taoist' aphorism, 'What's for ye won't pass ye by and what passes ye by was nay for ye', affirmation-doing will only clarify what you actually want and through clarification accelerate the process somewhat.

Let me leave you with a suggested affirmation for the upcoming week: 'Through the rigours of modern life, petrol shortages, unpredictable weather patterns and train timetables, I realise what a magnificent experience life can be and am uplifted!'

Directing mind power

According to a recent scientific discovery made by Dr John Gabrieli of Stanford University, California, certain people's brains don't appear to have the physical capacity to respond to pleasurable input, thus rendering them incapable of adopting a positive attitude, no matter what (they can't help it, in other words, and should therefore give up trying). I consider that conclusion defeatist, and would like to ride to the rescue with a few holistically minded ideas of my own.

It is my belief that when you discipline yourself to think positively or optimistically, you can alter brain function so that it lights up the appropriate 'emotion' centres whenever you have a positive thought, no matter how much of a grump you are by natural constitutional disposition.

Both in theory and practice, mind power is of paramount importance to holistic medicine. The ancient Taoists evolved the necessary techniques to develop and harness mind power in the service of healing self and others. They found that if one was able to collect one's consciousness into a tight ball, as it were, concentrated in the centre of one's brain, one could effect profound and radical changes in the physical structure of the body itself. Indeed the first acupuncture treatments were self-administered by early psychic explorers in a series of so-called trance patterns, comprising the insertion of 36 gold needles in various locations around the cranium. Effectively, these trance patterns would act as an inhibitor of forebrain activity, the site of one's internal dialogue, which otherwise would occlude the inner clarity prerequisite for self-healing. From this centre-brain vantage point, they found themselves able to command the actual cells of their bodies.

The Taoists also discovered that mind power was greatly amplified when harnessed to the breathing process. Once mind and breath are united, a form of psychically charged energy is generated, which the Taoists call 'chi' or light. When you send a thought to your right hand but at the same time breathe out imagining the breath to be travelling down your arm to your palm, for example, you are 'sending' chi or light to your hand. This can be applied to any body part of your choice. Sending chi is the essence of all Oriental healing practices, including acupuncture, shiatsu (acupressure), and chi-gung healing. Even herbology focuses on clearing the pathways for chi to flow through.

When you send chi to a particular part of your own body, semi-miraculous physical transformations can occur (I've seen it over and over in my own practice). So when it comes to rearranging the structure of the emotional centres of your brain, it is certainly possible (according to those Taoists) to do so successfully, if you're willing to dedicate a small amount of time each day to focusing on it.

As the unconscious mind tends to default to negative mode unless otherwise instructed, it is also crucial to insert positive commands along with the chi as this hones mind power. You may wish to inwardly command such sentiments as, 'I am now restructuring my brain cells on an atomic level to enable me to respond more readily to positive input.' Or you could simply say something like, 'Heal, you buggers!' It all depends on what kind of relationship you conduct with yourself.

In fact, the whole art of positive thinking, especially with regards to self-healing, depends entirely on forming a respectful, warm and loving relationship with your own mind and body. With that in mind, think of one body part that needs attention – any part will do – and with consciousness assembled in the centre of your brain, breathe out and feel the breath travel from centre brain to chosen body-part, along with the command to heal.

Adopting the holistic approach requires you make a choice between seeing yourself as a victim of circumstance or as a pro-active co-creator of your own reality. As a victim you say, 'This is how I was born. My brain composition is such that I am a naturally negative, pessimistic person.' As a pro-active co-creator you say, 'Whatever occurs within my body is under direct command of part of my own mind, however apparently inaccessible, and is therefore susceptible to suggestion.'

It's apparent to everyone by now that when you train yourself to meet the world with a positive attitude, the world treats you in much more magnanimous way, and at those times that it doesn't, you handle it better anyway.

Conversely, when you meet the world with a negative attitude, you'll get a negative result. Which is why it's so important that before even thinking about going out to meet the world every morning, you spend at least the minimum amount of time necessary to readjust your attitude towards the positive.

Tell your mind, 'This is my day, and I intend to enjoy it no matter what the external conditions!' (That's the spirit.)

Learning your true worth

I keep having this crazy thought. If someone inclined to such things winched an elephant up in the air above your head and offered you five grand to let them drop it on you, would you accept? Fifty grand? Five million?

Fifty billion? Of course you wouldn't. (I said it was crazy.) But how effectively (albeit simplistically) it serves as an indicator of your true sense of self-worth – £50bn is a lot of money to turn down, after all.

Where am I going with this, you ask. Well, it would seem to me that lack of self-worth is at the root of all evil. Not money, nor even greed for money – these are just effects.

For surely – and I'm asking you to jump in deep with me here – if you're fundamentally aware that your worth exceeds at least £50bn (in dollars, euros or whatever), you treat yourself differently. Or, to be more precise, to the extent that you're aware of your true worth, you treat yourself – and by extension, others – differently. This in turn will cause others, life in other words, to treat you differently, too.

If you go with the idea that you create the reality you experience with the ideas you follow and that the way you experience reality (within) directly affects the way others experience you, it follows that when you know your worth, others will experience you as worthy. A person regarded as one of worth or virtue (as the ancient Taoists described it) has a far easier time of it than the usual run-of-the-mill, unvirtuous so-and-so.

According to the Taoists, when you truly believe you're worth in excess of £50bn, wealth will come to you with ease and of itself. Not only wealth, but respect, status, renown, love and all the other goodies in life's temporal grab bag. This is because when you know your worth, your ego is complete. There is nothing in you reaching out for validation. No advertiser's hook that can snag your wallet. You are complete as you are. No longer need you buy into anyone else's brand (promise of completeness) to feel whole. Your ego, that nagging sense of 'I' that wants constant feeding, is healed and thus transcended. The internal niggling stops.

And because you're now so empty and peaceful, even gods and spirits come to you, not to mention mere mortals (if any purists out there will excuse me so crudely paraphrasing Chuang Tzu). And with them come all the opportunities necessary to achieve your healthy growth and total fulfilment.

There'll be no more need for greed, itself a manifestation of fear of not being able to get what you need (in case you don't deserve it). There'll be no need for road, desk, bed (or wherever else) rage because you will no longer take others' inadvertent disregard personally.

With your ego complete, you will no longer need to seek approval, validation or completion – professionally, socially, or personally. Imagine how different all your relationships will be.

But surely this blissful state would inevitably end up leading to complacency and laziness – surely without the nagging drive to prove yourself 'in the eyes of the world', you'd be completely without motivation?

No, because with all those gods and spirits coming to you on account of the spacious, peaceful (and unneedy) inner environment you offer, you'll be flooded with creative impulses appropriate to your field of endeavour begging for expression and will be driven to comply (or go mad). So no worries on that score.

Which is all well and good, provided you were blessed with parents, siblings and teachers wise and compassionate enough to nurture you carefully and thoroughly. All well and good for that tiny minority of naturally perfected beings in our culture. (So tiny, I've never met or heard tell of one.)

But what about the vast majority of us, with all our idiosyncratic chinks, kinks and foibles? How can we begin the ego-mending process and thus increase our sense of self-worth sufficiently to get our £50bn's worth?

Try this for starters: imagine that deep in your chest sits a little being (Tom or Tomella Thumb), a perfect little being – the you you would be, had you benefited from perfect childhood nurturing – the you without flaw. As you breathe gently in and out, imagine this being growing larger and larger. See the being expand past the bounds of your body, growing larger than the room, the building, the town, the county, the country, the continent, the planet, the solar system and all the way out until the entire universe 'fits' within your being's belly. Now, in this subtle state of expanded awareness, suggest sentiments to yourself along the lines of 'I contain the entire universe – all of it is mine – that's how worth it I am!' And then imagine the being diminish in size until it sits comfortably once again in your chest – and simply carry on as you were.

Well, it's a start, and if daily practice of that doesn't produce tangible external results within three weeks or so, there's always the elephant option. Frankly, I'd be tempted to go for the £50bn and run like the wind.

Remembering to remain focused

Every morning I go into the garden and spend a couple of hours running through a ritual of Taoist warm-up exercises, t'ai chi, hsing i and pa kua practice (Taoist internal boxing forms), followed by a while standing or sitting to meditate.

By the time I'm finished, I'm as clear as a bell, agile as a ballet dancer and ready for action. Then I walk back into the house. As I pass through the kitchen door, I kick over the dustpan and brush, knock the mop over, brush past all the washing so it falls on to the floor, and splash myself by turning the tap on too strongly causing it to bounce off the kettle and soak me.

Now how could someone so utterly centred and honed for the day ahead suddenly transform into such a bumbling fool?

It's easy. All you have to do is go unconscious for a moment, somewhere on the walk between garden and back door. And in that moment of forgetting about remaining centred, your mind is instantly distracted and flooded with thoughts, you come out of your body and into your head and then, no matter how centred you were a few seconds back, it's bang, clatter and splosh all over the kitchen and you're wasting precious early-morning nanoseconds clearing up the mess when you should be getting ready for work.

So I watch myself like watching a clown in the circus and I laugh, but it makes me wonder about continuity. It makes me wonder how to maintain an unbroken thread of 'now-centred' awareness, so that everything I do is t'ai chi, whether it's washing dishes or showing off on telly. But mostly I watch the process for clues so I can pass them on, as that's my job. So I'm always looking for new angles to explain the ancient wisdom in clearer ways.

What I have noticed is that, when I remember to remind myself, 'I choose to continue this thread of awareness unbroken through the day like a string of fine pearls,' I'm able to negotiate re-entry through the kitchen without incident.

If you remember to remain mindful, in other words, mindful you'll remain. But as soon as you forget and lose yourself, it could be days before you come back to yourself, having scattered who knows how many piles of fallen laundry in your wake.

Obviously I offer my bumbling fool-in-the-kitchen example as a metaphor. I'm sure you have your own version, where the mops and laundry are people you inadvertently let down, for instance, or deadlines you leave unmet. But other than reminding yourself to remember, how else can you anchor your mind in your body, so you maintain sight of the deeper plot as you go about your daily business?

Of course, regular daily practice of any psycho-physical discipline such as t'ai chi, yoga, Pilates, and so on will, over time, trigger an automatic consistent flow of awareness that lasts throughout the day like a good anti-antiperspirant and is strongly recommended.

But, with or without such practice, in order to enhance the anti-bumble factor, it's vital that you slow your breathing down to a sedate pace and regulate the length of the in and out breaths.

In fact, there is no more efficient way of getting a grip on your mental tempo. When mental tempo speeds up past a sedate 80BPM, it tends to draw the energy and heat of the body into your head, stimulating even more mental activity and decreasing synaesthetic awareness (body sense). Slowing the breathing tempo down so each inhalation lasts approximately five seconds and each exhalation likewise will return your mind to a workable speed and afford you more awareness of your body, enabling you to leave most (of life's) mops standing.

Finally, it pays to spend a moment morning and evening applying pressure to the centre of each heel. This has the effect of drawing energy and heat in a downward direction but also draws awareness to the heel, where you can visualise a small aperture through which you imagine yourself to be breathing.

Try it, and, as you breathe slowly in and out, tell yourself, 'By breathing through my heels like this, I reinforce my sense of groundedness and am able to go about my day without being a bumbling fool like (say) Barefoot Doctor. (But if I do find myself being a bumbling fool, I'll forgive myself for it.)'

Now we are six: avoiding self-pity

Have you noticed how the question of what it means to be an adult still sur-faces with some regularity as the years go by? One thing's for sure, it's nothing to do with age. I'm 49 and still enter the debate as a six-year-old pretender, sur-prised that all the grown-ups at the dinner table are talking so politely to me, a mere child. Then I remember that though they may look like my old headmaster or schoolfriends' mums, they're all at least five years younger than I am.

One benchmark I'm working on is the self-pity factor, or more precisely, the unclaimed self-pity factor. Obviously, having a good moan to a friend or loved one is essential therapy from time to time, and providing you get the moan over with and subsequently return fortified to the emotionally upright posi-tion, your adulthood is in no way diminished.

But whenever you default to self-pity mode without awareness, you're lost in playing the part of a whining child, no matter how you dress it up or justify it.

Whenever you carry your responsibilities without complaint, having reached a stage of personal development where you've now learned to value your life and everything it brings you, that's the point at which you enter the 'state of grace'. The Taoists call one who walks in a state of grace a person of true virtue, or 'te'. Te people (and I don't mean Tetley's) are the world's heroes.

But no one is in a state of virtue all the time. You flip in and out of it, hero to cur, adult to spoilt brat at the drop of a hat.

The art – and this is the second benchmark – is to remain mindful as you transit from one to the other. This gives you consistency, both in your internal dialogue and in your dialogue with others. Not consistency of behaviour, as in the hobgoblin of the middle classes sense, but consistency of presence of self as brought to bear on the moment, no matter what kind of moment it is, nor in whose company you're spending it.

Self-pity tends to arise when your spleen chi (energy) is weak. Just as your spleen chi governs the efficiency with which you process food and your ability to use it to your advantage, causing you to feel satisfied when replete, it also governs the efficiency with which your intellect processes information in order to reach a state of psycho-emotional satisfaction.

Self-pity is insidious. It disguises itself like a virus, attaching itself to the host body, your thoughts, colouring them with negativity, without you even realising, and before you know what's happening, you've succumbed and have fallen from the state of grace (yet again).

The main tell-tale sign is you find you're not enjoying yourself even though nothing awful has happened and conditions are pretty much the same as an hour ago when you were enjoying yourself. So, whenever you catch yourself moaning and complaining for example about how tough life is, how tired you feel, how much you have to do and how there's never any time for you to recharge, it indicates you've fallen off the skateboard, lost your ground; and your spleen chi, which is associated with the 'earth' element, is weak.

Moreover, consistency of mindfulness, (the second benchmark), is also governed by your spleen chi, which is said to 'house' your intellectual, hence discriminatory, faculties.

(Please note that, traditionally, Oriental medicine would say it was your spleen itself that is responsible for these functions, but as this would naturally elicit piles of harrumphing complaint letters from well-meaning members of the medical profession, I use the term 'spleen chi' instead, because how can you argue with something called 'chi'? It would be like picking a fight with a panda – or at least half a panda.)

Conversely, when your spleen chi is strong, you are far more energetically disposed to shouldering your burden without complaint and remaining aware of yourself through the pendulum swings between self-pitying and heroic modes.

Not that simply sticking your fingers under your ribs in the front on the left until producing a pleasantly winded feeling for 30 seconds three times a day will in itself prevent or cure self-pity and thus make you a person of true virtue, but it will help set up the right energetic conditions in which to retrain your mind along more naturally heroic lines.

Do it now, if you want to, and as you release the pressure, suggest to your unconscious mind: 'Nothing ever great was achieved through indulging in self-pity. I now choose to take my place among the adults and shoulder my burden with grace and aplomb!'

And now I'm rather tired, it's a tough life, I have loads too much to do and no time to rest and recharge, so I think I'll go and suck my thumb for a bit.

Life can be like a roller coaster, so enjoy the ride

I don't know about you, but I really hate scary fairground rides, where spinning on the big wheel, being hurled round impossibly sharp bends and slung down improbably steep slopes on the big dipper makes you feel like you've left your stomach behind, as you pray that the people paid to maintain the ride have been doing their job properly. So much so, in fact, that I vowed years ago to eschew such activities and save my energy for throwing myself more whole-heartedly into the bigger fairground ride of life itself.

Which is why I was surprised the other day to find myself just beneath that huge statue of Jesus that stands with arms outstretched on top of Tibidabo, that high hill above Barcelona, blessing all the people in the city below. I had just inexplicably willingly strapped myself into a rickety old swing, suspended by two 20m chains on one of those high-speed merry-go-rounds with the telescopic axles that elongate and shorten as you accelerate, causing such an intensification of sensation of centrifugal force you wonder if your stomach will dislocate from your upper body altogether.

To augment the sensation, as the ride gathered speed and height, three-quarters of the swing's orbital trajectory had me extended horizontally approximately 500m above a sheer drop over the city beneath, so that if one of those rusty old chainlinks were to snap, I would be catapulted far into the blue winter sky like a magnificent barefoot human cannonball to be finally splattered ignominiously among the mime artistes and late-afternoon strollers on the distant Ramblas below.

Call me a silly billy to make such a fuss, but being rather sceptical about the local maintenance standards – albeit probably far higher than Railtrack's – and reasoning that general wear and tear must eventually take its toll, I gripped hard on to the chains, prayed for salvation to the statue above, closed my eyes and pretended I wasn't there.

Meantime, I was willing the ride to stop and when it finally did I staggered away amazed to see my friend Nico Rhamodda, founder member of the Flying Dudes trapeze crew, stay on for a second ride. As the engine picked up speed, he stretched out his arms postmodern-day Jesus-style and literally flew above the city like a bird without a fear in the world.

'Man, you're so brave,' I told him when he caught up with me at the café later. 'No I'm not, I just love it,' he said. 'The haunted house scared the crap out of me!' Now the haunted house, even with the real-life actors and the most brilliant spine-chilling effects, was for me just silly nonsense.

Everyone's fear has a different face but, as I experienced viscerally on the swing, when in the midst of being afraid for your life, according to the Oriental understanding of energetics, your kidney energy becomes dislocated, causing a sensation of a falling-away belly. Conversely, when your kidney energy is dislocated or weak through illness, stress or overindulgence in alcohol, for instance, you fear consciously or unconsciously for your life (which in turn causes further weakening of kidney energy).

Because kidney energy is considered to provide the basis for your immune system, bone strength, reproductive system and will to survive, among other things, it is helpful for overall health and wellbeing to do everything possible to strengthen it in order to preclude the possibility of future dislocation, should you ever find yourself praying on a fairground ride or trembling in a haunted house, for example, but also to make you less timid of life in general.

To the furtherance of which end, start by pressing your thumb into the area immediately behind each inner ankle bone, with enough pressure to elicit a sharp but not unpleasant ache, fishing about for the most sensitive spots and surrendering to the sensation for about a minute on each foot. This stimulates the 'source' points on the kidney meridian, which encourages your kidneys to access more energy from their 'source element', water, or the moisture in the surrounding air.

Next, placing the fingertips of both hands pressed together on the centre of your chest, stroke lightly and slowly down your midline to the top of your pubic bone, separating your hands for your fingertips to stroke across your lower abdomen and then draw them up each side of your torso, over the breasts (chest) to meet once more at the centre to begin a new cycle. Repeat this cycle 18 times, breathing out as you stroke downwards and in as you pull back up. This is known as 'harmonising fire and water', a technique with myriad self-healing applications, ranging from the prevention and cure of indigestion to stimulation of sexual drive, which is why you'll no doubt see it popping up from time to time in this column in future. However, in relation to settling your stomach after a violent merry-go-round ride, or when just feeling discombobulated, it is unsurpassed.

And while on the subject of Nico Rhamodda and the Flying Dudes, you might like to close the session (which should be repeated daily for three weeks for lasting results), with a Taoist 'white crane' chi-gung move by raising both arms to the sides and, with palms facing down, gently flapping them in slow motion like the wings of a huge bird on sedatives while suggesting to yourself, 'I'm safe, I'm safe, I'm safe!'

An opportunity to think about nothing

There's an air of collective tension about, partly due to the rumbles of global tumult. On top of this, we feel the socio-economic tectonic plates shifting beneath our feet and it naturally makes us feel insecure. At times like this we do all need a place to think – a place to internally regroup – somewhere far from the madding crowd, away from all the media noise, where we can retrieve a balanced perspective and thus return to the affray renewed, loins neatly girded and ready for whatever the Tao may bring – or take away.

As it happens, I'm sitting in the place I come to think. Not the loo, but a spot I call Daisy's Rock, which perches discreetly on an outcrop at the edge of a craggy Catalan cove wearing a pine forest on its head like an unruly hippie hairdo, cocking a snook at the white-topped turquoise Mediterranean waves that slap it soundly and remorselessly about the cheeks.

I come here whenever I get the slightest chance. I'm not being flash – clichéd maybe – and anyway there's nothing flash about queuing at Luton airport at 5.30am for an 'easyJet' to Barcelona (the whole process of which is anything but easy) as I did this morning. But in fact to say I come here to think is not strictly true. I come here more precisely not to think, which is the concept I'm about to pitch you today.

Imagine being forced to run every waking moment for the rest of your life – picture your poor legs, the chafing between your thighs, the strain on your knee joints, the blisters on your feet, not to mention the indigestion due to eating late-night kebabs or nori on the hoof, as well as the general wear and tear to your system.

Well, that's exactly what most of us are doing with our minds: thinking, thinking, until we become mentally and hence physically exhausted. Even the fittest runner has to stop and take a break – you can't run one marathon after another without collapsing – at least without a rest in between (the remarkable recent feats of Sir Ranulph Fiennes notwithstanding). Same with the mind. As any great thinker will tell you, if you want to entertain truly momentous thoughts, you, just like Einstein, have to let them come to you unbidden, of themselves, which they can't do if your mind is full to the rafters with habitual internal chatter – there'd simply be no space for them to dock.

So if you fancy having a really good think, the first thing to do is stop thinking. The Taoists call it taming your monkey mind or reining in the running horse of intellect, and the way you do it is to draw all your attention into the dead centre of your brain like a little Buddha withdrawing and sitting cross-legged inside your cranium, and observe as thoughts traverse your forebrain (in front of your point of awareness) – usually from right to left (but there's no fixed rule).

The trick is not to follow any particular thought however visually enticing, but simply to watch each one pass like another cloud in the sky of your mind. Keep watching patiently, and as always happens eventually, even in the UK, all clouds will pass to reveal untarnished endless azure stretched out majestically before you. To assist the process, maintain your breathing at a slow, even, steady pace.

Initially, practise this sitting quietly with eyes closed for three minutes or more at least once daily to give the legs of your mind a break, and over time you'll find yourself able to do it with eyes open as you go about your business, even in the midst of the most stressful day, by which point your mental and hence physical energy will be absolutely boundless, rendering you far more adroit at managing whatever life throws in your path.

And I swear, all that came from not thinking a single thought.

All you need is a good map to navigate your way through life

I've noticed a marked increase recently of people in my immediate orbit deeply engrossed in loud conversation with themselves, totally oblivious to the world around them, ranting, mumbling and shouting at ghosts. Lost souls, perhaps, but then consider the ongoing internal dialogue occurring in your own mind at any one time. Consider the more jagged edges of that dialogue, the darker thoughts you'd share with no one but a trained therapist or priest, and you quickly appreciate that the dividing line between care in the community and pillar of society is merely a diaphanous veil at best.

So what separates the hinged from the unhinged? You could put it all down to orientation. Knowing where you are – which requires a good map and proficient map-reading skills. This applies as much to placing yourself geographically as psycho-emotionally. When trying to find your way around in a strange city, it helps immensely to know the north, south, east and west of things, so you know how to place yourself and thus save yourself the anguish of getting lost down the back streets.

Same with your inner world. If you wish to avoid losing yourself in an inner maze, you need a sound cosmological map, good map-reading skills (insight) and a clear sense of orientation. Most of us grow up with enough acquired bits and pieces of maps to navigate our way through most city streets of the soul, but often when the inner landscape suddenly changes – earthquakes, volcanic eruptions or tidal waves caused by, say, death, separation, illness, redundancy or bankruptcy – we find the map inaccurate, outdated and inadequate. At this point, without map-making tools, the options are cracking up, entering a dream-state where you talk aloud to ghosts, antidepressants, psychotherapy, religion or self-numbing through compulsive disorder behaviour, alcohol, drugs, sex or shopping.

To prevent you reaching this state, and to some extent to heal it if you do reach it, it is essential to get yourself a map that works, and that is achieved through meditation. Basically, meditation means to still your thinking mind, so that with clarity of consciousness you viscerally feel where you are and what you're doing. Sounds like nothing much, but daily practice collects you into one joined-up piece, unshakeable in the midst of external events, no matter how wildly they swirl about you. There are thousands of schools of meditation – and finding the one for you is a matter of trial and error or destiny.

Perhaps the most popular form of meditation is TM, transcendental meditation, made famous by the Maharishi (guru, not clothing label) and Beatles connection. This involves inwardly repeating your own sacred sound or mantra, given you in an initiation ritual, 20 minutes morning and night. At advanced stages, practitioners are actually seen to levitate while they meditate.

At the other extreme, there's Zen, where the very most you do with your mind is count your breaths up to nine and start again, ad infinitum, and occasionally let your mind be blown by koans, impossible abstractions like the infamous one-hand-clapping sound, but mostly just sitting thinking absolutely nothing and being hit on the back with a stick by the roshi, or master, whenever spied falling into somnolence.

Give me a couple of pages and I'll regale you with descriptions of many more, but meantime, try this little Taoist-Buddhist gem. It's short, simple, and will leave you feeling sharp as a diamond.

Picture, in the dark cavern of your skull, a magnificent diamond, magically lit from within, rotating slowly in the centre of your brain for the next six minutes or so.

I'll leave you with that while I go off to mutter at some windmills.

You don't have to bare your belly to change your life

Call me a navel gazer, but I've seen a lot of bellies around lately. Have you noticed them, too? Women the length and breadth of the land are proudly letting the air get to their midriffs. And not just the ones with washboard stomachs, but with all kinds, including pregnant ones.

It's reassuring, and inspiring, to see that the grip of the body fascists may be over. Women, some as voluptuous as a Rubens painting, are proudly displaying their most vulnerable part without a care for conventional ideals of the so-called perfect body. This indicates, from a sociological perspective, a more accepting stance towards self and hence towards others. In fact, at a t'ai chi camp I just taught in Wales, one participant, who by her own admission is no Twiggy, spontaneously gave such a graceful and unabashed flesh-wobbling belly-dancing demonstration, it inspired me to write this piece. It suggests that we in the West are slowly changing our understanding of our relationship with the body along more Oriental lines.

According to Taoist wisdom, your belly, and particularly your lower belly, is the centre not just of your body, but of your physical universe. In t'ai chi and most other martial arts, you're taught to manoeuvre your body from the lower belly if you want your moves to have grace and power. If you constantly keep a few degrees of awareness just below your navel – at work, rest or play – your words and deeds will ring more true, you'll feel mentally as well as physically more balanced, and your will to succeed in whatever you're doing will increase.

Also, because keeping awareness here helps activate kidney energy, which governs sexuality, you'll find yourself feeling and being far more sexy. At first it seems alien, even slightly naughty, to be mindful of your lower belly because we've been trained to locate ourselves, as it were, in the head and chest, but once you start centring yourself further down, you realise how natural it is.

The Taoists call it your tantien, meaning, literally, the field of heaven – that point in your body through which the spiritual real, or Tao, finds expression within you. Keeping it relaxed so the energy flows is considered key to health, longevity and enlightenment. On a practical level, it helps reduce discomfort from all kinds of bowel problems.

To help get your mind down there, six or seven times a day, gently, purpose-fully press in with a finger 2in below the navel to produce a pleasant yet pointed ache that radiates throughout the belly. Hold for a minute or so while breathing naturally and tell yourself, 'By pressing here, I unleash a torrent of chi (energy) and become 10 times more powerful, effective and altogether damn sexy immediately!' (or words to that effect).

Now visualise a channel running from the tip of the spine over the top of the head down the front of your body to form a loop. Breathe in very gently and visualise the breath travelling up the rear channel to the top of the head. As you breathe out, feel the breath dropping down the front part of the channel and accumulating with quite some pressure around the tantien region. Do this nine times.

Think of yourself moving from this point, talking from it, making love from it, generally experiencing life from it. Let heaven move your belly. Even take up belly dancing or t'ai chi to cement the relationship. But a slight note of caution. Only expose it when the weather's warm or you could risk triggering illness. Many Oriental women wear silk sashes around their waist in winter to ensure the heat stays in, so go easy on the jeans with no waistband as autumn draws near.

Meantime, I'm predicting a Rubens-look revival on a large scale (excuse the pun). You heard it here first.

Drugs aren't the only way of keeping pain at bay

So there I was, writhing on the bed, with a searing pain in my gum where a dodgy dentist had done a bogus root-canal treatment 20 years previously, which had apparently become infected. As the night wore on, the pain grew worse till, hallelujah, 9am finally came around, whereupon I stumbled round the corner to see my mate Frederik, the enlightened dentist – you may remember me mentioning him and Janice, the dynamic dental duo, a year or so back and how enjoyable it always is to visit them – and he didn't let me down this time.

The sheer, unadulterated pleasure of the anaesthetic numbing my mouth was indescribable and the extraction like scratching an itch of apocalyptic proportions.

Anaesthetics, however, wear off eventually, and as you know if you have ever had a tooth out, the after-pain provides a constant mid-level hum of acute discomfort for a good few days and, being so close to the brain, causes a skewed perspective on everything.

Fortunately, though, it also afforded me a perfect hands-on opportunity to put a few Taoist pain-control strategies to the test and pass on what worked in the hope that it will help some of the people who write to me complaining of chronic pain of one form or another.

Enter into the heart of the pain, using all your intellectual focus, and if you can remain there long enough the pain will disappear altogether for as long as you can maintain focus.

Push the pain to one side of your mind, so to speak, thus enabling you to continue with your schedule – you're still aware of it but you're bigger than it is now.

Dispel the pain by exhaling into it like a woman in labour breathing out into the contractions.

Imagine the pain as a friend (a terrible one, like, say, Attila the Hun) who's come to teach you something important, perhaps to remind you of your mortality and help you see your life in clearer perspective. Accept it without self-pity, using it as an opportunity to strengthen your soul.

Resist giving way to panic as this drains kidney energy, which weakens your willpower and immune response. Instead, keep breathing as evenly, slowly and purposefully as possible.

Resist whimpering, as this jerks your breath, energy and mind around, which dissipates mental focus. Groan instead – but make it musical, starting on a high note and sliding down to as low a note as you can. This relaxes you, while nasty-sounding groaning makes you feel miserable, which weakens you.

Relax whichever parts of your body you can – ideally, even the painful part. Watch out for a build-up of tension in unaffected parts. If, say, the pain's in your belly, make sure your shoulders and neck aren't tensing in sympathy. The more relaxed you are, the more your blood and energy can flow, which is what soothes and heals you.

Regularly massage your kidneys (in the soft part of your lower back) with your fists in circular motions, 18 times in each direction. This helps strengthen your kidney energy, which helps boost immune response and willpower levels (you need buckets of that to get you through the pain).

Rub your palms together to produce heat and place on the affected part, visualising the warmth penetrate and dispel the pain.

Don't call it pain – call it sensation.

If you must take painkillers to help you relax, be aware that their high toxicity levels weaken kidney energy, thus reducing immune response and draining your willpower.

The above is in no way intended as a glib antidote to the awful suffering endured by millions, but if just one person finds only momentary relief, I'll feel my ex-tooth has made its contribution to the world.

Your unused consciousness knows what we're thinking

I had a wonderful time running a workshop the other evening at the College of Psychic Studies, an august establishment in South Kensington, founded in 1874 and of which Sir Arthur Conan Doyle was once president. Not that its solid, old-school, Victorian roots make it fusty. Far from it – a lighter-hearted, more contemporary-minded bunch of people would be hard to find.

I was teaching the Taoist approach to developing psychic power, which has led me to have all kinds of interesting premonitions over the years. For the ancient Taoists, for whom self-realisation or enlightenment was the central thrust, developing psychic ability was never an end in itself, but a welcome by-product of engaging in regular meditation. It gives you an edge when making decisions or helping others to do so, can provide you with a nifty party trick, and may even provide a source of income.

The approach is simple: the psyche, soul or unconscious, knows everything that ever was, is and will be. This infinite span of information is then filtered by the conscious or local mind so that you can carry on your day-to-day agenda without overload. Developing more psychic awareness is merely a matter of widening the filter, while detaching from the internal chatter enough to be aware of what's being presented.

This infinite field of knowledge can be accessed 'physically' in the back of your brain, while the internal dialogue (shall I wear a different shirt, does so-and-so like me, I feel hungry, etc) occurs in the forebrain. So the first thing is to relocate yourself, as it were, in the back of your head.

You know you've arrived there when the rear section of your skull starts tingling. To help it along, press your thumb into the depression under the base of your skull, just where your spine meets the skullbone, with light but purposeful pressure for 30 seconds.

To still the activity in the forebrain, press a finger on a point slightly above your eyebrow line in the dead centre above the bridge of the nose.

To energise the back of your brain and encourage it to throw forth information freely, squeeze your perineum, the muscle between your legs, by pulling it gently upwards from within, and keep squeezing until you feel a shuddery sensation pushing up along your spine and into the back of your brain. You can reinforce this by simultaneously pushing your tongue firmly on to the roof of your mouth and rolling your eyes slightly upwards as if looking up through the top of your head.

Finally, make a strongman arm posture, bending at the elbow, and press firmly into that indentation where the deltoid (shoulder-cap) muscle meets the biceps to produce a pointed but pleasant ache. This has been found to increase psychic awareness by at least 30 per cent if practised three times a day.

After doing this, 120 participants then paired off, with one of each pair placing their palms on their partner's head, one at the back, one at the front (sitting or standing sideways on), then waiting with empty minds until a picture, colour, smell, word or shape popped up.

Over half the pairs reported success. For example, one man saw children's building blocks with letters forming words, many of which were misspelled. It turned out that his partner was a special-needs teacher specialising in dyslexia.

Within a month of regularly pinging your energy as above, you'll be so impressed with the way it expands your everyday awareness and affords you a deeper glimpse into what makes you and others tick, you'll be rushing down to Brighton beach to rent a stall.

Meanwhile, I'm going to send you a message telepathically now and you have to tell me what it is. Answers on an email, please.

Learn to suppress those primal urges

Today, I have nothing to say.

The temptation to leave the rest of the page blank is fairly strong, though I know I wouldn't get away with it. It would be sent back with, 'Write a piece, you lazy Barefoot!' scrawled across it in red ink. And fair enough – I get paid for saying something. But is that enough of a reason to write words empty of substance? Of course not. So then I dig a little deeper and what I find there is a layer of resistance, beneath which lies a veritable maelstrom of conversation waiting to burst through to the surface, a layer thick with unarticulated passions, fears and primal urges. And as I catch a glimpse of it, I recognise an almost overwhelming compulsion to communicate with you at that level – to talk to the part of you that, beneath your own layer of resistance, is screaming to be communicated with.

Normally, a neat device springs to mind, a conversational opening gambit from which to launch into a neo-Taoist rationalisation, something to take the edge off any hint of Sunday blues that may be nagging at you, along with one foolproof remedy or another. But not today. Today no device will do, no easy rationalisation will suffice, and no instant self-help remedy will fit as a handy antidote. Because for a start, there's nothing to antidote.

The existential soup bubbling away in the deeper recesses of your mind is not a disease, though suppressing it or managing it in faulty ways can lead to all kinds of disease, both physical and mental. To the contrary, that primal swamp within is the wellspring of all your creativity, generative power and motivation to succeed in your life.

The question is how to harness its power without it sending you into a kaleidoscopic spin. How do you channel the deep, dark fears of obliteration, whether by terrorist or disease; the painful yearnings for love, romantic or otherwise; the craving for respect at work or at home; the lust for fulfilment in your career and life in general, along with all the other primal longings shouting for recognition in your soul – how do you channel all that into enough of an orderly configuration to deal with it at all?

Now you've got me. Which is why I say I have nothing to say. Because at this moment, the nation's cheekiest and possibly most verbose self-help teacher and people's healer doesn't have the answer. Not that I'm sitting here overwhelmed by existential angst – far from it. As I said, my layer of resistance provides a well-formed shield, enabling me to carry on as if nothing's happening – just as it does with most of us as we go about our busy lives. And, of course, it's so tempting to say that whenever you find the cries from the swamp threatening to engulf your mind to the detriment of your ability to carry on effectively, this indicates a deficiency of heart energy, which can be remedied by eating lots of radishes, taking hawthorn-berry tincture and pressing firmly on the underside of your wrist in line with the base of your little finger on a heart meridian point known as the 'spirit door' – and that would be no lie – damn useful information, in fact.

But that's not what I'm on about here – I don't want even to suggest that you do anything to change it. We're always trying to change things just because they feel a trifle uncomfortable for a second. What I'm more interested in now, and am sure you are too, is how to sit with the gurgling existential primal mush within, complete with all your worst primal fears, yearnings and reachings out; how to sit with that without holding your breath or tensing yourself against it, and so drink of its juices, so to speak, that you may be refreshed and remotivated by their primal power, so you can go out there and give it some (welly) for the week ahead.

But other than suggesting that you breathe, relax and let it happen without trying to pass comment, I don't know what else to add. As I said, today I have nothing to say.

Make your mind up

Choices, choices – voices, voices.

Doesn't that seem to be the substance of your reality these days – decisions needing constantly to be made – should you go this way, should you go that – one voice telling you one thing, another voice telling you the opposite. Look beneath the surface of your internal dialogue and you see that every nanosecond you're unconsciously choosing something – relax the muscle in your hand or keep it tense, turn your eyes to the right or to the left, hold your breath or exhale – and so on all the way up to the apparently huge decisions involving relationships, career, lifestyle and ethical issues. The bigger the decision, the more conscious it becomes, of course, but the same mechanism underlies all of them from unconsciously deciding on the smallest twitch of a muscle to deciding whether to tell your partner, boss or significant other to jump in the proverbial lake (or not).

The ability to make decisions, apart from having an intellect developed through education and experience and all the other subtle aspects of a well-tuned psyche, is supported, according to those Taoist doctors of old, by the energy of your gall bladder. When your gall bladder, that repository of natural detergent that sits politely upon your liver under the ribs on your right side, is working smoothly, choosing this over that comes as easy as punch – as if your thoughts have wings that fly them to the right decision without effort – you see the vista clearly, the voices inside are all singing in harmony and choices are made effortlessly. When your gall bladder overheats, however, due to mismanagement of food, drink or other substances, you become variously hot-headed, deluded, confused and afraid and hence unable to make sense of whichever dilemma you're presented with.

Rather than attempting at this point to come to any conclusion, it may actually be wiser therefore to mentally step away from the issue at hand and focus your thoughts instead on directing the hot air in your head to subside.

Hot air is a pretty accurate description, because when your gall bladder overheats through having to overwork in its digestive functions, that heat rises as disruptive energy through the gall bladder meridian (energy channel), which runs bilaterally through your shoulders, neck, base of skull, over the brain and into your forebrain where all the chatter takes place, steaming things up in there so you can't think straight any more.

So the way you direct it back down again is to manually give signals to the meridian by gently pressing a series of acupressure points. Start on your forehead on points directly in line with each pupil about 1cm above the eyebrows and hold for a moment. Now press in likewise at the base of your skull just where the muscle ridges bordering the spine meet the skullbone. Next press, one side at a time, on the ridges of your shoulders, those tension points known as your karmic golf balls. Now moving down the meridian to draw the heat away from the upper parts, press in the depression formed between the bone of the little toes and the next ones in up at the base of the foot bone. Finally, place your palm over your upper abdomen a little to the right, imagining a light blue cooling mist permeating your insides, and address your gall bladder respectfully, 'Cool it you little bugger!'

The effects should be noticeable after an hour or so, whereupon you are able to return to your dilemma with renewed clarity and gusto and will no doubt find yourself deciding which course to take without strain.

Obviously, it helps to maintain your gall bladder at an even temperature – go easy on rich food, alcohol and drugs. Generally, drinking a glass of warm water with half a lemon squeezed in, morning and night, is all the tonic your gall bladder needs, and seeing as I really can't decide how to finish this piece, I think I may go and drink one right now. On the other hand...

If you're growing your confidence, be sure to shave your head

So I got hauled up to see the boss because a few of my biggest fans were concerned I'd gone off the boil a bit on this page a short while back, and he wanted to be sure I was still with sufficient inner flame to turn the heat back up. And it's true, I'd known it myself. There were a few weeks when no matter how hard I tried, I just couldn't get the magic to flow out of my fingertips.

You could blame it on the war, which certainly caused a dip in my confidence – people violating each other, no matter what the reason, always does that to me. You could blame it on the fact I was writing a book and simultaneously coming to the end of an 18-month stint of making an album and wasn't able to switch to column mode with enough dexterity. You could blame it on the endless trickle of complaint letters which I elicit – amazingly – finally reaching critical mass and suddenly weighing down on me, making me self-conscious. You could blame it on me struggling out the painful back end of a four-year relationship, as I was at the time. You could just say it was due to life's normal and natural cycle of yin and yang, dark and light. And no doubt it was a combination of all those things and many other factors besides.

But underlying was (and of course always is) the struggle with myself to be authentic, here and now, with you, in the moment. It's all well and good being able to craft clever sentences, construct the odd gag here and there to distract you and make you giggle, and laudable indeed to furnish you with easily explained ancient techniques for self-development and pain relief, but if I'm using that in any way to hide behind, the transmission will only be skin deep.

So I explained all the above factors and the boss's answer was: 'Be more confident, Barefoot!'

I love it when someone does a hammer-nail-head, as my mate Mad J Riley would put it, and smashes through all the crap in my forebrain. By being more confident about who you are, what you bring to the mix will be more authentic.

But how do you instantaneously manifest more confidence? At the end of an often painful process, I'd say you start by noticing which areas of self have been lacking in confidence – which areas, in therapy-speak, have been split off or disowned through some sense of shame. The next step seems to be a softening towards those parts of you, an acceptance and forgiving that dissolves the shame, a welcoming of those ugly bits and a willingness to walk forth from here, perhaps not as pretty as you'd hitherto imagined you were, but certainly more complete, hence natural, hence, presumably beautiful. For this part of the action, I was compelled to have my head shaved just two days before going on stage at a soul jazz festival down in Banyuls-sur-Mer, billed – not my doing – as 'Barefoot Doctor, Damn Sexy Worldwide Healer, Londres', but looking instead like Nosferatu, the bald Dracula, but with an incongruously tanned face – very yin and yang – and very ugly (believe me). To aid my confidence in this, I bought a hat.

Next stage is to rally yourself with positive thoughts such as 'I am relevant to my culture – what I bring to the mix is unique and valid – I am valid because I believe I am and I have every reason to feel confident now', which you should repeat with great frequency for at least one day.

Finally, increase your daily exercise regimen to include new challenges – swimming 50 lengths, adopting hitherto untried yoga postures in great profusion or standing 20 minutes in any chi-gung posture of your choice. The more trust you develop in your body, the more trust you develop in your deeper self.

And the reason for shaving the head? As your hair grows back, your confidence grows with it. And it's working – I have a noticeable stubble adorning my scalp already and am feeling more confident and authentic by the minute. Is it showing yet?

Love, Sex and Personal Matters

The art of health-enhancing flirtation

'Sometimes it just takes a lady to smile and make your day complete.' So sang Jerry Jeff Walker, the country-singing roué of 'Mr Bojangles' fame. For PC purposes, obviously feel free to substitute 'gentleman' for 'lady', for it is this subject of the everyday social intercourse between us that I wish to expound upon today, or at least that aspect of it so finely developed by our cousins at the other end of the Channel Tunnel: flirting. The French have mastered this (fine) art almost to the point of it being a national cultural institution. But why, you may ask, in the context of alternative health, would I mention such a thing? Were I to be pontificating instead on the benefits of those other Gallic staples, red wine and garlic, you would hardly look askance, but if I posit the idea of flirting as invaluable for your self-esteem and hence your general wellbeing and by extension your immune system, I wonder whether your eyebrow starts spoiling for some self-raising action.

We, the natives of these Great British Isles, are not normally comfortable with flirting. Perhaps island life breeds insularity and a fundamental unease over personal boundaries, which makes full eye contact (the basic currency of flirting) uncomfortable for us. Perhaps we are still unwittingly held hostage by Victorian prudishness or maybe it's just the weather that makes us shy and reticent to reach out from our souls to strangers in the street or in a café. Because, let's face it, without alcoholic support we do tend to be a socially timid bunch. Not that I'm criticising – I find our awkward ways quite fetching and indeed indulge in them all too often myself.

Intrinsically, we all want to be acknowledged. Road, air, trolley and all the other newfangled 'rages' we are now said to subscribe to result from feeling unacknowledged by strangers. As any driving instructor will tell you, a lot of this can be offset by initially establishing eye contact, for once eye contact is made, souls connect and you feel acknowledged. Once acknowledged, your basic sense of decency is evoked and it is hard to feel anger.

Not wishing to stray here into negative territory, however, let me return to my theme, namely that flirting is good for your immune system. As attested to by the vast sums of money spent annually in the UK by both ladies and gentlemen on cosmetics, toiletries, clothing, grooming, and even cars and interior design and other lifestyle accoutrements, that aspect of ourselves we most wish to be acknowledged for – whether consciously or otherwise – is our essential desirability, and yes, of course, status... which again leads back to desirability.

And what better way, other than becoming a celebrity or media star, which uses up inordinate amounts of valuable energy, to get your daily acknowledgment dose than from a bit of harmless flirting. I'm not in any way suggesting promiscuity or a new sexual revolution, simply the willingness to indulge in eye-to-eye contact and the occasional smile to make your day and theirs complete.

Flirting is the expression of the sexy part of your character. It doesn't make you a slut or libertine. There is a clear distinction between a brief soul-to-soul connection through the eyes, facial expression and general body language, and giving someone the come-on. Obviously the extent to which you take things is your business, but that is not the point. I'm well aware of the possible dangers of 'flirt signals' being misinterpreted and resulting in trouble, for which I deeply recommend proper self-defence training, yet I'd suggest that the benefits are worth the risk.

The beauty of a good flirt is that it need lead nowhere. You are neither being unfaithful to your partner nor to your better instincts when you smile and let flutter those lashes. You are merely bouncing a bit of harmless sexual energy between you that will help you each feel better about yourself, as a living artform, if you like, and more able to infuse any real-time relationships with more spark. In a long-term, monogamous relationship, it is also crucial that you flirt with each other, connecting your erotic selves through a moment of (heart-felt) eye contact as often as you can.

The French, from whom we stand to learn much in these matters, are sophis-ticated enough to flirt without self-consciousness, prudishness or feigned coyness, even (and often especially) when in the company of partners, who never seem to display jealousy. They simply accept that, like fine wine, garlic (and possibly skin creams), it's good for your health.

Now if you find my suggestion in any way scandalous, do not read what follows, as it describes an ancient Oriental Taoist method for moving internal energy in such a way as to render you more sexually magnetic to others, and which, if practised every day for 90 days or so, will increase your personal flirta-bility factor to near Parisian levels.

Imagine being able to inhale through the soles of your feet, up the inside of your legs, into your perineum (between your legs), and up to the tip of your uterus or penis, and then being able to exhale from there, back down to your perineum, across the top of your thighs, and down the outside of your legs to the soles of your feet. Repeat this with mind and breath in unison up to nine times. Additionally, supplement it with some basic auto-suggestion along the lines of, 'I am sexy!', 'I'm so sexy!' or even, 'God, I'm so sexy!'

And please remember that feeling sexy and desirable is for everyone, as the ongoing iconic status of such (august) folk as Sir Sean Connery and Catherine Deneuve would confirm. I would say in closing, however, that for the sake of both propriety and basic aesthetics, winking should be eschewed, if at all possible.

Unite sensual pleasure and spirituality

The light outside is reminding me of a day many years ago. It was January 1968. I was 14, I'd become smitten with a girl I'd just met on holiday, and was giving her a private DJ performance in my bedroom, as you do (or did). To win her heart I started with Pink Floyd's 'Interstellar Overdrive', moving on through Love's 'Forever Changes', Cream's 'Crossroads', and because she was a bit of a soul girl, James Brown's 'Cold Sweat'. It was then that I threw the crescendo of Tchaikovsky's '1812 Overture' into the mix. 'What the hell do you listen to this shit for?' she wondered in that innocent way peculiar to 14-year-olds, and I could tell I was about to lose her to this other guy who was into Smokey Robinson and the Miracles.

That was my first taste of being thought a bit left of centre as far as the mainstream was concerned, and though Smokey was 'fab' (in a retro-kitsch kind of way), I figured left field was the place for me and settled into a happy cultural slipstream.

When I stumbled upon Taoism and became addicted a short while after, it was just another of those quirky things my peers had come to expect of me, so you can imagine my surprise 30-odd years later to find myself with a column in the best broadsheet on the planet, flinging out pieces of Taoist advice left, right and centre. Then it occurred to me that many people may not have the slightest clue what Taoism is and may be wondering if I've been subliminally co-opting them into a secret cult, or worse. So I thought I'd best make it clear.

Taoism is a philosophy that developed in China before the Buddha or Confucius left their stamp on the culture. So effective is it as a template for successful living that it's survived the transition from East to West, ancient to postmodern, and is now almost the height of fashion (in a philosophical sense) throughout Europe, America and even on our own wee, wild, woolly isles.

It is not a religion, but provides a personal operating system which you install in your body-mind's hard disk by regular practice of psychophysical exercises ranging from t'ai chi and the other internal boxing forms, chi-gung, calisthenics, meditation and inner 'alchemy' all the way through to observing the correct feng shui in your home and workplace, clearing your meridians with acupuncture or shiatsu and even how you make love with your partner.

Religions, as well as providing a cosmological map, dictate moral standards by instituting rules and threats of divine or temporal punishment. Taoism has no rules or enforceable morals. Instead, you are advised that your body is a temple, hence access point to divine realms, which you reach by generating a psychically charged version of your physical energy, or 'chi'. Once you get the chi flowing in your body and environment, you are both soothed and energised. You feel balanced and at one with your true nature and surroundings. Your true nature is one of virtue, or 'te', which when accessed has you treating others and yourself with empathy and respect, rendering you far less likely to wilfully act in hurtful ways. Hence rules and morals become redundant. So rather than tie yourself in moral knots, you simply practise the techniques every day.

Chi, once activated, will heal and energise you and enable you to do so for others. But it's also known to make you damn sexy. Your body may be your temple, but that doesn't mean it's not your nightclub, too. Indeed, there are many techniques used to amplify the pleasure of the senses. The way a Taoist sees it, sensual pleasure is not wrong, nor is it right. It just is (if you let it). And the more you can get (and give), the better, providing you're not forcing the flow and causing damage. Generally, it's only in the West that we think sensual pleasure and spirituality must be divorced. However, the Taoist way is to marry the two, and in that marriage will your enlightenment be found.

You might like to experience the flavour now. Start by holding your palms together at chest height and moving them in slow motion apart and together, as if playing a concertina. After about 18 passes, you'll begin feeling a build-up of chi between your hands as if the air has suddenly become much thicker and warmer.

Now place both palms over your lower abdomen with fingers pointing downwards, one hand either side of your external genitalia. Be sensitive, and you'll feel the chi permeating into your pelvic bowl like a warm fragrant mix, soothing, energising and making you feel damn sexy.

You might even like to reinforce that consciously by affirming with controlled gusto, 'My, I (don't half) feel soothed, energised and damn sexy!' (Should have used that instead of the '1812'.)

Nurture the seat of your being

Racing round the UK on a book tour, I was fetched and carried over 3,000 miles in planes, trains and automobiles like an overgrown little emperor for three entire weeks. On a mission to spread unconditional love in the nation's book-shops and assorted venues from sea to shining sea – from the magical western edge of Wales, across the borders to the rich atmosphere of Glasgow, down among the good people of Liverpool, Manchester, Leeds, Birmingham, Southampton, Bristol, Brighton, Canterbury and finally to London – I found to my surprise and delight, a palpable willingness of everyone to partake of that love.

Sound all a bit hippie-romantic? Not a bit of it. I stood before every crowd, open and vulnerable, without a clue what would come out of my mouth as I took the microphone. Some people go skydiving; for my extreme sport I talk to crowds without knowing what I'm going to say. And though I was there, as I explained to them, ostensibly to promote a book, I was actually there to share love. Simply knowing that and holding it as an intention makes words pour out in just the right way to touch people's hearts (worth bearing in mind before doing any public speaking).

You can use it in normal social situations, too. Rather than allowing yourself to be conned into believing in the superficial reason for a gathering, see below to the subtext, which is always essentially people gathering for whatever excuse, simply because people need to gather. The reason is love. And we do it through information – the currency of love. If it's carnal love, the information is touch. If it's universal love, it can be anything from music to vaudeville.

How you develop the ability to radiate love in such a way as to make something wonderful happen in a crowd, is to relax your chest and express yourself warmly, looking people in the eyes as you do.

This ability can be enhanced by pressing firmly on the 'stigmata' points on your palms, which lie on the 'heart protector' meridian. Pressing for a few moments on each palm a few times a day will cause your spirit to grow more generous and more receptive to the generosity of others, as well as lend your aura an extra shine, as if you travel with your own spotlight.

However, to exude charisma and radiate love so people feel it, you must source the energy from deep within. Your hips are the seat of your being, physically in terms of supporting your torso of course, but psycho-emotionally, existentially and spiritually, too – the entire multidimensional complex you think of as you, all has to function as a unit for you to be in optimum fettle. Too much heart or love energy flowing without you being firmly anchored in your hips will drain your energy, weaken your spirit and leave you feeling flat at the end of the party.

One highly effective way to ensure this doesn't happen (and one which is also extremely effective for strengthening the lower back), and which works a treat to calm you at the end of a frantic day, is to lie on your front on the carpet, forehead nestled in your cupped palms so your spine is straight and you can breathe easily through your nose. Place your knees 18in apart, legs bent at the knees and feet sticking in the air. Criss-cross your legs alternately like a pair of scissors cutting the air over and over, with first your left foot nearest your bum, then your right. Keep your ankles and feet loose so they can flick about freely as you move. After a while, the movement picks up momentum as if happening by itself and you find yourself falling into a relaxing trance akin to those familiar altered states of early childhood. Counting helps to still the mind while you do it, so feel free to count up to 1,008 flicks back and forth.

One thousand and eight blessings on all the people of the UK – may we live long and prosper!

Viagra is marketed as man's best friend, but is it really necessary?

It worries me, all this use of Viagra. I've never tried it and doubt I would, not because at the innocent and tender age of 49 I'm such a swell guy – excuse the pun – in fact, I'm usually too busy teaching the world to relax to even consider such things (indeed, I'm not far off being a male nun these days), but because it scares me to imagine becoming dependent on a pill to enjoy sex.

Yet you only have to mention such things to any well-meaning friend and he offers you a spare Viagra he just happens to have lying around, its use seems so endemic these days.

Having treated people for many years for sexual dysfunction in the tradition both of Taoist doctors and Wilhelm Reich – who believed sexual dysfunction was at the core of all physical, emotional and psychological problems – I've seen that except for physical impediment, erectile dysfunction and its female equiv-alent, including problems ranging from lack of interest to vaginismus, can usually be sorted by a combination of psychotherapeutic and energy work involving herbs and point stimulation.

This may seem a one-sided chat, with an emphasis on the boys – maybe inspired by the recent overkill of images of phallic symbols moving rapidly across and exploding in the corner of our TV screens – but the issue is of equal importance to both sexes. It seems from conversations with many men that nervousness about the ability to achieve and sustain a full erection is wide-spread. Perhaps with women being more financially independent, socially confident and hence sexually more predatory, the boys feel off-balanced, unclear as to strategy, and hence more sexually insecure. Moreover, the stress of war-torn, economically uncertain, ecologically shaky modern life, as well as the long hours necessary to stay in the game, wears down your kidney energy, which controls your libido levels. On top of that lies the confusion on the male part about politically correct behaviour – how far to let their maleness shine through or play the 'new man', along with the pressure of living up to the multi-orgasmic expectations of the media-saturated modern woman.

So Willy is nervous but short of Viagra – what to do? While there's no short cut to get to the deep-seated reasons for the low self-esteem patterns that undermine your sexual confidence, or to root out the latent sexual shame that makes you withdraw – for this you need a competent therapist – you can certainly make a start by using affirmations. Keep repeating: 'I am a fully functioning, healthy sexual being, able to express my deepest sexuality during the sexual act to the highest degree at all times!' and notice the negative thoughts your mind throws up in response – 'No I'm not, I'm always too tired', or 'No I'm not, I'm too fat', for example. Simply noticing the negative beliefs you've been holding on to about yourself helps dislodge the pattern. As it slowly infiltrates your unconscious, constant repetition of the affirmation will gradually instil in you more sexual confidence. Keep it up daily for three months for best results (so many puns...).

As for herbs, while I've tried most well-known sexual remedies over the years, the one that seems to have the most effect is the sustainable-crop Brazilian rainforest tree bark Catuaba, two to six capsules of which taken daily for three months strengthens sexual response for men and women and also helps soothe your nerves because it affects kidney energy, which as well as fuelling your rising sap also controls the nerves.

Finally, to trigger kidney energy appropriately to enhance your sexuality, press with the fingers of one hand into your perineum, the muscle between your legs, between genitals and anus, and massage gently but firmly by turning in clockwise circles 81 times, twice a day, for three months.

I hope you didn't find my writing style too stiff.

When a partner leaves, the first person to fall in love with is yourself

'What would you recommend for the torturous pain of a broken heart?

In addition to emotional pain, I suffer from a feeling of intense claustrophobia when I think I'll never talk to my former partner again. Please help, Linda.'

Thousands of emails come every week, but this one stopped me because treating broken hearts is one of my specialities. I remember as a student of Oriental medicine being utterly amazed watching my teacher successfully treat someone for a broken heart using acupuncture.

It was proof that adjusting the levels of energy in your various vital organs can positively affect your emotional and mental state. But, as the expression 'broken heart' demonstrates, this is not just an Oriental concept. In the West we talk, for example, about being livid when angry, as in being overheated in the liver, the cause of anger, according to the Taoists, or giving vent to one's spleen, as in speaking your mind, the spleen being thought responsible for providing you with intellectual power, and we talk about having a broken heart.

But, in fact, your heart cannot get broken – what actually happens, energetically at least, is a major disruption in the flow of so-called 'heart-protector' energy. This, if you go with the Taoist approach, is an energetic sheath surrounding your heart, akin in Western medical thought, to your pericardium – there to protect your heart from painful information, as occurs when you're forced to part company permanently with someone you love deeply.

Your heart is said to support your spirit, or consciousness, and to hold it in your body. When the energy of your heart protector becomes momentarily ruptured by trauma and shock, the heart energy itself is effectively weakened and loses control of your consciousness, which moves up out of your body and into your brain, where it gets stuck in a claustrophobic loop of self-punishing thoughts.

'I'll never meet anyone who loves me or who I'll love again; I'm useless, undesirable and unworthy; my life (which was probably perfectly fine before I met this person) will fall apart now; my life is meaningless; the light's gone out of it; I'd rather be dead' – these are all perfectly understandable thoughts for someone whose spirit, the font of life itself, has gone Awol.

In fact, it is your own spirit leaving, not the other person, which actually causes these feelings, and as soon as you mend the break in the heart-protector energy and your spirit returns to your body, those awful feelings and thoughts evaporate.

One way to do it is as follows: start off by spending 50 quid on a damn good massage as this will instantly draw you out of your head and back into your body. Then spend a few moments roughly six times a day, pressing fairly firmly between the two tendons that run up the midline of the underneath part of each forearm approximately three watchstraps' width up from the wrist bracelet. When you hit it accurately your hand will feel pleasantly paralysed. Stimulate this point (on the heart-protector meridian) as above for three days and the energy will mend itself.

More crucially, though, use this whole episode as an opportunity for you to reacquaint yourself with yourself. For after all, it's you you came on to the planet with, it's you you experience all the ups and downs of life with, and it's you you leave the planet with when the story's finally over. In other words, it's you with whom you have your primary relationship, however distracted from it you may have been by any secondary relationships with others, so spend some time falling in love with yourself again. Then pick yourself up, dust yourself down, put on your finest party outfit, go out and dance (metaphorically and literally), and before you know it, those suitors will be banging on your door once more and the whole chest-churning fairground ride can start all over again.

The Body

Sit up and take notice

Stop slouching and sit up straight! When I say that, do you find yourself reflex-ively pulling in your stomach, puffing up your chest, closing up the back of your neck and contracting your lower back in an uncomfortable facsimile of correct posture?

Few of us have been instructed from an early age in achieving optimum physical self-positioning in relation to space and gravity, ie good posture. Hence we have little idea of what it is, how to achieve it or the benefits it bestows. Indeed, any interest taken in attaining it usually comes about when we experience insufferable pain in the back, neck or shoulders, caused by a lack of it.

Our technologically oriented culture has us sitting for protracted periods, bent over keyboards, stuffed into car seats and lounging on sofas. Whether you look to the yoga of India or martial arts of the Orient, or to the work of postural correction pioneers FM Alexander, Moshe Feldenkrais and Ida Rolf, it quickly becomes apparent that the reflexive action most of us make when reminded to sit up straight is not the best way to use our bodies.

With optimum posture, you can breathe more freely (the first requisite for relaxation and stress control), think more clearly (your head sits lightly on your body) and feel more cheerful (your vital organs have proper space in which to function). But firstly we must develop our proprioceptive sense – the ability to feel from the inside out. Attaining 'the true and virtuous' posture of the Taoists requires thinking yourself into the right shape rather than forcing your muscles to produce it.

As you sit now, become aware of your hip region and especially your 'sit' bones, deep within your buttocks. As you breathe in and out, visualise them spreading out sideways. Having mentally broadened your base, visualise your spinal column growing upwards out of your hips, creating the sensation that the top of your head is reaching for the sky. Imagine your skull is a balloon-like vessel filled with helium, elongating your spine. Or picture a silver thread attached at one end to the crown of your head and the other to the ceiling, asserting a gentle upward pull. To assist this lengthening sensation, tilt your sacrum, the triangular bone at the base of the spine, slightly forward. Pay special attention to (mentally) elongating the back of your neck. Now imagine your shoulders and upper back broadening outwards and allow your breast-bone to lift and your chin to drop a little.

If you've managed to follow that, you should find yourself sitting in optimum posture and may already be feeling lighter, more physically relaxed and clearer headed. Notice how the stress is taken off the trapezius muscles that work so hard holding up the weight of your head. Notice also that your lungs can operate more freely and your organs of digestion are far less cramped.

As well as the obvious advantages of increased blood and cerebro-spinal fluid circulation and improved cardiovascular, respiratory and digestive func-tions, sporting yourself in optimum posture confers not-so-obvious psycho-emotional benefits. With head held high, chest lifted but relaxed and feeling supported by a broad back, it is hard to feel other than totally confident and positive. Negative thoughts literally pull you down. Low self-esteem makes you want to curl up (your spine) and become invisible. By reversing the effect through postural self-adjustment, you also reverse the psycho-emotional cause.

Moreover, as we age, we shrink. Succumbing to the pull of gravity, the spine becomes compressed and the torso caves in. By adjusting your posture, you actually regain some level of control over the ageing process. Not that this will happen in one sitting, so to speak. No change worth its salt happens overnight. Lasting change takes diligent, consistent application of the above principles.

Many well-trodden paths provide a reliable map or structure to help you achieve this. Alexander Technique is perhaps the most comprehensive approach to postural correction. Rolfing (deep connective-tissue massage) releases blocks in the fascia, or binding of the structure. T'ai chi (which is based on the same principles as is the Alexander Technique) is an effective way to translate good posture into movement, and yoga, the undisputed mother of all exercise, provides the perfect medium for self-correction.

I bet by now you're already beginning to slump in your seat again, so let me leave you with those familiar words ringing in your ears: Stop slouching and sit up straight! (Except now you know how to do it.)

Avoiding sudden back pain

I don't know if you've ever 'done your lower back in' – if not, I hope you never do, or if you have, may you never do so again. I'm not on about chronic backache – this is about the sudden variety, the skewed sacro-iliac joint affair, the kind that seems to come out of almost nowhere – perhaps bending over the sink, or even stretching before getting out of bed. The sort that has you walking completely lop-sided and bent over, emitting a series of grunts, groans and stifled screams as you valiantly attempt the sharply painful transition between one position and another.

At first you go into denial. You didn't really make that movement. This pain isn't really there. It's all in the mind. It'll pass in a moment if you stretch like this or like that. Then you realise it's not imaginary at all and you start thinking about your schedule for the next few days and reconciling it with your current physical state. Denial gives way to anger.

'How could this happen to me now?' You bang your fist on the nearest object, causing pain now in your hand as well. After a few futile moments throwing toys from your pram, anger gives over to self-pity. You feel helpless and want to cry (like a child). Schedule-awareness then returns and you start making practical decisions. Have you got time to visit the osteopath? But the pain is growing sharper with every tiny movement and making fast-track shifts in your priorities. So you shuffle slowly and bent, tail between your legs, to the phone and beg emotionally for an urgent appointment.

Either by eye and palpation or by X-ray as well, the osteopath ascertains it's not a disc problem, simply the sacrum (triangular bone at base of spine) sheering off on a rebellious angle, causing spasm in the muscles around the sacro-iliac (hip-bone) joints. Lying on the treatment couch now at the mercy of the gods, you surrender your body to a series of mind- and heart-stopping 'keklunks', get dressed, pay your money and hobble out, hopefully to full recovery within a couple of days.

However, if you look back, you may notice this crisis did not just occur out of the blue. There were signs: perhaps stiff shoulders and niggling pains in the middle back, headaches, stomach, bowel or kidney pains the week before. Maybe you were under extreme pressure at work or confused and unhappy at home, or both. Perhaps you were worried about money. Almost for sure, you were doing too much for one person to reasonably handle at that time.

It's hard to accept in this fast-moving, over-exciting world that you're not superhuman. Sometimes your inner-self, struggling to keep up with the pace, has to give you slow-down signals you can't ignore.

If an acute back crisis should occur, osteopathy (or chiropractic) is perhaps the most effective way to set the bones back into proper alignment. Acupuncture or acupressure (shiatsu) can be helpful to release the muscular spasm. Normal massage tends to aggravate the condition when at its most acute and should really only be used once symptoms have settled and subsequently as a preventative. Take painkillers, if you feel the need – it's no crime to mix natural medicine with allopathic – the overall relaxing effect can help the healing process.

Obviously, if you don't have complete faith in alternative practitioners to correctly diagnose the fault, do visit a GP and back specialist, but don't be too quick to agree to surgery. Instead, take the medical diagnosis to a competent or recommended osteopath or chiropractor, whose arts originally date back to the bone-setters of ancient India and China, and have them 'klunk' you back into shape the natural way.

Above all, use the entire experience as an opportunity to examine how you could better restructure your life and agenda, however minimally, to make the adventure slightly easier for you from now on. You deserve that.

Growing old gracefully

Anyone over the age of 29 must be familiar with those days when the sighting of a new grey hair or facial line triggers an 'ageing crisis'. We all know, intellectually, that we're getting older with every breath and that eventually we will die, but are perhaps thankfully able to ignore the process most of the time and get on with the ramshackle business of living. But on those days when no matter how much you squint into the mirror you can't dispel the proof of ageing, the process becomes suddenly urgent.

Of course, vanity is not the only trigger. Residual aches, pains, or worse, flare up due to unbalanced diet or overindulgence and, instead of feeling at one with your inner child, you feel at one instead with your inner old wrinkly. Naturally, this gives rise to anxiety. Anxiety gives rise to increased spending on hair colour, emotionally soothing face creams, vitamins and even, occasionally, to the making of resolutions to change dietary habits, take up yoga, join the gym or start cycling to work.

But why wait until you're quaking in your boots with mortal fear to make the change? That's like being in a long-term, worsening financial position and ignoring it until the bank shuts off your credit line. Just as with a healthy bank account, it's not so much about always being in credit as it is about keeping a steady flow of cash in and out, and trying to remain in credit most of the time. Bank managers love an account with high activity.

And so it is with your person which, if it isn't to degenerate, stagnate or run out of funds altogether, needs consistent high-level input-output – physically, mentally, emotionally and spiritually.

To prevent atrophy, stimulate your mind daily by studying – as informally as you like – something that makes your brain hum with intellectual excitement. Prevent yourself from becoming bored and boring. Keep an active eye on cultural trends and spend regular time interacting with younger people. Discipline your thought patterns to run on positive choices. Whether or not you believe the mind controls the body's self-regenerative powers, you may as well hedge your bets by suggesting to yourself, 'I choose health. I choose longevity. I choose my mind to reprogramme all my cells for health and longevity now.'

Stimulate your body and all its sub-systems by treating it to a daily session of intelligent exercise, meaning exercise performed in such a way as to allow your natural intelligence to travel to all parts and sub-systems of the body simultaneously, as in t'ai chi or yoga, for example, but no less so in running or using free weights if performed correctly. Any Olympic champion will tell you it's not the muscles that win the medal, it's the mind that informs those muscles. This involves breathing efficiently and relaxing the muscles to allow the joints to open and the blood and 'chi' (energy) to flow. In Oriental thought, to leave your daily exercise undone is tantamount to not washing, so do at least 20 minutes' intelligent exercise every day.

Try to have a steady seven hours' sleep a night, preferably embarked upon before midnight or soon after and do more to consciously forbid yourself to succumb to stressing yourself about anything – ever.

To prevent your emotions from curdling or becoming stultified with age, avoid smothering your feelings with the errant belief that you know all the answers. Be open, be vulnerable. Love those around you as you would have done before kindergarten. Love everyone more, even and especially yourself. Let yourself feel the pain of love – the exercise keeps your heart young. Take up some form of daily meditation, if only for a few minutes a day, to provide instant access to the more peaceful inner realms and give the spirit a bath, so to speak.

None of the above, nor indeed any intervention by healer, doctor, geneticist, nutritionist, pharmacist or life-assurance company can guarantee you freedom from infirmity and eventual death. But you stand to gain immeasurable long-term benefits by taking the game into your own hands.

In the meantime, a most closely guarded Taoist (Chinese) secret of longevity is to ensure a profuse daily intake of thyme which, as well as being a powerful anti-oxidant, is considered by some to be the mystic 'elixir of youth' itself – live long and prosper.

How to handle PMS

Any man will to some extent agree that a rudimentary understanding of the condition commonly known as PMS (pre-menstrual syndrome) is essential. For a man, to be forewarned and forearmed means to be better able to understand and possibly be of worthwhile help. For a woman, to be able to justify why all hell breaks loose once a month might make her feel more in control of the situation – for feeling out of control is the crux of the problem.

The process of menstruation is complex, involving three major, and inextricably linked, organs. First, according to those Oriental doctors of old, your spleen (which is under your ribs on the left) is integrally connected to your pituitary gland, master-switch of the endocrine system. This controls your appetite (especially for sweet things), your short-term memory, your feelings of satisfaction with life on a moment-by-moment basis and, most importantly, the overall production of blood. In the few days leading up to menstruation, the spleen has to work twice as hard to build blood to replace that which will be lost during the period. That's why you crave more sweet food, can't remember where you left your keys, and whatever someone says or does is not good enough.

Second, your liver, whose job it is to store, purify and release the blood on demand, is also in charge of your 'animal soul' – the wild one within, with all its potential for unbridled emotional chaos, including and especially the expression of rage. Just before the period, as the liver cranks up to work overtime on the new blood load, it strains, overheats and, in so doing, loses control of the wild woman. Hence the sudden bursts of unprovoked anger and feelings of frustration: whether in your relationships or your work. When added to a maladjusted spleen, this can produce an inflammatory mix.

Third, the kidneys, responsible for overall maintenance of the womb and reproductive system, are also in charge of eliminating waste (through urination), regulating body fluids, maintaining body temperature, stabilising the emotional landscape in general and the flow of tears in particular, and keeping you feeling safe in the world. The kidneys are, with the help of the spleen and liver, in charge of providing, circulating and regenerating the yin or female energy for the entire system, itself intricately interlinked with all internal functions and especially the 100 per cent, no-men-need-apply menstrual process.

Just before the period, the kidneys tend to suffer an appreciable loss of energy through the extra exertion, potentially leaving you weepy, bloated, temperamental, anxious, occasionally spotty, clammy, hot and cold, fraught and feeling like you can't cope. So when you throw depleted kidney energy into the equation, you have the full three-dimensional horror of full-blown PMS, complete with anguish, hurled plates and household nuclear war.

To suggest a universal remedy is as impossible as suggesting which colour T-shirt would suit everyone in the UK. It all depends on the constitutional state of the liver, spleen, kidneys, reproductive system, hormone levels and temperament of the individual.

However, it is fair to say that agnus castus can work wonders in reducing water retention and often all other symptoms, too. Mega B complex with extra B6 can be helpful in supporting the liver.

Donquai is effective for keeping the kidneys strong and supporting the general yin energy of the body, and raw beets can be good for supporting the spleen and strengthening the blood. Acupuncture works well for some people, as does cranio-sacral therapy, as in fact do most alternative methods aimed at rebalancing energy flow. But with all these suggestions, it's important to remember that rebalancing requires time – perhaps many menstrual cycles – and hence patience.

As for the men, it's important for us to recognise the signs early and, above all, be willing not to take things personally. As you've no doubt heard countless times before, the best you can do when caught in hormonal crossfire is to ignore all missiles and shrapnel and go over and give her a tender, loving cuddle. Just don't expect a reward.

Unknotting your spinal pathway

I'm about to extol the virtues of lying on the floor with a good book under your head. So, if you have an aversion to floors, lying down, good books or all three, stop reading now. If, however, you might be even slightly interested in the enormous benefits of this simplest of recreational activities, or indeed already know all about it but could use a little propaganda to remind you of its inestimable value, bear with me as I unravel. For unravelling is the main purpose of this exercise. Unravelling the build-up of stress that comes with every life story. Unravelling the misconceptions about life that cause you unnecessary grief. But mostly just unravelling the knots around your spine, so you can walk, sit, run, dance and even hop, skip and jump if the mood takes you, with greater ease and range of movement.

Though adopted by practitioners of the Alexander Technique as a way to experience fully the advantages of a lengthened spine and broadened torso, lying inert and supine was originally developed by practitioners of hatha yoga in India and Taoist nei kung (inner development work) in China at least 5,000 years ago. Naturally, lying on one's back in its raw form has been around since the start of human commerce and is nothing extraordinary in itself. What is extraordinary is when you practise it mindfully. In yoga it's called the 'death' or 'corpse' pose and is practised with legs straight, heels together and without a book.

In Taoism, it's called 'taking a rest' and is practised with knees bent, soles flat on the floor, feet shoulder-width apart, both feet facing forwards as if on parallel train tracks and head resting on a copy of something of the (physical) depth of say, *Captain Corelli's Mandolin* or even *Return of the Urban Warrior*, if you can bear to put it down. This head-raising effect was originally provided by a bamboo neck support to prevent the back of the neck closing up and hindering circulation to the brain. The bent knees mimic the way you'd stand if performing chi-gung or t'ai chi, and enable your lower back to sink properly 'into' the floor.

The idea is to become totally inert as if dead, except of course for the rise and fall of your belly as the breath enters and leaves (at a slow, even pace).

So, having arranged your physical form appropriately, ensuring an absence of draught or damp, use your mind to extend (uncrumple) your spine from the sacrum (at the base) to the back of your skull. Simultaneously, mentally broaden your torso across the hips, middle back and shoulder blades. Let your arms rest naturally by your sides, palms up, and allow your genitals, belly, chest, throat and face to relax.

With each successive round of inhalation and exhalation, feel as if you are sinking progressively more deeply into the floor as if magnetised towards the core of the earth. Focus attention on your spine and working your mind upwards from the base to the head, imagine you are mentally unpicking all the little knots that have accumulated along your spinal pathway.

When you feel fully relaxed and sunk to the max, start to focus on your breath, which by now should have decelerated considerably and be entering and leaving your body effortlessly through both nostrils in absolute silence. This increases your natural joie de vivre and frees your mind to appreciate the miracle of your moment-to-moment existence.

But if you find that hard to believe, try this Taoist meditation. As you inhale, imagine your entire self dissolve so that all that remains is that pure consciousness without past or future which simply watches. If it thinks anything at all, it thinks, 'I am dissolved!' With every outbreath, conversely, imagine yourself to be outpouring the unique essence of your life, complete with past and future, into the world around you in order to infuse it with fresh energy.

By practising this for, say, 30 days every day, you'll find yourself breathing into a space that is more accurately described as eternal life, which can be very reassuring. And now for a spot of 'taking a rest'.

Devising a daily exercise regime

Hanging out with Nico Rhamodda, one of the Flying Dudes trapeze outfit, the other day, talking over the state of the world, I was impressed by his solution to achieving personal balance, courage, calm and the ability to 'shine the light' during such potentially dark and tricky times in human history. His view is that we should redouble our efforts as a warrior to strengthen and prepare our mind, body and spirit to meet the day with grace come what may, by increasing whatever we do for daily training.

This made me realise that adopting a daily training routine does not come naturally to many people, and so I thought I'd remind you how important for peace of mind as well as health of body it is to adopt a form of psycho-physical exercise and stick to it every day.

Before engaging in battle, the much feared warriors of Genghis Khan's Mongolian hordes would sit up all night practising 'churka', a form of intense kneading massage using a small implement, applied by self or fellow warrior to all parts of the body systematically. It is an extreme sensation which would normally be described as utterly painful, but that puts a negative slant on it, as pain is only an opinion and this kind of pain is highly beneficial, arising as it does from releasing stagnant energy and tension from the muscles. By going through this pain, each warrior would become fearless and thus near invincible.

While most of us fortunately are not called upon to enter into direct battle with our 'enemies', we still find our bio-emotional wiring responding to global events as if we do, at least on an unconscious level. And though it would prob-ably be taking things a bit far to sit up all night kneading ourselves till we scream, it would certainly behove us all to rise an hour or two earlier and devote that privileged early morning period before the world wakes up to indulging in a session of self-strengthening. The result after only a few days will be increased alertness, perceptiveness, clarity, emotional stability and a reduced tendency to worry or fret.

The psychological benefit of feeling physically ready for whatever the day may bring is so tangible that it is well worth the effort required to addict yourself to daily training. Like other addictions, exercise alters your state of mind, but unlike other mind-altering substances which eventually get the better of you, exercise – if performed with sensitivity – is an addiction that does you good. See it as your morning meeting with the internal troops, a time to focus on what kind of day you wish for.

Whichever form of exercise you choose, there are various factors which are best kept in mind throughout the session. Keep the breathing as slow, deep and steady as possible. Keep all muscles, other than ones directly being used, soft; lengthen your spine – especially at the back of your neck and lumbar region – and focus your awareness entirely on what you're doing rather than on what you have to do later (it may help to keep a notepad handy for any brainwaves you have while exercising).

Personally, I know of no other form of all-round personal training so effective as martial arts and of those none so efficacious as the Taoist internal forms of t'ai chi, pa kua and hsing i, but then I'm biased and there are many who swear by practising karate or tae kwon do or capoiera. However, if investing time, energy and money in learning any of these is difficult for you, you may wish to experiment with the following Taoist push-up exercise, which as well as loosening your hips, strengthening your arms and loosening your shoulders also generates an increase in emotional stability. It can be practised by anyone, strong or weak. If you do suspect you may suffer from any cardio-vascular condition, you should consult your doctor first, however.

Stand legs apart, feet at double the width of your shoulders, bend forward at the hips and place your palms on the floor three feet in front of you.

Inhale. As you do, bend your elbows and move from a point just below your belly button, forward and diagonally downwards so that your chest hovers just above the floor between your palms. Now exhale and, straightening your arms, move backwards and diagonally back upwards from that same point below your navel to return your body to the starting position. Start with three repetitions and gradually work up to 18 at a go, maintaining total relaxation throughout.

This is a useful addition to any routine but even in itself will help boost strength and stability levels and render you more amenable to view world events on the lateral plane where so-called miracles occur, or unexpected quantum events such as the sudden unexpected universal declaration of world peace and prosperity we all so need right now.

It is possible to transcend day-to-day reality

Recently, I started the morning in the most wonderful way by paying a visit to Frederick and Janice, the most entertaining dental duet on the planet, for a clean and polish. Though deft of drill and all other arcane metal bits and pieces of the dental world, Frederick is blessed with a superb sense of humour, which works a synergistic treat with his nurse Janice's – they have you cracking up with their mad gags and surreal dialogue fired incessantly over your face against a backing track of zany tunes blaring much too loud for 'normal' dentistry protocol. If one could insert a camera in one's mouth, there'd be a Channel 4 commission in the offing in no time – reality, fly-in-the-mouth comedy soap (*In the Mouth with Jan and Fred?*).

Like all great comedians, Frederick's blessed with innate wisdom. He points out that lying there, offering your mouth, is tantamount to surrendering control for 20 minutes or so – something we don't like to do. When you're gripping on to control, he suggests (and the oral region is one of our most controlled 'bits'), you're not available to receive true education from events around you. But when you let go, you are invariably gifted with the next portion of enlightenment due you on the path.

Then he started with the metallic scraper thing that makes the nerves in your teeth go into overdrive, so I pressed into the 'great eliminator' point between thumb and forefinger on the opposite hand to the side he was working on to numb the sensation (I'll explain later). Focusing on my breathing, giggling a bit with Frederick reminding me to 'Move that little tummy up and down and let the breath roll in and out!' I slowed it down, exhaling strongly, like a woman in labour (but not as pretty), whenever the sensation nudged red on the internal pain meter. Within three breaths, I'd managed to alter my relationship with the pain to the extent that it disappeared altogether. Helped along by more uncontrollable fits of incongruous belly-laughter with each gag that sailed between Jan and Fred across my upturned face, I was now free to enjoy the meditation.

I say meditation because when you surrender control to a 'higher force', in this case personified by Frederick, thus disidentifying with your habitual 'daily self', relax your breathing and focus awareness in your skull (which having your teeth messed about with forces you to do), you enter a deep state of meditation, a sort of dental nirvana, and great revelations unfold in your mind. I accept this is a rather extreme way to engineer a good meditation session, or indeed to watch a bit of close-up comedy, but if you have to go to the dentist or any other activity involving sensations normally associated with torture, you might as well grow into and through the experience, rather than resist it and miss any jewels it may conceal.

I was actually doing part of an old Taoist meditation which was initially explained to me in a heavy Beijing accent (some 25 years ago) thus: 'First you bones – just bones. Next you muscles – just muscles. Next you fluids – nothing else. Next you nerves. Next you chi [energy]. Last, you spirit!'

Contemplate yourself as being nothing more than a skeleton – even as you sit here reading this. Once you've had a moment feeling that, contemplate yourself being nothing but soft tissue. You then 'become' fluid – blood, digestive juices, hormonal secretions, urine, etc. Then see yourself as nothing more than a nerve network, then an energy field and finally (disembodied) consciousness. If you manage a moment of that, you're doing well – in fact, you're doing well to achieve pure awareness of any of these states – it takes time and practice. To re-enter a normal waking state, simply contemplate yourself as a fully integrated network of bones, muscles, fluids, nerves, energy and consciousness, focus on your breathing, internally shout 'Hurrah!' for the miracle of it all, and carry on as you were.

The effects of this practised over a few weeks can cause you to see everything from a more grounded perspective, resulting in more unshakable inner composure.

As for the 'great eliminator' point to numb your mouth at the dentist's, it can be found at the end of the crack on the side of each hand formed by holding thumb to index finger. Press in with the thumb (of your other hand) until it produces a strong but pleasant, almost paralysing ache that radiates through the palm. The large intestine meridian (of which this is the fourth point along) runs up both arms and into the oral region, but crosses over at the mouth, so press the left hand to numb the right side of the mouth and vice versa. This point is helpful in relieving some forms of constipation and associated headaches, so bear that in mind if suffering from such a condition when using this at the dentist, in case it works instantaneously while you've still a mouthful of metal instruments. Mind you, I'm sure that would trigger the ultimate crack-up round at Jan and Fred's.

Stay supple in mind, body and spirit, and the older you are the better

I am in a recording studio in Cheshire working on my album (being a compulsive musician as well as writer, for my sins), waiting for Justin, the engineer, to finish fiddling around with my disembodied voice so I can put some new guitar parts down, and writing this in case the moment passes. You see, I've been watching moments passing at great speed lately.

Do you have phases like that, when you're acutely aware of your egg timer spilling its sand? Such phases usually last 72 hours and invariably begin for me with a bad face day – I would say bad hair but mine's too short to cause any significant mood fluctuations. I gaze in the mirror and think: I really am looking like an old bastard and there I was thinking I was just 17. Then I walk down the street and wonder how I fit in. Do people see me as a middle-aged man poorly disguised as a carefree youth; am I still attractive or desirable in any way (commercially as well as romantically); shall I settle suavely into being a sexy older man or just lie down graciously and wait for one of my kids to have a child so I can play Grandpa and find fulfilment like that?

The way I see it, I've only just begun, and though at 49 I may have already gone through half the sand in my egg timer, I nevertheless feel myself to be merely at the start of a limitless adventure. Or maybe that's just the t'ai chi I practise each day giving me delusions of mortal grandeur.

Yet TT Liang, one of the great t'ai chi masters of the last century, said (at the age of 83) that life begins at 70. That's because he was savvy to the fact that daily practice of t'ai chi keeps you young by boosting your blood and energy circulation, massaging your internal organs and exercising your muscles and joints in its uniquely bendy-stretchy fashion. So by the time you reach 70 you feel as young as a spring rose and hopefully have the wisdom of experience to lend you some psycho-emotional weight to provide a ballast as you finally embark on the beginning of your life.

Talking of weight as a ballast, the other night I saw Sam Moore in concert – he's the Sam from Sam and Dave, the killer duo who as well as singing the classic 'Soul Man' in the late 60s were the inspiration for John Belushi's *Blues Brothers*. Pushing 70, and with a stately pot belly to show for it, he's loveable and can still out-soul anyone I've heard on MTV Base. This dude is seriously funky. And when you watch him dance, you realise how suppleness is key to youthfulness. The singing helps. Children sing spontaneously, so singing puts you back in touch with your childlike nature, but also exercises your lungs and gets more oxygen to the brain.

Then there's my dear friend and guiding light, Raja Ram, the undisputed king of the global trance (dance) scene. He's on a different continent every weekend, DJing to audiences of tens of thousands from Rio to Tokyo, or New York to Ibiza (think first class, think limos). He's also the boss of the world's leading trance label and has more energy in his little toe than most nuclear power stations. He's 61. From him I see how important it is to be mentally challenged to keep your brain active, and to be challenged you need to be creatively engaged with a project that fires your fascination to the quick.

So forget about retirement. Your dreams of permanent armchair vegetation won't make you happy and will more likely accelerate your demise. Change paths at 60 or 65, sure, but don't think of giving up on your meaningful inter-action with the world. Instead think of using that time to learn a new art or develop one, whether it's t'ai chi, singing, dancing, DJing, painting, mountaineering or whatever, and allow that to be the vehicle to carry you on your adventure. Never say die to the adventure, and let it be one that others are inspired by. Keep your body strong and supple, and your mind will follow. Keep your mind strong and supple, and your body will follow.

A strong and supple thought-stream there, and totally out of nowhere. Really, I was just sitting here listening to my voice go round and round, and suddenly before I knew it this piece was written. I didn't even know I was thinking all that stuff. Maybe just an undisciplined rant, maybe a channelling from the gods Akai and Rolland. I get internally anarchistic like this when I'm making music – it brings out the teenager in me. Take it as a post-adolescent rallying cry to (myself and) everyone who has even vaguely considered their ageing, not to be seduced into the idea of giving up and putting themselves out to pasture, but to embrace the thought of beginning life anew at 70 and start preparing for it straightaway – the younger the better.

And now if you'll excuse me, Justin's holding out the guitar and gesturing me to come and drop a chop or two on to the old hard disk, because I'm not such an unfunky old geezer myself. (Move over, TT, Sam and Raja Ram!)

Give yourself a gentle, drug-free pick-me-up and your GP a break

Consult your GP before reading this! I say that because I've been told that I rarely preface my advice with the above. I admit I have felt free to drop it recently, being of the opinion that the majority of readers understand when and when not to visit a GP. Also, counting more than a few GPs as close friends, I know that for a fact, in their already overstretched state, it would be counter-productive to suggest that every time someone experiments with self-help, they should visit their GP first – sadly, there just isn't the person-power available.

Which is exactly why so many of us have made the bold decision to take responsibility for our own wellbeing and do all we can to prevent conditions occurring or becoming unmanageable. Obviously, the downside of this is that sometimes alleviating symptoms may blind you to a serious problem needing medical attention. But this can also be the case if you take the allopathic route. The point is, even with the best equipment and minds at our disposal, there is always an element of guesswork or intuition involved in diagnosis and disease detection.

The upside, though, is that by engaging in self-help you become more intuitive and sensitive to the workings of your body, hence more likely to detect the warning signs.

Furthermore, if someone doubts their own ability to balance themselves in a particular state, there are battalions of well-trained holistic practitioners covering a myriad of effective disciplines just waiting to help them.

True, when so-called alternative medicine first started surfacing as a viable option, people still treated practitioners as they did their GPs – gods, with the power of life or death, to whom they could hand over responsibility for their health. But now the take-responsibility-for-your-own-health message espoused by every holistic practitioner in the land is common currency, and people are far more receptive to the idea of triggering their own rebalancing.

Of course there's a downside to this as well – overdosing on various supplements or mixing the wrong herbal and allopathic remedies, though rare, can be extremely dangerous. Most, however, manage to conduct their self-help experiments without major mishap and, indeed, with great benefit, not least to overworked GPs.

But it is an experiment. How else could it be? We are not machines, and healing of any kind is an art as well as a science. Hence, outcomes are slightly unpredictable. The same holds true for all kinds of medicine.

However, the fail-safe is your body's own innate intelligence, which if given even half a shove in the right direction tends to work miracles or quantum-healing events in your person. It's all in knowing how and where to shove.

So saying, try this as a general subtle pick-me-up (however, if in any doubt, of course do consult your GP first). Sitting relatively upright, back comfortably supported, body relaxed, with breathing slow, even, soft and fluid, place a forefinger directly on your crown (the uppermost point on your head), and with arm and shoulder relaxed, gently, using no more than 110g of pressure, make circles of 1in diameter, moving skin against bone, 18 clockwise, 18 counter-clockwise. As you do, feel, or imagine you can feel, a line of energy snaking up your spine from the base to the crown of your head at the command of your circling fingertips. Then lower your arm slowly and relax, visualising the energy settling again at the base of your spine and within minutes you should feel lighter and more optimistic about keeping yourself in good balance – rather than feeling you need to visit the doctor. (That's right – give those guys a break.)

Forget the yoga mat, all you need is the floor

During a deeply introspective moment just now, I realised I have a thing about, indeed am harbouring an out-and-out prejudice against, of all things, rubber yoga mats.

When I took up this ancient discipline in the early 70s, people didn't use rubber yoga mats, nor did they wear so-called yoga clothes to practise. The loose-fitting hippie attire peculiar to most early yoga-adopters was sufficient, as was a good old-fashioned floor, whether covered in carpet or just bare boards. People didn't use accessories. Sure, the odd karate belt was employed to tie up limbs to ease passage into a particular posture. Perhaps one would even lie back over a bench covered with cushions to stretch open the chest, while holding a couple of heavy books to add torque, but there were no specially con-structed back-arch supports, no ropes or pulleys.

Yoga originated in India with aesthetes who plonked themselves wherever they found themselves and dropped into whichever posture was appropriate, without a thought for equipment. Then, in the late 70s, along came an enter-prising German who found that if you bought high-quality, light-green carpet underlay at wholesale prices and cut it into rectangles, you could sell them on at a profit to the burgeoning number of yoga students who liked to take a suck-a-thumb blanket to their yoga lessons lest they make facial contact with the floor.

Before long, not an ethnically decorated living room in all of bohemia was without its rolled-up strip of green-rubber carpet underlay in the corner. And that was fine by me, as long as these mats remained confined to the home or yoga studio.

But as I saw more and more photographs in daft celebrity magazines of scrubbed-up, mineral-water-toting, goody-two-shoes celebrities with mats rolled up under their arms like an accessory – and no longer hospital-green but sea-blue, too – a prejudice took root in my soul.

You see, to me, yoga mats have a smell about them: not just of sweaty feet, but, more sinister, the smell of the control freak. Put your cheek against the floor, for heaven's sake. Merge your features with the humble ground, be it carpeted or bare boards. Be one with the underfoot filth of the human race – it helps build up your immunity.

Yoga is a psycho-spiritual discipline of such profundity that it needs no yoga equipment marketed by yogic entrepreneurs. On the contrary, its very name means union – union with all that is, and that means carpets and floorboards, too.

But to be fair, the mats were sold on the premise that rubber underfoot would prevent your feet from slipping in standing poses, though if you stand correctly with proper placement of foot on floor, a mat shouldn't be necessary. If it is, you're probably straining. And of course, using cushions to support yourself if particularly stiff or challenged by illness or disability is obviously bona fide.

When I started yoga as a teenager, my legs and hips were so stiff I had to use cushions just to sit down on my heels. But you should never go beyond what you can do naturally, even if that's limited. Yoga grows inside you slowly over time with practice – it's never something to rush. It's all this rushing on our yoga mats that's causing the unprecedented rise in yoga-related injuries in the UK since the mid-90s.

The most advanced and difficult yoga posture, and the one that all others are designed to facilitate optimum practice of, is the 'corpse pose' – lying on your back on the floor like a corpse, absolutely still but for extremely slow, gentle, deep breathing, so relaxed it's as if you're not here at all.

So I say, leave your suck-a-thumb blankets at home and let's have an end to the rubberisation of not just yoga but life as we know it.

Warming up can be bad for you

I saw one of those things in the papers the other day that attempts to throw your worldview on its head, and which for dearth of real news somehow made it to front-page headline position, giving it the near-divine status of unassailable fact, and I really think that as a responsible barefoot doctor, I should air it here in case anyone was confused or misled by it.

Not that in the light of the current potentially tumultuous world events – the ecological crisis, geopolitical brinksmanship games and the economic-meltdown scenario – it would appear to be particularly dramatic news, but it seems a team of Australian scientists have determined after years of careful, costly research, that stretching before and after exercising in the gym does you no good whatsoever.

You may sympathise with them for jumping like kangaroos to this patently absurd conclusion if you've ever observed people stretching in the gym, bouncing up and down, huffing and puffing, po-faced with straining jaw and bulging veins, because that does you no good. Huffing and puffing constricts your blood circulation, straining stresses your organs, grimness of face makes you feel glum, hence lowering immune response, and bouncing like a demented jack-in-the-box traumatises your muscles, which can't cope with the mixed messages being sent them: 'Relax – I hate myself – relax – I hate myself', etc. Your muscles require clear messages from you, just like anyone you're having an intimate relationship with.

Stretching as we know it originates from hatha yoga, which, it must be categorically stated, does more good for your muscles before or after exercise, or any other activity, than just about anything else on the planet short of a damn good pro massage after a day's soaking in a sulphur hot spring with a Martini.

In yoga, you don't so much stretch your muscles as elongate them gracefully, using your mind rather than brute force. In fact, you never use brute force because that's working against your body rather than with it. You must entice your body to co-operate. This, though, requires patience, mindfulness and humility, three qualities often hard to access in the gym environment. So perhaps do your stretching at home, where it is hopefully warm and cosy. Give yourself five minutes for each stretch, which is adequate to ease yourself slowly into position, hang there for a bit and come out of it slowly. And on no account bounce.

The point of stretching, or any of the internal forms of exercise – t'ai chi and chi-gung, for example – is to build an increasingly better working relationship with your own body. The injuries you do yourself exercising occur because somewhere in the hidden recesses of your mind you've actually (unconsciously, of course, unless you're incredibly weird) issued the command for an injury to happen. So the more conscious connection you have with the workings of your body, the more you can supervise the commands being issued.

For example (and only try this if free of back or hip injury or impediment), stand with feet just over a metre apart, both feet facing forwards, and very gently and slowly lower your trunk from the hips, supporting yourself with palms on the floor in front of you or holding your lower legs, and simply hang there luxuriating in the stretch along your hamstrings and inner thighs for nine breaths. Now slowly allow your trunk to come upright, starting at the hips and bringing your head up last, keeping your breath flowing throughout.

When you've done that, do it again and you'll notice it comes more easily.

Then go out for a brisk, bouncy walk round the block, arms swinging and head held high, and if you don't feel more springy of step, young of hip and fleet of foot than usual, I'll eat my shoes.

Smelly, sweaty and unsightly... toes don't deserve their bad press

Be honest, if I asked you to imagine yourself covered from head to toe in a mystical golden healing light that made you immune to illness and pain and caused your coffers to be instantly filled with wealth, apart from thinking this piece is going to turn out extra hippie-like, which bits of yourself do you spend most time seeing so covered?

I bet it's not your toes! In fact, and I'm not just saying this as part of a barefoot propaganda campaign, in all my years of working at fixing people's bodies and souls, I'd say the bit that the majority of people despise about their bodies the most is their toes. People are actively ashamed of them.

It starts off with wearing shoes that cramp the toes as a child, progresses to never taking your trainers off indoors in case the smell overwhelms you or your company, and by the time you're a fully formed adult, the poor things are mangled so out of shape, you can hardly bear to look at them.

As a young lad, I used to mow the grass and do the shopping for an elderly lady called Mrs Stenlake (which, as a silly schoolboy, I used to change to Mrs Swanlake), who unfortunately could hardly walk, on account of having had most of her toes amputated. This left a big impression on me, so that even before I got into yoga or healing, where much emphasis is placed on them, I was always sharply aware of the importance of toes. We weren't given them for nothing, after all.

In fact, the Taoists claim that only when your toes are relaxed and uncramped, spreadable and flexible, can your energy and life force find full expression. Cast your mind back to walking barefoot over rocks on the beach, feeling your toes grip to balance you, and you'll appreciate this.

Anyway, back to the plot. As well as being more crucial to your wellbeing than you thought, not to mention their usefulness in helping hold you upright on rocks and urban streets, there's nothing that aesthetically rounds off a nice pair of feet better than 10 (if you're lucky) beautiful toes. But if, through years of neglect and misuse, you find yours a trifle ugly, don't despair. Help is herein at hand.

By gentle stretching performed on a semi-regular basis, say once every few days, your toes will regain their original beauty within just a few weeks, ready, hopefully, to be displayed with pride on the beach next summer.

Start by lovingly taking hold of the little toe on your right foot between thumb and forefinger and pulling it slowly back towards your leg till you feel a powerful little stretch through the underside of the toe and the ball of the foot. Hold this for half a minute breathing freely as you do, and release slowly, luxuriating in the sense of relief flooding the toe. Repeat on the next toe, the next toe and the one after that, but when you get to the big toe, press the other toes down away from you with one hand while using thumb and forefinger of the other to pull the toe back in order to achieve a proper stretch. Then use thumb and forefinger as best you can to stretch the little toe away from the next, then that from the next and so on, in order to maximise their spreadability. Spend a few loving moments massaging up the length of each toe between thumb and forefinger, and when finished, repeat the whole ritual on the other foot.

Finally, look down at all 10 toes at once and, wriggling them joyfully, now all full of pulsing energy, tell them sincerely, 'I love you, my toes!' and carry on as you were.

See, that wasn't as hippie-like as you'd suspected it might be, was it? So now if I suggest you visualise yourself covered from head to toe in a healing golden light bringing you immunity from illness as well as great prosperity in spite of the economic forecasts, I wager you'll see a greater preponderance of light down below than before. And when they shout, 'Oy, Twinkletoes!' in the street, you'll now have the quiet confidence of knowing they mean you – Twinkletoes!

Tune in to the sounds around you

How precisely do you listen to what people say to you? Do you actually hear what's being said? Indeed, how often do you listen to the multitude of sounds around you? Hearing is a miracle, but how fully do you allow yourself to enjoy the magnificent cacophonous symphony of life being played entirely for your benefit even now?

We all employ selective listening, and necessarily so – were we to actually focus on all the sound assailing us, our minds would probably implode. However, left unchecked, selective listening progressively becomes so acute that you stop hearing and become stone deaf. According to Taoist medical wisdom, your ears are the so-called flower or expression of your kidneys – that is, your hearing abilities are directly influenced by the amount of energy in your kidneys. Hence hearing diminishes with age as your kidneys naturally grow weaker.

Kidney energy also determines emotional resilience levels. When your emotions are disturbed, say as a child by your parents arguing, your kidney region subtly contracts, thus reducing energy flow. This triggers a subtle closing down of the hearing on an energetic and emotional level. You unconsciously choose to block it out. This process embeds itself as a pattern, eventually severely limiting what you can hear, and has you all tied up finding the best price on a ridiculously expensive newfangled digital hearing aid.

To counteract this tendency, there's a Taoist meditation exercise known as listening behind you. Simply close your eyes and, gathering your awareness in the dead centre of your brain, allow all the sounds behind you to fill your mind. Don't analyse or categorise – simply allow the sound to enter without comment. The behind-you bit is just a metaphor, a trick to trip the mind into shutting up, as you're actually hearing to the sides and front as well. Practising this, it quickly becomes evident that you've been seriously limiting the range of sounds on offer. If you can manage a few minutes a day, within just one week or so, your hearing will become noticeably more acute.

Opening yourself to this panoramic soundscape also helps your directional hearing abilities. Directional hearing is becoming more problematic these days as we sit around in noisy restaurants and walk along noisy streets. To assist directional hearing in such environments, cup a hand over one ear to block out peripheral noise and help capture the sound you require from the appropriate direction instead, even if this does make you look like an old biddy.

You can also augment your hearing abilities by stimulating energy flow topically. Massage each ear between thumb and forefinger gently yet vigorously for a minute or so, paying careful attention to every nook and cranny. Then close your ears by covering them with your palms and rhythmically release and increase the pressure alternately 81 times, so that outside sounds rise and fall like ocean waves. Not only is it relaxing, but practised on a daily basis, it will also make you more resilient to noise as well as help prevent, and sometimes cure, deafness, tinnitus and ear infection.

According to spiritual traditions worth their salt, as well as to the big-bang progenitors of physics, the world began with sound. In the Bible, the first words of Genesis are, 'God spoke, and said let there be light.' The Hindus call this divine generative speaking 'shabd', the subtle holy sound for which yogis spend years quieting their minds enough to hear, believing correctly that this will bring enlightenment. The Taoists say shut up and listen properly and all will be revealed.

So, if this is what you seek, quieten yourself for a moment now, massage your ears, do the opening and closing exercise, then relax your arms, close your eyes and allow the plethora of sound around you to fill your consciousness until at the very core of all sounds you hear the faint traces of the one subtle sound underlying all others. And if that gives you any serious revelations, let me know. Sound sound?

Take your foot off the gas and you'll find you travel further

Up in the studio mixing my tunes, I noticed after a couple of hours of intense concentration came to an end, that particular job done, with 'Bernie the Journey', the mixer who came over from Germany especially, getting on with his bit, I had nothing to do for a moment – no phone calls, no tasks, no decisions to be made, yet instead of consciously taking command of the situation and allowing myself a little rest, so caught up in the buzz of being busy was I, addicted of course to the endorphins, I caught myself holding my body quite tense and thus wasting precious energy for no reason. It made me reflect on how, according to those reflective Taoist sages of yore, the interplay between action and rest is governed by the motion of yin and yang, and so instead of actually resting I was compelled to share my reflections with you.

The dance of the two primal forces of existence, the yin representing contraction, hence rest, and the yang expansion, hence action, occurs universally, affects all known phenomena and is intrinsic to the human condition. You can take advantage of it to optimise your energy and stamina and thereby increase your effectiveness.

The first stage is to observe yourself during those times in the course of a busy day between phases of intense (yang) activity when there's nothing actually needing to be done for a second or two, where hitherto you wouldn't have believed it's worth changing mode for such a short yin time between tasks – this is like revving your engine at the top of the gauge and keeping the clutch pedal down near the floor even when moving at 10mph – it strains the machine

– in this case, your vital organs, which, in the long run, shortens your life.

Between tasks give yourself the luxury of decelerating momentarily and letting yourself creep along very slowly for a few yards. It's really rather pleasant when you get used to it – but not only pleasurable, essential if you're at all interested in increasing your longevity, as it's the only way in a busy world like this to refresh your energy. Failing to do so winds you up tighter and tighter, increasing inner heat until you internally combust and die.

Catch yourself now, if you have a moment, and check your body. Are you relaxed or holding your musculature unnecessarily tense? Is your breathing shallow or deep?

The simple act of noticing it tends to slow and deepen it, thus increasing relaxation levels immediately, though you help it along by consciously telling your breathing pattern to decelerate and deepen.

Finally, adjust your body positioning. The more perfectly aligned you are in relation to the ground, the less strain occurs in the muscles and hence everything else.

The dance of yin and yang plays itself out between your rear and frontal aspects – your back being yang and your front yin. Being perfectly perpendicular to the floor balances the yin and yang which makes you feel immediately lighter and more in the present moment.

Too far forwards on the balls of your feet or too far backwards on your heels places unnecessary strain on your psychophysical complex, thus wasting precious life-force.

Take a moment to stand up with feet shoulder-width apart and rock gently on your soles from heel to toe until you find the optimum point of balance.

Then check left-right balance. Again with feet at shoulder-width, gently rock your weight from side to side from left foot to right until you feel the optimum point of balance.

Which isn't half a long-winded way of saying, relax, breathe, straighten yourself up and you'll feel a lot better immediately. Meantime, having taken my ear off the ball in a semi yin way, it now sounds like 'Bernie the Journey' and the mix may have gone a bit off the beaten track, so I'll be off now in a fairly yang way to rectify things.

We don't have to take the weight of the world on our shoulders

As I sit gazing out at the South Atlantic from my window in Cape Town, instead of working like I should be – two weeks of engagements nearly done, 14 days of being extremely responsible in fulfilling my obligations – my eye alights on a coach below with 'Atlas' emblazoned on its side, along with a picture of that crazy Greek hero of old holding up the world on his shoulders. I check my own shoulders and am gratified and (still) surprised to see how 40 years of yoga and t'ai chi have paid off on finding them and me supple and loose as a long-legged barefoot goose.

I chuckle as I recall someone at a workshop this week asking if I had any short-cut moves for releasing chronic shoulder tension, and me quipping back: '15 years of yoga!' Chuckling almost leads to smugness, so I halt the process for fear of descending into complacency and notice that, by focusing, I can actually get my shoulders to drop a good inch more, which makes me think of you and how I might be able to entice you to do likewise, such a fine feeling of relief does it encourage in my being.

But before I do, consider how much psychological weight you've been carrying around since you were old enough to think for yourself – the weight of all those decisions, all that pondering about life and death, not to mention bank balances, the weight of unresolved guilt for all the bad things done, the weight of love, of missing, the weight of existential fear, of unexpressed rage, of regrets for things never done, the dreams you fear you'll never realise, the lies, the weight of trying to fulfil other people's expectations. Feel it resting on your shoulders now and ask yourself, 'Do I really need to be carrying this weight around all day and night? Do I really want to?'

It may momentarily surprise you to remember you have a choice in the matter. But if you don't, then who does? Of course, if you feel it suits your make-up to carry the world on your shoulders to give you ballast, then carry on. But if you have a sneaking doubt that life might be better were you to drop your load, so to speak, then don't hold back.

Which brings me back to enticing you. Imagine yourself as Atlas now, with the weight of your entire lifetime resting on your shoulders – the tonnage of all those experiences, feelings, people, situations, all those buildings, all those vast vistas that comprise the story of you. Feel that weight. Now breathe in and, as you breathe out, see yourself drop it on the ground behind you and say affirmatively, in Ayn Rand's immortal words, 'Atlas shrugged'!

Do it again and again until your shoulders have fully dropped and you feel broad as a (very large) bean across your upper body.

As I implied to the person so eager for an instant fix, there are no short cuts. It's a matter of patiently training your body through your mind. Real training takes years to penetrate the fog of the body-mind complex with its years of bogus postural habits. So start shrugging repeatedly now and every day for the rest of your life if you want to achieve full, ongoing lightness of being.

And here's a Taoist trick to help: sitting comfortably, back straight and perpendicular to the ground, breathing slowly and evenly, hold your arms out in front of you, palms facing your chest, as if holding a bail of cotton slightly too wide for your hands to meet. Now, very slowly, turn your head from side to side as if saying no in slow motion 18 times in each direction. Avoid straining or stretching – simply let that old hunk of bone, brain and sense organs swivel as if mounted on a ball bearing. Slowly lower your arms, rest, revel in the delightful sense of relief in your shoulders as the blood and energy start to rush to the region and declare with pride, 'No longer do I carry the world upon my back!'

I just looked outside this very moment to see Atlas's coach drive off into the sunset. It bodes well.

Spend a few more minutes in the shower and you'll walk taller

You may remember me recently extolling the virtues of multitasking in the shower or bath, specifically in letting the soaping process double up as a healing and energising self-massage routine in the Taoist style. Rather than allow your daily soaping ritual to be a random affair, it takes exactly the same amount of time to order your moves to conform with an ancient Oriental routine, which entails stroking up the inside of each leg and down the outside, down the inside of each arm and back up the outside, down the centre line of your chest and belly and up the sides into your armpits, each circuit to be repeated about nine times before rinsing off. Daily practice will not only leave you thoroughly soaped and spankingly clean, but also build up a tangible flow of internal energy that within only three weeks will produce noticeable strengthening of your immune system, a prudent investment in the light of Sars.

The above routine doesn't cover your entire body, but I was saving the more contorted techniques, including how to massage your own back and shoulders, for when I was feeling more verbally dextrous and muscular. This is not one of those times, having just completed a solid nine-day run of workshops, talks, TV and radio in Cape Town, which almost used up all the words I own. However, while performing my own soaping routine this morning in the shower, I was so excited by the hamstrings technique I am compelled to use what words I have left to share it with you.

You may only think of them as natural cushions that make sitting on the loo more comfortable, but hamstrings are fairly crucial in holding you upright.

Additionally, Taoist medicine also ascribes various functions in the psycho-emotional realm to the different muscle groups, and in the case of your hamstrings it's your ability to stand your ground, to dig your heels in and say 'No!' if you need to. During 20 years of observations while healing on the front line, it was patently clear that people with tight hamstrings had a hard time letting go into the unknown and tended towards stubbornness in their lives, while people with weak and floppy ones found it hard to be assertive or say no to anything. Conversely, those with well-toned, yet supple ones found it easy to display healthy assertiveness and were more likely to go with opportunities as they arose along the path.

Weak hamstrings come about through sitting or lying around too much and not walking, running or exercising enough, or after a protracted illness, and can usually be swiftly corrected by a few sturdy marches round the block. Tight hamstrings occur because you haven't been stretching them, which usually seems to go along with being intrinsically fearful of change and thus inclined to dig in your heels and say no. Yes, it's a bold statement, but it makes sense if you go along with the Taoist idea that unresolved, unconscious fear of life gradually causes your kidney region to contract. It's then only a simple matter of body-mechanics to see how that contraction travels over time down either side of your spine, through your buttocks and into your hamstrings and calves, thence to lodge in rigid stubbornness.

But the briefest moment of interplay between soap, hand and hamstring on a daily basis will instigate a subtly powerful energy flow to the region promoting more flop to the rigid and more ridge to the floppy, thus helping balance your assertiveness and go-grab-it levels.

It goes like this: place your right palm just below your right buttock, push lovingly yet firmly down the muscle, pressing more firmly on the outside, down to the back of the knee, then pull up likewise from knee to buttock, pressing more firmly on the inside. Complete nine full passes and repeat with left palm and left hamstrings. After three weeks you will feel more assertive and adventurous and less fearful.

Energy, Health and the Immune System

Are you persistently tired for no apparent reason?

Does your energy flag in the afternoon? After a good night's sleep, do you still find it hard to clear your head? Visit your GP and you'll be told to take more exercise, cut down on caffeine, avoid fatty foods, and be less stressed. All valid advice, but what they don't tell you is why they give it.

During periods of stress, perhaps due to feeling overworked, unfulfilled, or unable to effect necessary changes in your life, you tend to be more self-abusive. A sedentary lifestyle, together with comfort eating and drinking, puts strain on your liver, causing it to become cramped, thus impairing its function. This causes fatigue.

This contraction pattern is an amoeba-like response to an environment perceived as hostile to your aims and represents a closing down of your spontaneous impulses. Over time, if left unchecked, it can produce chronic depression. Other possible signs include sore eyes, migraines, headaches, neck and shoulder tension, bloating, lassitude, irritability, low sex-interest and finding yourself repeating the 'I'm so tired!' mantra.

When manifesting any of these symptoms, don't panic. It is likely that you're capable of safely effecting your own cure by exploring the following technique from Taoist medicine.

Relax. Inhale fully. Exhale fully. Place the fingers of your upturned right hand just under the front ribs on your right side. Using your left hand to give some weight to your right, gently push in, up and under until you meet resistance. Relax more and maintain light pressure, visualising your resistance melting like butter – until it does. Keep breathing. At first touch it's usual to feel slightly though not unpleasantly winded. This is the contraction pattern releasing. After about a minute, withdraw your hand slowly. The entire process can be conducted while engaged in other activities.

To prevent future liver blockage and increase your energy, stamina and confidence, repeat three times a week.

Following the path of least resistance

'Trust in the Tao and it'll all work out somehow,' goes the ancient song of the itinerant barefoot doctor, meaning be confident, trust yourself and trust in the innate benevolence of life, as it unwinds through its unbroken sequential process of cause and effect, and your personal fairy tale will have a happy ending (if you don't mind dying, that is).

Pre-dating Buddhism and Confucianism, Taoism evolved in the ancient Orient as a philosophy, code and way of life at least 5,000 years ago (some believe 12,000). It was said to have been passed down by the so-called 'sons of reflected light'. Taoist folklore has it that these beings were 7ft tall, wore unusual clothing, lived in the mountains between Tibet and China and one day disappeared without trace. But not without first sharing their secrets with the locals.

They taught how energy and consciousness flows and works – both microcosmically in the human body and macrocosmically through time and space – and how to take command of that process in order to reach your optimum potential.

Taoism is not actually an 'ism' at all and is definitely not a religion, though in more recent centuries, its practice has been mildly subverted by some who have managed to twist it into a neo-religious form.

The art in sampling or exploring this rich yet simple seam of metaphysical gold lies in identifying with the minds of the original Taoist practitioners. I say 'practitioners' because Taoism consists merely of a series of mind-body-spirit practices designed to maintain in harmony all aspects of your life and how it stands in relation to others and to your environment. These practices include t'ai chi, chi-gung, feng shui and acupuncture, as well as many other lesser-known arts.

Using Taoist methods to your advantage would not run counter to any religious or nonreligious belief you may or may not hold, but would rather augment it. The Tao is not an alternative to God, the Buddha, or any other manner of label we attach to the unlabellable. It's just a big, friendly, all-encompassing idea that can help make sense of the nonsense of life.

And it's got a clean history. No one, to my knowledge, has ever fought, killed, conquered, savaged, raped, plundered, or had done to them likewise in its name. As far as I know, no other concept of the inconceivable has managed to thrive through 5,000 years with such a spotless record.

This may be because a fundamental tenet of Taoism is not to arouse contention in your fellow humans. This is not to suggest giving way and getting trampled on in the jungle of postmodern life. Indeed, t'ai chi and its older Taoist sister arts, hsing i and pa kua, are the three most respected boxing (and self-defence) systems in the Orient. The ideal to aspire to is the round-based wobbly doll, which, no matter how hard you push it, always circles and returns upright without ever losing its equilibrium or dignity.

This implies always following the path of least resistance while remaining centred and collected internally. Done with a particular intention in mind, you flow like water, easily, effortlessly and, when necessary, powerfully from your centre towards your goal, never expending wasteful energy in worry or giving way to frustration, self-pity or panic.

This requires a trusting willingness to surrender to the flow, letting go of the fruits of your labours, deriving all your satisfaction from the action of doing itself, rather than the results. The Taoists call this phenomenon of effortless achieving wu wei .

To become adept at practising wu wei you first have to teach yourself to relax. First, tense the muscles of your scalp for a brief instant, gently without straining, then release. Repeat likewise through your neck and shoulder girdle and so on, progressively downwards through your body in lateral 'chunks', until you've tensed and released more or less every muscle group. Finally, remembering to breathe in and out smoothly throughout and to maintain effortlessness, tense your entire muscular network at once from head to toe and release. Now spend a 'quality' instant luxuriating in this brief interlude of inner peace and basking in awareness of your intrinsic virtue. Virtuousness, the quality Taoists call te , also means authenticity, or being in the flow of what actually is.

This means being willing to accept the conditions of your life as they present themselves and to let go of trying to change them with your metaphorical remote control. But even following these strictures diligently will prove to be a dry affair without the wilful exercise of compassion – your inbuilt faculty for feeling into the pain and suffering of self and others, knowing you can't help everyone, yet helping rather than hindering whoever you can. In this way we will feel a little comfort every now and then as we wander along this often ferocious but quite magnificent boulevard of broken dreams.

Hitting your stride with a regenerative walk

With summer starting to announce its imminent arrival, it's time to devote some thought to giving your energy a good airing through exercise. Don't groan. As well as feeding yourself correctly, there is no other agent through which health and longevity can be promoted so effectively than regular exercise.

It's not just for the sake of vanity (though looking good is something we all aspire to, and why not be the prettiest flowers we can be?) but for the sake of giving yourself the opportunity of spending truly constructive time with your-self, in order to reconstitute your worldview and reposition yourself in relation to that world. And there is no better way to do this than by consciously training your body (in motion) to follow the commands of your mind. Nothing yokes you to yourself in the same way. And though some would say yoga is the mother of all exercise, surely there is nothing more natural and primal than walking.

While it's true that running takes you higher, in endorphin-release terms, it can also easily aggravate chronic joint problems relating to spinal misalign-ment or knee weakness. Walking, by contrast, provides a perfect opportunity to consciously release bodily and mental tension without jarring your joints, yet still engenders a significantly profound altered state. Walking's benefits on the cardio-vascular, digestive and eliminative systems are well documented, but the spiritual, character-building and energetic ones are less well known.

Many myths exist of Taoist masters said to have walked 100 miles a day without effort, which are no doubt exaggerated, though it's true to say that when adhering to the 'flying' rules, you'll startle yourself by how far you can self-propel with ease.

Before starting out, be sure to wear appropriately comfortable, supportive footwear and easily removable and tieable-round-waist layers, as well as suitable chattel-transporters (bags or backpacks) where appropriate. Before your first foot has crossed the threshold into the world of the '10,000 things' outside, however, hold a vision of your destination and your successful arrival there in mind and make a compact with yourself to fulfil that vision honourably, no matter how many buses, trains or available cabs tempt you off your feet and on to your bum. Then say something to yourself along the lines of: 'I can do this. I will do this. I am doing this!' as foot crosses threshold and the door is shut behind you.

Out on the street, your mind will at first tend to wander – stimulated by the energy of cars, road-sign culture, billboards and passers-by – to thoughts of schedules, commitments, resentments, fantasies, hopes and fears. You could instead gather awareness into your body, starting with the soles of your feet, which must be relaxed, toes spread optimally within shoes, arches lifted without strain and a sense of rolling from heel to toe with each forward step. To facilitate the roll, allow your knees to be mildly bent at all times. To accommodate the bent-knee posture, gently tuck your pelvis under and feel your lower back angled perpendicular to the ground. Relax your buttocks completely and let them swing. It is a great misconception that clenching them tones the muscles and makes you look sexier. The muscles in fact get far more exercise and hence circulation through swinging freely than through clenching. At the same time, elongate the back of your neck (using your mind rather than force), allowing your chin to drop slightly and imagine an invisible thread pulling your crown up towards the sky. This is the Taoist version of walking with a book balanced on your head, but is spine-lengthening rather than spine-compressing.

Relax your belly, back, chest and shoulders, so your organs have room to enjoy the walk too. Rest the tip of your tongue on your upper palate. This helps conduct mental energy back down the front of your body into your belly, where it is regenerated as previously stated.

Organise yourself around a point 2in below your navel, known as your tantien, and let this be the centre of the universe within you. Imagine all movement originating here.

Pay attention to your breathing. It helps to synchronise your breath tempo with your footsteps in order to stop breathing becoming random. Start off at an easy pace without forcing anything. This way you don't send your body into revolt. With arms swinging freely, and all the above attended to, you may start to feel a heavy sensation in your palms and fingers, as if they're filling with blood and heat. This is quite natural and is an indication that your chi, or life force, is flowing with more velocity.

There will be some initial resistance from the more mutinous sub-personalities within, and the lure of passing cabs may be strong. This is due to your liver not having released the extra quantity of blood required for a good 'flight'. Overriding this resistance usually coincides with the liver kicking in, however, and is worth the effort of will.

Who needs Kyoto summits?! If enough of us get with this 'flying on land' fad, we may just save the planet yet.

Reward yourself with regeneration

Exhausted? Feel like every movement of your body is powered by will alone? Out of breath and dragging your legs up the hill? Notice your reaction to life tends towards the negative? So tired you can't even be bothered to go to bed? You need a holiday, mate!

But seriously (seeing as holidays don't fall off trees), we can take the core mechanism of a good holiday and use it as a template for a discrete 24-hour instant self-regeneration programme. The first stage of a holiday comprises the wind-down and unravelling process – being willing to pull your foot off the gas pedal to reduce idling speed altogether.

This tends to cause the release of a hundred different random thought-streams and consequent disorientation as your familiar internal reference points become blurred and momentarily irrelevant. Instead of fixing your location on the metaphysical map by such reference points as your interpersonal relationships, what you do for a living, how you do it, how (you think) others perceive you, social status (as you see it), financial status, hopes, dreams and expectations, you can only fix it by reference to being in a state of unwinding. The Taoists of the ancient Orient, field leaders in burden relinquishment, called this process of self-voiding 'investing in loss', the rationale being that it's hard for life to fill you with its goodies when you're already full (of yourself) and damn tired from it to boot.

The unnerving thing about letting go like this is an inevitable sense of having lost the overview. Suddenly, all the demons that have been obscured by activity come rushing up to the surface. That's the second stage: facing your demons. So you grapple with your fears of failure, illness and death; you wrestle with your resentments and inadequacies. You wonder whether it may have been better just to keep going.

But you're so exhausted, you haven't even the stamina to keep this up for long, and eventually you succumb to the pull of TV, a good book or just plain gravity, and fall fast asleep. You don't even care that the sun is shining, albeit very intermittently. You just want to sleep. And you do. You sleep and sleep (for a good hour or more – remember, we only have one day). And you dream, and your dreams unleash a torrent of twisted images, like the dross in a waste-disposal unit.

But after a while, as you come to – and this is the third stage of regeneration – you do start to wonder if it might be nice to experience the sun on your face, and the thought of interacting with others live, by phone or email mildly excites rather than terrifies you. Be careful, now, because you mustn't rush this stage. Slowly, you stumble from your bed (or couch) and, with mind fresh, instil a positive thought, such as 'I access limitless energy now!', because we all know you can't self-regenerate successfully with a negative attitude – that would only reinforce the exhaustion.

Next you attend to your liver, because though all organs and indeed systems are intimately involved in the exhaustion-emptying-regeneration process, it's your liver that does the living, and which provides the key to re-energising yourself. So saying, take hold of your lower front ribs on both sides (one side per hand) and gently prise apart, breathing deeply throughout. Keep prising till you feel you have reached full lateral extension. Hold for a minute or until you grow bored of it and release slowly. This will not only reduce stress in your liver region and increase circulation of blood and energy, but will also help your diaphragm relax and hence increase breath capacity – crucial in energy production.

Finally comes re-entry. Swallow a few drops of Bach Flower Remedy of Olive, and gird your loins with such sentiments as 'I am fully regenerated now (though a proper holiday would've been nice), and ready for anything! I'm so regenerated I can hardly bear it!' Too gung ho? Oh, forget it. Let's pull a sicky and stay in bed.

Boosting the immune system begins with the mind

How many times have you been to a GP with a list of seemingly unconnected debilitating symptoms to be told after perfunctory examination, 'It's probably a virus'?

To be fair, it probably is.

With the proliferation of people on the planet has come a proliferation of viruses. From the Latin *virus* (meaning the poisonous sap in weeds), viruses are primal slime looking for a friendly host-body to colonise. Don't take it personally – it's just nature's basic urge to thrive on every level.

There's currently a particularly interesting slimeball virus circulating the length and breadth of the land. It 'invades' the liver, causing sudden extreme tiredness, headaches, bloated stomach, indigestion, mild depression or disorientation, grouchiness, fever, intestinal cramps and sometimes sore throats. Its symptoms reoccur every fortnight or so for at least a few months. They are almost indistinguishable from glandular fever or Epstein-Barr syndrome and not dissimilar to hepatitis.

The intense stress of going through your daily paces – work, travel, social networking and technology-accelerated communications – pounds the nerves, liver, kidneys, heart and digestive organs hourly. Air-, water- and food-borne pollutants are increasing exponentially, making the liver work far harder to detoxify your system. The constant self-assessment necessary to adjust to the daily marketplace, along with the insidious bombarding of the senses with product advertisement, upsets your sense of self-esteem. This expends and diverts vast amounts of energy normally used to maintain the immune system.

More than ever, our defences are strained, leaving us increasingly vulnerable to virus invasion.

To build your immune system, you first need to start with the mind, which then relays the message to the body. Make a clear choice and intention to attain all the health and longevity within your power. This will mobilise the necessary energy to stabilise your system and protect you against 'invasion'.

Daily exercise is crucial in helping this regulatory energy circulate. It should be a combination of hard and soft, external and internal exercise. Running and yoga. Weight-training and t'ai chi.

Avoid rich, greasy, stodgy food and stimulants – this will help to take the strain off the liver. Relax, breathe and remember that you feel far stronger when you know you're loved, so love yourself as best as you can. Above all, factor in time for unbridled joy. Take yourself out to the nearest good party and dance. Dance till your socks fall off. For in that uninhibited, childlike state, your true strength will be revealed.

Attaining the ultimate high

What is the ultimate high? And why do so many of us expend so much time, energy and money looking for it? Being catapulted 1,000ft in the air in the front seat of a glider, bungee jumping from a bridge or abseiling off a cliff are all adequate metaphors for the ultimate high. Any external experience that pushes you up against death will trigger the release of adrenalin, the internally produced chemical most associated with the high of a peak experience.

Others are more inclined to take their brush with death less dramatically, by ingesting psychotropic substances or meditating. Le petit mort , the little death experienced during orgasm, is a big favourite, as is the momentary loss of self while dancing or playing live music. Even clinching business deals can produce an ecstatic effect.

But unless you've learned to defy the basic laws of gravity, the problem with an ultimate high is that it is inevitably succeeded by an ultimate low. Which is fine as long as you have the time and will to process it.

The ancient Taoists, together with all practitioners of authentic spiritual paths, keenly observed the perpetual interplay between peak and trough, calling it yin and yang. They then decided to eschew chasing the jagged peaks, aspiring instead to attaining a high mountain plateau state, affecting mind, body and spirit simultaneously. This sustainable high they called the t'ai chi – literally, the supreme ultimate.

As we are all subject to pressurised lifestyles, we might find it desirable to aspire to this plateau, which incorporates all our daily activities.

What it boils down to is training yourself to relax your body and breathing.

Then step behind the thoughts in your mind so that you can preside over them, like a general observing the troops.

At the same time, relax your chest. This will enable you to feel love for others: not an airy fairy, romanticised love where you idealise people, ignoring their thorns or missiles, but a grounded compassion for the essential being within each of us, behind all the various disguises (bank manager, artist, IT expert, etc).

In this state of love, you feel connected and at one with all aspects of your environment. With practice you will learn to sustain a consistent state of moment-by-moment, manageable 'highness'.

Examine your behaviour of late. If you've been overly cynical, pessimistic or downright nasty, you might wish to experiment with the following perceptual reframing technique.

Greet everyone you meet with the thought: 'I am willing to look beyond the role this person is playing and love them rather than fear them.'

It's an experiment, requiring you to temporarily suspend your belief system. Don't judge the results before three days are up. Simply repeat the thought as often as you can remember, regardless of whether you think you mean it or not. The likely outcome will be enough of a taste of the t'ai chi reality to inspire you further.

In praise of the common cold

It is rare to speak out in praise of the common cold – one of the scourges of postmodern centrally heated life – but, along with the fantastical new world order of the hustling, bustling 21st century, I believe its time has come.

The first signs you've landed one can begin to show up to a month before – the sudden catching pain between your ribs in the middle back, a sore spot on the back of your head near the ear, an increase of mucus on waking, aching knees, sore shoulders, stiff neck, unexpected tiredness in the afternoon or various combinations of these, not in chronological sequence. Eventually, you catch yourself muttering, 'Damn – I've got a cold!', until that thought becomes an undeniable reality.

At this point, the 'Western' tendency is to panic mildly about likely agenda disruptions and the probability of a few awful hair and runny-mascara days, and to make every attempt to stuff the cold down with various combinations of allopathic and alternative 'remedies', according to your bent. But the common cold virus, according to Taoist (Chinese) medical philosophy, is not necessarily malevolent. In fact, if allowed to run its course, a cold can do you the world of good.

Trying to resist a cold once it has taken hold is futile – you're simply wasting valuable energy. Don't be afraid of it, as fear makes your kidneys contract, which weakens your immune system. Instead, surrender gracefully and let the cold take you into that wonderful soft, fuzzy, altered state where, with ears and Eustachian tubes semi-blocked, you feel as if you're swaddled in cotton wool. This is the 'yin', or feminine state, that makes you withdraw to the interior.

If you can afford the time (a big if, indeed), grant yourself a couple of days mooching round the house taking full advantage of the revelations that often accompany such withdrawal. If you are compelled, for whatever reason, to go out and mingle in the workplace and thus spread the germs of your blessing with others, do what you can to preserve the sense of internal softness, so as not to expend energy you can't afford. The Taoists believe that enduring strength only arises from this 'soft' state. Specifically, the common cold is one of nature's highly efficient ways of giving your immune system a bit of exercise to make it grow stronger. Welcome the cold as a benevolent force and, just as any guest who's made to feel comfortable in your house, the cold will treat you well in return.

Denying the cold its due respect by pushing on regardless and resorting to chemical suppressants often causes more complicated inflammatory conditions in the respiratory tract later on. Of course, where the respiratory tract is weak initially, complications can arise, even if you do surrender to the cold — everyone's cold is different, and generalisations are limited in scope. But there are a few rudimentary steps you can take without changing your whole life that will make the cold's passage both more swift and enjoyable.

To clear your Eustachian tubes, throat and sinuses, eat a slice or two of raw ginger or take a dab of mustard on your tongue. The explosive reaction, though startling, is hugely relieving and the heat is useful for boosting kidney energy and hence the immune system.

Use natural decongestants (eucalyptus and menthol) at night to prevent breathing in dust through your mouth while sleeping. To clear the air passages and prevent the cold going on to your chest, drink mullein tea and steam your face over a bowl of friar's balsam in boiling water. To move 'dirty' blood and energy from your chest and thus strengthen your lungs, do a lot of arm swinging and push-ups, if you can manage them. Do what you can to ensure your body temperature remains constant to ease the strain on your kidneys and, above all, relax.

The lungs traditionally correspond to the emotion of grief or clinging unhealthily to people or situations from the past. Colds often seem to take hold when you're in transition between one significant phase and another and need to let go of something or someone to be able to move on in your life. Some say a cold appears when you need to have a good cry but haven't had time or inclination. Use the time to examine what needs letting go of and resolve to make the necessary changes. If you find this frightening, simply suggest to yourself repeatedly till you start to feel a sense of equipoise, 'All change is good!' Good!

Anxiety, Stress and Letting Off Steam

Quelling anxiety

You've got a deadline to meet. You're being squeezed in a cash-flow crunch. Your partner's threatening to run off with another unless you suddenly get more sexy. The deal you've been slaving over might not come off. The promotion you've been counting on may never come your way. Your children are acting up at school and show signs of delinquency. The exchange rate may rocket against you before you have time to buy your second home in France. And, yes, you may die before fulfilling your life's dream.

Anxiety has overtaken you. Your breathing is shallow. You can't or won't focus on the very job at hand that could pull you out of this chicane, which is compounding your anxiety.

So you have a drink, smoke a cigarette, spend money you haven't got on frivolous whims or regress to vegetable state, further compounding the anxiety. And it has to stop.

Anxiety is endemic. We have grown accustomed to going through our daily paces in a state of low-grade anxiety, as if it is the natural state.

Originally, anxiety is a chosen or learned response, a bogus coping mechanism usually adopted in infancy from an anxious parent. The anxiety response soon embeds itself in your psyche as a pattern, whereupon it assumes the status of an a priori truth: of course I get anxious – I've got deadlines to meet, bills to pay, etc. Sounds plausible, quite grown up, in fact.

But as any martial artist, flying trapeze artist or commercial airline pilot will tell you, your mind and body perform to optimum levels only when you're relaxed.

Anxiety causes the area surrounding your kidneys and adrenal glands to contract, thus impairing their functions. This leads to symptoms including lower-back ache, cystitis, headaches, tinnitus, nervous stomach, poor digestion, significant drop in sexual interest or performance, and more anxiety.

Now you could run to your GP and attempt to stuff the feeling down with various chemicals, or you could take the self-help option: slow the tempo of your breathing down to half-time. This means relaxing your belly so your diaphragm can pull the lungs down efficiently.

Breathe in fully. Breathe out fully. If so inclined, tell yourself you're exhaling the anxiety and inhaling calm and clarity.

Using your fists, massage in circular motion the soft area of your lower and middle back until you feel it soften.

Drink small amounts of valerian tea.

Take Bach Flower Remedy of Mimulus.

Eschew coffee and other adrenalin stimulators.

Long-term, take up chi-gung or t'ai chi, as these work intensively on strengthening the kidneys and adrenals.

If you are suffering from extreme anxiety, visit an acupuncturist one week, a homeopath the next and a shiatsu specialist the next, repeated in rotation over a six-week period. It'll be worth the investment.

Finally, remain mindful of your body, at work, rest and play. Whenever you find yourself in a state of unnecessary muscular gripping, get a grip with your mind instead and ask, 'Don't I deserve to feel better than this?'

Beating the blues

Depression is endemic. We've grown accustomed to believing it to be a disease, which in one sense it is – dis-ease. In fact, the term 'depression' is just that – a term: in one way precise, in that one's natural, joyful self is being pushed down (de-pressed), in another, too vague to adequately describe the myriad aspects of anguished existential experience lurking beneath the surface exterior we all present to the world.

I'm not suggesting that we're all 'depressives' (another overly confining term), merely stating, heretically perhaps, that what we term depression is not a disease, but a natural state, given the immense pain (inevitably and inextricably bound to the immense joy) of living life. Or at least a natural state to which our systems default whenever the pressure of life overcomes our natural ebullience and we can't see our way forward, or, if we can, don't feel possessed of the energy or will to go there.

Every day, we are required to manage all the pressures of survival in the modern workplace. Our bodies have to cope with, among other things, fast-moving climate changes, pollution, microwaves, viruses, infections, poor diet, possible substance abuse and media overload. All this while dealing with a complex balance of inherent, genetic, constitutional tendencies.

The stress this generates is huge, and though most of us seem to manage to muddle through most of the time appearing cheerful, if we were all to come together in a large auditorium for a nationwide encounter group, I suggest it wouldn't take long for us to ascertain that we all, beneath our brave exteriors, suffer. Some, hopefully the majority, have found efficient-enough strategies to overcome this natural tendency to default to depressed mode. They somehow create adequate 'space' within for expression of their 'natural, joyful selves', to the extent that most of the time, they feel mostly satisfied with life.

Others, however, find themselves temporarily, and sometimes permanently, without the appropriate inner 'technology' to rise up against the pressure, and are diagnosed as depressed.

Attempting to accurately pin down the cause for any particular individual's depression is like looking for a needle in a haystack. However, Oriental medicine has always recognised that depression, whatever its cause, is in fact often perpetuated by so-called flattened liver energy or depressed liver functions. These may not show up in clinical tests, but will certainly be apparent to anyone trained in Oriental pulse-taking and tongue-inspection forms of diagnosis.

What this implies, both in theory and in (alternative) clinical practice, is no matter the actual cause of depression, treating the liver through acupuncture, herbs, massage, diet and various forms of exercise will, in time, alleviate all the symptoms of depression and facilitate a state of mind positive enough to make the necessary changes for the patient's healthy growth. At the same time, attention would probably be also applied to strengthening the kidneys (thought to generate the will) and the heart (thought to strengthen intention).

Obviously, it is not enough to simply correct the liver energy and hope the cause for depression will be forever banished. The usual stresses and strains of life will still be there, and a workable strategy must be developed to deal with them. The Taoists recognise the perpetual alternation between opposing forces (yin and yang), according to which principle, a period of darkness, if left to the natural course of events, will be followed by a period of light. The Buddhists discipline themselves to always think positively about every situation. In other words, on finding yourself in a slump phase, chronic or acute, have faith that the condition can be reversed. Secondly, apply all the attention you can muster to training your mind to start thinking in a positive manner. Learning to meditate is often the most effective way to grow this positive mindframe and, finally, remember there are no neutral thoughts. As you believe it to be, so it shall be. Make a mental or written list of everything you want to change in your life, then start telling yourself repeatedly, 'I have the intention, will and power to rise up and overcome all negativity. I'm willing to believe I can achieve inner peace.'

And if none of that works, hit the St John's Wort.

Taking the stress out of life

Even as late as the mid-50s, the people of the UK still abided by a social order laid down by the Victorians. Those were the days when Aunt Ethel would disappear mysteriously for a couple of weeks to 'hospital' every now and then with a so-called nervous breakdown, treated mostly by sedation heavy enough to numb her into forgetfulness. Uncle Arthur would simply make do with a stiff glass of Scotch and a cigarette from one of those silver-plated cigarette boxes kept on the mantlepiece. As he puffed, he would rhythmically tense and relax his jaw in the way 'real men' did in those days, mimicking a Jack Hawkins hero stereotype playing captain of the ship as it sailed into the eye of the storm.

No one questioned the established order of life, except poets and eccentrics. You went to work at a job you could just about count on holding on to for life. The promotional ladder was clearly defined, mass tourism, avocado pears and designer perfume hadn't yet arrived in the high street, and everyone knew where they stood. And, short of the odd world war, there wasn't much that could appear on the horizon to shake the apple tree.

Then Bing Crosby gave way to Bill Haley and all hell broke loose. Suddenly rock 'n' roll whipped up the teenage angst of a generation into a whirlwind of social revolt. Then Elvis gave way to the Beatles, the Beatles gave way to the Maharishi and black bombers and purple hearts gave way to pot and acid, just around the time the Kerouac-reading beatniks started reading Leary instead and the hippie movement was born.

As the hippies turned on, tuned in and dropped out, a wave of new therapies emerged (in the San Francisco Bay Area), christened collectively as 'the human potential movement'. 'Let it out!' was what you now did with your angst. Nervous breakdowns were a thing of the past, while inflation and the Americanisation of the working culture, with its short-term contracts and insecurity of tenure, were rapidly becoming a thing of the present.

Then Thatcher's reign reinforced the 'me, me, me' culture, and suddenly any lip service paid to altruism, religion or queen and country stopped dead. Around this time, the Bay Area human potential movement had grown into a global self-help industry, known euphemistically as the 'new age'. The new age got married to IT and now you can get enlightenment from logging on to various websites. It's that simple. So we've solved it. No more nervous breakdowns (you're out, Auntie Ethel), no more stiff upper lips (unless you've had too much collagen injected), no more staying up all night taking drugs and having your upper brain stem rattled by digital jackhammers. Now the answer to life on a planet of dwindling resources fast nearing the point of not being able to sustain us any longer, where there are no new frontiers to explore (except dread and dreary places like Mars and the moon), can be found on a website. Sorted.

Except obviously we're not. Otherwise why are so many of us so angry that we resort to violence at the drop of a hat? Why do we consume enough alcohol every week to fill all the craters of the moon? The fact is that no one ever taught us how to communicate – with ourselves and each other – and we no longer have any memory of the old-school social protocol that kept the world glued together in Ethel and Arthur's era.

In the light of the vast wealth of self-development knowledge readily available, it would be easy for every schoolchild to be instructed in rudimentary communication skills and martial arts (to sublimate the violent urge). How wonderful it would be if every parent were obliged to train in basic ethics and induced by tax breaks to pass on a simple code of human decency or at least good manners to their kids.

In the meantime, however, we have to deal with our own bad selves, stamping our feet because we want more and we want it now. All this anger causes problems with our liver energy and needs a safe outlet before we all start losing the collective plot. The stress of external life will only increase now, especially as that naughty old recession starts biting our trouser legs. It is therefore crucial, if we wish to maintain a semblance of social propriety that enables us to get along with each other, that we quickly learn to relax more internally as individuals and with each other.

One way to let off steam safely and promote inner peace is to go out for a walk every day to your nearest park or open space, breathing deeply and letting your mind take a brief holiday. If you have no close canine friends to accompany you, take an imaginary one and, when you get to the park, yell his or her name a few times at the top of your lungs. No one will know you don't have an actual dog, so there's no need to feel embarrassed about it. If you're very vain, take a dog lead to make it look more authentic. My imaginary dog's name is Rowley, by the way. I find it a wholesome sound to yell – the 'ow' bit helps release any emotional pain that's been accruing. So if you see a funny-looking bloke with no shoes yelling 'Rowley' on Hampstead Heath, keep it to yourself.

Deep breathing to soothe the spirits

How do you clear your head when you're busy, so busy you can't think in a straight line long enough to attend to the next important thing you have to do? How, in this brave new world of always-on communications, do you manage to get any meaningful downtime with yourself? And how, in the midst of this accelerating madness, do you manage to apportion fairly any spare moments you do have among partners, children, friends, let alone helping strangers in the street?

I bet you were expecting me to come up with an answer, weren't you. No. I was asking you! Because I haven't got a clue.

However, as I sit at my trusty workstation pumping these keys, I realise that I am sitting at my workstation. I don't make this as an obvious existential state-ment, but as one of surprise. Surprise that – even with brain cells spinning on their axes at goodness knows how many million miles an hour as they defy all logic and uncomplainingly process the slew of incoming information that assails them moment after moment so that my entire head feels like the inside of a washing machine on fast rinse – I am still able to think at all, let alone sit upright at a workstation.

So, in the more-than-likely event that you find yourself similarly afflicted (from time to time), I feel it only fair to share with you the few sanity- and clarity-maintaining methods I have and practise.

As I said, I am sitting at my workstation. Ergo, I am alive. This is the first point. An obvious one, perhaps. But as any hypnotherapist used to treating depression will tell you, having the simple thought of your own aliveness reinforced is one of the most effective triggers for releasing any form of self-pity that may be blocking you.

For surely, succumbing to this stressful feeling of being snowed under by the demands of life to the point that one's head spins is a cleverly disguised manifestation of self-pity. There are, in other words, many dead people who would probably have loved to still be sitting (with beating heart) at a workstation now. So number one is to perform whatever mental acrobatics you have to get over the self-pity. If nothing better springs to mind, just keep repeating, 'I am alive!' (until you mean it).

Secondly, and I know I use this platform to promote this theme a lot but it's a theme vital to the above – you have to remember to keep breathing. And yes, the basic mechanism is autonomous, but the quality of breathing – and it is the quality, according to the Taoist good-time masters of old that determines the quality of your experience of life in any moment – is entirely under your command. Let the breath be soft flowing, deep and smooth, and that's how life will feel for you.

Paradoxically, during stressful moments, we tend to breathe shallowly and hold back the exhalation, even though this exacerbates stress. Take the bull by the horns, however, and slow your breathing down, ensuring full exhalation, and magically the stress begins to dissolve. But don't take my word for it. Exhale fully now, generally decelerate your breath tempo and see how it instantaneously relaxes and clears your mind a little more.

Third, when nearly flattened by the force of moment-to-moment responsibility, have the behavioural panache to simply laugh with a hearty 'Ha Haah!' and walk away from it for a brief interlude. Go outside, and with the confidence of one who rules the world, albeit a world rushing by so fast you can hardly see it, open your arms in a wide embrace, and declare: 'All this is my world, my life, and no matter how hard it is to keep up with at times, it's my choice to enjoy it to the full!'

But if you really want to work transformative magic on yourself, there is an acupuncture point in the centre of your forehead, a couple of centimetres above the eyebrow line and just above the bridge of your nose, known as 'the happy point', so called because regular manual stimulation of it causes bouts of unstoppable happiness even when you don't want it to. So apply with caution! Push the tip of an index finger on to the point with approximately 110g of pressure until you feel a mildly tingling sensation. Keep pushing for about 30 seconds then release slowly, so slowly that you can't quite tell when contact has been broken, and spend a brief moment enjoying your forehead.

Which brings us to the final aspect of today's 'treatment' – reminding yourself to take some time at least once an hour to enjoy nothing but the sensations in your body, for like all those dead guys that would love to be at workstations right now, you'll probably miss the opportunity when you're gone. Sold? Now what was I meant to be doing...

Facing up to the modern condition

There's much talk around these days about opting out of the 'rat-race', down-shifting, about how the pressure of life has never been so great and that the stress is killing us. Poor us, eh? The disaffected, disenchanted of the developed world suffering the terrible stress of deprivation, while surrounded by enough labour-saving devices to make a 19th-century science-fiction writer's side-whiskers curl with excitement.

No longer being able to wash our clothes down by the river, we are forced to use washing machines in our own homes. No longer able to roam the plains, dodging savage predators, we are forced to drive cars, dodging speed cameras. No longer able to undergo the deprivations of hunger when the crops fail, we are now forced to drive to the supermarket and fret over genetic modifications or worry ourselves sick as to how organic the food may or may not be.

Stripped of our rights to experience the scurvy-ridden rigours of open-ended sea voyages, we are forced to suffer the indignity of long-haul flights lasting a mere 14 hours or so, and rise up in national clamour against the horrors of inflight bloodclots. Denied the laborious task of training carrier pigeons or riding on horses for days to deliver a message, we freak out from the stress of having to deal with a few emails and text messages each day.

Has it escaped everyone's notice that we have become spoilt, whingeing babies? I'm not suggesting we all need a good war or other such catastrophe to make us grow up and get real, but isn't it time we stopped moaning and groaning under the strain, and started appreciating the world we've created?

Wouldn't you rather a bit of stress to deal with than return to the days and ways of the pre-industrial era? Yes, there are some deluded social romantics who claim we'd all be better off that way, but how many could survive without the conveniences of postmodern life?

Destroy all the computers and mobile phones and let's get back to basics and put an end to this awful stress? Excuse me while I just kick my scribe for not writing my ideas fast enough, so I can jump on my horse and deliver this copy in time.

But our stress is not caused by the technological wonders of our age. Our stress arises because we still run on the same internal programmes as we did when we lived in caves. We walk down the street to work with the same fear-knotted stomachs and clenched buttocks as our forebears, when having to ward off sabre-toothed tigers. No one has told us to update the programme in line with our new, easier conditions. We no longer need the same stress levels now. We have created the possibility for everyone to be housed and fed to a greater or lesser extent, have the ability more or less to manage disease enough for most of us to live past 60, and have enough in-house entertainment to prevent ennui on even the darkest night. Yet we still live with the same stress levels as if having to negotiate with clubs.

The stress is generated within, not without, and it's time to stop generating it. In short, it's time for us to evolve to a level commensurate with our technology.

Worry and stress are a choice we make. Not worrying and relaxing about everything are also choices we make. The ancient Taoists were experts in stress-management. They encapsulated the method for dealing with stress in two words: acceptance and breathing.

First comes acceptance of one's conditions in the moment. Finding yourself with a thousand emails in the in-tray for example, don't give way to panic.

Don't resist being in front of the computer. Instead, welcome it as what's meant to be happening right now. Celebrate what's happening in the moment as if it's your birthday party, no matter how challenging. Surrender to the moment. This requires you stop whingeing on about the stress of it all, take a moment to appreciate the fact that no errant asteroids have dropped on your head today, and gratefully surrender to the flow of the action. Because in the present moment, that's all there is to your life. The rest is all in your imagination.

Acceptance requires relaxation, so check your body now – not to see if it matches up to the media-dictated standards of beauty (oh, the stress) – but for any unnecessary holding in the soft tissue. This requires developing synaesthetic sense to identify the holding and common sense to stop it.

Initially, this is developed by spending 10 minutes or so lying down, feeling into your body with your mind, starting at the feet and slowly moving up to the head, taking as long as you need to identify and disperse. In a matter of days, you'll be able to shorthand the process so it can be done while otherwise engaged in worldly pursuits. But the key to all this is breathing, especially the outbreath, which helps you release the toxicity from both your body and your thoughts. So don't play with that unnecessary stress a moment longer. Exhale fully now and as you inhale, think to yourself, 'I am an evolved being, able to handle whatever life throws in my path!'

Facing the abyss

You're sailing along, singing a song, without a care in the world. It's one of those rare confluences of events in time and space where all your externals are in good enough order not to be a bother, and you're actually feeling quite pleased with yourself. You congratulate yourself on how well you're managing things these days. Whoops, you shouldn't have done that (as you know). Because suddenly, like smashing into the bus you didn't see, you run headlong into a crisis.

It could be your health, it could be your wealth, it could be your love life, it could be a build-up of unresolved personal issues bursting like a summer storm over your clear, blue sky. It doesn't matter – crisis is crisis.

As I'm sure you've heard a thousand times in new-age circles, the Chinese character for crisis means danger and opportunity. The English word itself literally means cross or crossroads, a point of choice, in other words. And the choice is between the danger of sinking into the abyss or rising like a phoenix from the ashes of the past.

But before I drag us through the mire of excessive metaphor, let's examine the Taoist view on the stages of, and the way of handling oneself during, crisis.

First stage is denial – I didn't really just slip my disc, I don't care if my partner did just leave me (I'll be all right), it doesn't really matter that I've just realised my entire cosmological map was completely wrong and it actually turns out I'm a raving fruitcake unfit for civilised society, etc.

The quicker you are at grasping reality, the less time you're able to keep up the pretence and it soon gives way to anger – stupid me for getting in this mess, stupid life for doing this to me; damn, I'll have to totally reorganise my schedule, etc. The less of a spoilt brat you are, however, the quicker you stop throwing your toys all over the nursery, and anger gives way to humiliation, shame and remorse for not being the flawless being who would have managed to avert this disaster.

The more resilient you are, though, the sooner you stop berating yourself and remorse gives way to terror. Terror because you suddenly realise how fragile your construct of reality is in the midst of this ferociously infinite universe. Fear that you might not pull out of the spin this time.

The less of a drama merchant you are, the sooner you stop shaking and your existential terror (that nasty underlying, recurring stuff) gives way to acceptance – the moment of grace where it's just you and your maker. This is when you choose whether to languish in the pit of the old and die (one way or another, sooner or later) or climb out on the back of the new and create yourself afresh. Give up or give in.

Though it's your call from start to finish, a Taoist would always advise you to go with the latter – surrender to the story, stop resisting the flow of events and ask yourself what can be learned or gained from this that you can use to empower yourself in order to start the next chapter of the book.

And according to that same Taoist, the most valuable asset acquirable at this stage is an increased capacity for compassionate detachment, which enables you to observe and even enjoy observing yourself handling life's vicissitudes, as if watching your favourite hero in an adventure movie. The suspense and drama are just there to give the storyline a bit of edge, to keep you juiced up, but you know really that the hero (or heroine) will win out in the end and will be back starring in a new movie in the twinkling of an eye. This gives you space to relax in your seat and not become unnecessarily tense. This gives the details space to work themselves out.

But to pull this storyline-regulating stunt off correctly, it's essential to spend a minimum of 12 minutes a day (arbitrary figure) in the following mode in order to enjoy some quality self-observation time. Sitting comfortably, with back reasonably straight, heart open and belly full of life, decelerate and regulate your breathing tempo and consciously relax all your muscles.

Now, notice the internal dialogue running in your forebrain, all the chat you give yourself about your current position and possible strategies, and draw yourself back behind it until you're sitting like a little Bodhisattva bang in the centre of your brain. Centre brain is known to the Taoists as the 'original cave of spirit', and learning to locate yourself there permanently is considered a major key to enlightenment.

Once observing from there, all the forebrain chatter transforms into so much swirling nonsense going on behind your frontal bone, and all you do is breathe and watch. Be alert, because it will try to suck you in like quicksand. Remain centrally poised, aware of your breathing and body below and refuse to allow yourself to be enticed. Keep pulling back until you establish at least one moment of absolutely pure consciousness without a shred of interference from your local self.

To achieve this is no mean feat, but perseverance will pay off, not to the extent that you'll avoid all future crises – that's impossible and undesirable, for without them there'd be no growth – but so that they'll pass more swiftly and painlessly. And furthermore, the next time someone asks you at a dinner party whether you meditate, you'll be able to say, yep, been there, done that.

Rewriting the script of your inner drama

When you watch a stranger walking down the street, you see a body (in movement) dressed according to its inhabitant's whim, facial features animated according to their wearer's mood. It doesn't make much more impact on you than passing a flower in the garden, because you don't see the entire personal universe that person is accommodating within their Tardis of a skull, complete with all its myths, stories, failures and glories. This is because the universes we transport cranially are invisible and imaginary, but we become so attached to them, we mistake them for objective reality – whereas in fact the nearest any of us get to objective reality is in someone else's eyes, when we're playing the role of stranger walking down the street. And if we were able to be as detached about ourselves as we are about passing strangers, we would be so tranquil and free of suffering we'd have nothing to complain about, and would have to invent things (because we love complaining). Which is, in fact, exactly what we do.

Deep inside, we all know the truth: our personal universes – the ones we defend to the death – are mere illusions. At the core of our consciousness, we know that our hopes, fears and memories are merely devices, arbitrary reference points we use to give ourselves a sense of place in a chaotic universe – something from which to create a personal drama. Drama gives us something to fret about, get excited about, moan about or shout about. In short, the drama we construct internally gives our life meaning. Or so we think.

But as any ancient Taoist or Buddhist sage will tell you, none of this is really happening. It's all invisible and imaginary. And if you don't believe me, look at any stranger passing in the street and tell me where their drama is. The Taoists call this everyday reality we each of us construct in our mind 'the world of the 10,000 things', and while it is only proper – just as in any polite game of charades – to honour the illusory existence of every one of the 10,000, the way to enlightenment (including the boons of clarity, wisdom and inner peace) lies in holding fast to the unchanging core within, your 'Tao'.

Buddha said all suffering comes from attachment; Lao Tsu (heavily paraphrased) said, shut up a your face. Jesus said be in the world but not of it, and Jack Benny said, your money or your life. But they were all talking about differentiating between the constant within and the passing ephemera of 'daily existence'.

Fine words, perhaps. A crude existential meander for sure, but pointless without some suck-it-and-see factor. For this retrieval of the inner-core consciousness is no mere intellectual concept, hence a spot of pragmatic Taoism. In ancient China, people who followed Taoist ways would arrange their temporal affairs to afford themselves regular stints in the mountains, where they could retreat from the cacophony of local street life long enough to recapture their perspective. To speed things along, they used to stimulate a particular series of acupuncture points – around (their own) head, neck, shoulders and upper arms – using fingertip, needle or kneading instruments. This collection of points is poetically named 'windows of the sky'. Working their way through them in various prescribed sequences would put them instantaneously into detached mode, so they could enter directly into the undifferentiated absolute within – the constant in the equation – without a moment wasted.

By practising the following version now, and once a day after that, you may find yourself suffering from unpredictable, uncontrollable, though minor, bouts of inner peace and enlightenment, so only indulge if your fascination and agenda permit. Stimulate these points by pressing with approximately 110g of pressure using your fingertip or a small, round pebble or crystal, three times each in quick succession, and always follow the given order for optimal results: centre of forehead just above bridge of nose, crown of head, under base of skull (in the middle), 3cm directly above the apex of each ear, behind the mastoid processes (sticking-out bone handles behind each ear), and tip of each deltoid (shoulder-cap muscle where it meets the biceps and forms an indentation on your upper arm). This will help momentarily reposition your consciousness so that it identifies with the unchanging Tao, rather than with the disposable world of form.

You can reinforce the effect by choosing consciously to release your hold on the inner drama with every exhalation, while choosing to step anew, and unencumbered by personal myth, into the mystery of (your) life with every inhalation. 'Hello, stranger' takes on a whole new meaning now, doesn't it?

Life getting frantic? A few minutes' hand massage will keep you on top

What a morning! It's a miracle I'm still in the ring. Talking of rings, in the midst of a thousand-mile-an-hourer, with 'urgent' emails flooding in like the broadband cyberdam has burst, and a list-load of phone calls to make, as well as a radio phone interview to do, my landline has just decided to tease me by going stone dead.

And though the thoughtful cable operators spend millions making us aware of their special packages, they don't seem to have paid anyone to operate their helpline, which blurts an extremely irritating and irrelevant recorded message for no less than 50 minutes on my mobile before I finally hang up and email them instead. And, of course, this is the moment that my mobile has chosen to keep losing its signal every two seconds to add to the mix of the morning's entertainment.

And yes, I know that to a Victorian this would hardly be cause for concern. Indeed, were she even to have one brief second of coverage on a mobile phone, she would feel blessed beyond measure. And in light of the fact that the oil on which our lives have come to depend is apparently due to run out within 40 years, and that terrorists stalk the earth looking for somewhere to detonate their radiologically enhanced explosives, my trifling challenges this moment are truly risible by contrast.

Nevertheless I, like you, am faced with innumerable tests to my sanity each and every day, and am required to handle them with a minimum of dexterity just to stay in the game.

According to the Taoists, your ability to handle events, big or small, is in a large part controlled by the amount of intelligence reaching your hands. If your brain mapped out what was important to it, in terms of where it spent its energy each day, your hands would take up about 90 per cent of that map.

By exercising your hands in the appropriate way, you not only help re-energise your brain, you also increase your ability to handle life, metaphorically speaking, but with very tangible results.

Start now, by looking at your left palm, fingers pointing to the heavens and, grasping your little finger with the other hand, exert gentle downward pressure, pulling the finger back away from the palm until you feel a stretch through the left palm and along the length of the little finger. Breathe slowly and evenly for, say, three cycles, and return the finger slowly upright. Now push it the other way to close with the left palm, and straighten it slowly. Repeat this in turn with all other fingers of your left hand.

Now turn your left palm away from you and let it flop at the wrist in the ancient Taoist letting-your-nails-dry posture and, using your right hand, gently pull your left thumb back towards the palm-side of your forearm until it almost touches it. You will feel a pleasant stretch across the top of your wrist. Slowly release and pull the thumb away from the palm until perpendicular to it. Finally, take it across the palm by gently pushing on the bone at the base of the thumb.

Repeat this entire procedure now on your right hand. Next, grasping the base of the little finger on your left hand between thumb and forefinger of the right, massage up towards the little fingertip as if milking a cow. Again, do this with the other fingers and thumb and repeat on the right hand.

By now your hands should be feeling full of energy, more alive and happier than they have for a while. Within 10 minutes, if sensitive to it, you'll feel a subtle upsurge of energy all over your body, a mild rush of clarity in the brain and an increase in calmness.

Which is all well and good, but if only I'd taken the telephone engineering module along with my Taoist studies, I'd really be laughing now.

When feelings of disaffection overtake you, it's time to call in Dr Huuu

A disaffected-looking young man in the post-Gothic tradition crossed the road, pale-faced, in front of my car as I waited at the lights. On his mostly shaven head was what looked like a small, black skullcap with a nine-inch feather sticking up from its centre, but which on closer inspection turned out to be part of his hairstyle. In itself unremarkable in these aesthetically random times, but his air of general dissatisfaction struck a dissonant chord in my soul. I'd been grappling with a feeling of dissatisfaction of my own as I drove along, noticing how it was unrelated to external conditions, for I had, at that moment, no cause for anything but relative peace within.

Yet internal friction was clearly palpable. Granted I'd not been long off a 12-hour flight and hadn't fully landed yet, itself significant as you'll see, but there was no actual reason to feel disgruntled with life.

Dissatisfaction is intrinsic to the human condition. Indeed, it is the major driving force of progress. However, in light of rapidly dwindling resources, it's obvious we have to address the issue and learn to assuage our hunger for more, more, more (money, houses, food, sex, experiences, travel, etc) in different ways.

As it happens, those wily old Taoists may just have the solution. As I've often said, every possible mind-state correlates to an energetic balance or imbalance in one or more of your five vital organs – kidneys, liver, heart, spleen and lungs – and that whether that mind-state is triggered by external events or by weakness in the relevant organ, it can be adjusted by rebalancing the energy in that organ.

In the case of dissatisfaction, it's your spleen energy that needs attending to. Though in Western thought the spleen is fairly underrated, in the Taoist scheme, it's responsible for, among other things, your entire digestive system, including regulating body weight by letting your mind know when you've eaten enough. It does this by signalling satisfaction as soon as you reach optimum levels of food intake. If it happens to be weak and its energy deficient, it will require no end of shovelling food in your mouth to reach that point. When severely weakened, you never reach that point and are prone to obesity. But food is not just the stuff you eat, it's also the information you constantly take in and process, as in the food of life, which according to the Taoists is also under control of your spleen. So when weak, no matter how grand your external conditions may be, no matter how little there may actually be to complain about, you feel dissatisfied.

At this point, the normal reaction is to try and work out what's bothering you and attempt to resolve it intellectually, which as you know often just ties you in knots.

The Taoist way, though, is to adjust the energy in your spleen and allow the dissatisfaction to evaporate, without analysing the practical or psychological factors involved. This isn't a cop-out, for as soon as your energy normalises and your natural contentment returns, the practical and psychological reasons for the discontent reveal themselves and can be addressed in a calm, orderly and energy-efficient way.

Each of the five organs, incidentally, is related to one of the five elements – water, wood, fire, earth and metal, respectively – the spleen being related to earth, which explains my own attack. Any time you leave the ground, to fly in a metal tube through the sky, your spleen energy becomes dislodged, and obviously the longer you're up there the stronger the effect.

To remedy the situation energetically, should you be suffering a dissatisfaction attack you wish to resolve in a hurry, massage with gusto in the instep of each foot, firmly circling your thumb just behind the edge of the ball of the foot, completing 36 circles on each foot. Now placing your palm over your lower left-hand ribs, resonantly chant the Taoist spleen-healing sound, 'huuuu!' and feel it vibrating through the organ. Finally declare, 'Dissatisfaction be gone and let the good times roll!'

Feeling better? Maybe I should change my name to Dr Huuu.

We all hide our hurts but there can be ecstasy in our agonies

Working on my new book recently, I'd been sitting hunched over for 50 hours or so, bashing away at the keys. Yes, hunched, even with all my experience of postural adjustment – so call me a fake, but I defy anyone to find a posture that works for your back when you're typing for extended periods. The upshot was that I managed to weaken my lumbar region so much I could barely walk, barefoot or shod, more than a few steps without causing myself rip-roaring agony.

As fate would have it, I was sequestered in my windy hillside hideaway in Catalunya, many kilometres from the nearest chiropractor, and was thus forced to make the best of a bad job, taking each small step with utmost gingerness as I went about my business in the nearby town, eliciting looks of deep empathy from very old men.

With a fair amount of time spent lying on my back, head supported by a book, knees bent and facing skywards, allowing my lower back to settle into the floor, along with a few self-administered acupuncture treatments and a couple of half-effective spinal adjustments, I fixed it enough to get back to London and am now almost right as rain.

But what it showed me, yet again, was how amazingly arrogant I'd become – how much I'd been taking my health for granted, but also how little compassion I'd been feeling for the pain of others. If you'd seen me driving along you'd have just thought I was driving slowly to be irritating. So it made me think: if every time I was stuck behind someone of latter years driving slowly it was because they were in pain, then what an impatient, unfeeling git I was to get irritated.

And what if it wasn't a physical pain – what if they'd just lost a job, a home, a reputation, a partner? Compassion, I thought – I must develop more compassion.

Now I'm not suggesting we all go around with bleeding hearts – no, the show must go on and we all have our parts to play without having to worry about others – but how fine it could be for the show in general if we all developed a bit more tolerance and understanding – or even just if I did, for that matter.

It also reminded me (and this was something I learnt as a healer) that most of the time most of us are in pain – physical, mental or emotional – to varying degrees.

We tend not to show it, perhaps as a reflex from the days our ancestors lived in caves: if you showed weakness you got left behind.

And what do you do if, in the throes of such extreme pain, you feel immobilised? The first thing is to resist the urge to panic. Stop thinking too far ahead – take it one small step at a time, paying attention to every micro-movement of your body. To help you in this, also pay attention to your breath.

I know I've said it countless times, but it's crucial to ongoing existence. When you slow your breathing down, your mind slows down, enabling it to direct the body's actions in the most effective way under the circumstances. As you slow your breathing down, also pay attention to relaxing your entire body as much as is humanly possible. Tensing the body, though the normal reaction to severe pain, restricts blood and energy flow. Relaxing it encourages the flow of pain-relieving healing energy, which can be augmented by pressing a point directly below the small round bone that juts out at the very outermost edge of your knee joints into the muscle that runs down the outside of your shin, until you feel an ache radiating towards the ankle for about 15 seconds on each leg.

While this will not act as a painkiller, it will alter your relationship with the pain enough to stop you freaking out about it — and surely that's the main thing in this crazy old world, whether in pain or not: to be able to avoid freaking out. I wish you a cool, clear head, a strong, warm heart and a body, mind and soul free of pain.

The Outside World

Stress-busting exercises for the 21st century

If anything's certain today, it's that nothing's certain. It has always been this way for us human earth-dwellers, but until recently news travelled slowly. If you were going to cop it from a sabre-toothed tiger, you'd probably be the first and last to know. You wouldn't have been able to access a 'dangerous predator early-warning sign' by WAP. Nor would you have been any better forewarned of a plague or freak tidal wave, town-criers with bells ringing notwithstanding.

These tumultuous days, however, not an iceberg can melt, nor a dietary staple show signs of running scarce or becoming contaminated without us being bombarded by early warnings, dire prognoses and processions of experts pontificating from a plethora of 24-hour news services.

So, we've been warned – not just by anybody, mind you, but by the United Nations themselves, surely the closest we have to a global authority figure (no long-haired, sack-clothed prophets they, in other words). In the unlikely event that we mend our wicked ways, we must all prepare for increasing amounts of so-called freak weather – such as our own homegrown variety of flood as witnessed this very year on a grand scale, tidal flooding of vast tracts of inhabited land, including most of the world's major infrastructurally crucial metropolitan hubs, as well as drought, famine and unprecedented spreading of disease. They tell us euphemistically, in an attempt to be unalarmist, that this 'could' result in large-scale human death and suffering. And, to top it all, the markets are wobbling, mostly downwards, corruption is rife at the highest levels, social trends absurd and unpredictable, violence on the increase and substance abuse at an all-time high.

Let's face it, the very structure of life as we know it is entirely up for grabs. Our world is falling apart, in other words, or at least undergoing radical transformation in a way that may well upset your morning breakfast. Indeed, daily breakfast is no longer guaranteed, nor even is the solid ground upon which to stand the kitchen table.

And what do we do? Ignore it, of course. We go fully into collective denial and immerse ourselves in piffling details about which politician didn't manage to cover up a lie, which It-girl's marriage has just broken up or which bit of retro fashion has been rehashed yet again by the latest fly-by-night London designer. We become obsessed with the newest nutritional discovery or yoga style – especially if it's endorsed by one of the usual gaggle of mediocre celebrities.

Of course we do. What other course of action is there? Running away isn't an option. Nor is trying to change the situation (it's too late). So we focus on the minutiae of our daily lives as if sticking to our agendas will grant immortality. And in the midst of all this potential mega-mayhem, you have characters like this columnist telling you that you have to learn to relax.

Which is good advice at such uncertain times. After all, uncertainty fuels insecurity and insecurity fuels stress and no matter how well you hide it from yourself and others, this fundamental survival stress affects us all. Specifically, stress weakens your vital organs, which have to work twice as hard just to maintain equilibrium. This, in turn, leads to an increasing loss of stamina and, without stamina, every action, every thought even, presents a major challenge. Stamina is what enables you to keep going for the duration, no matter the challenge facing you – from running to the shops before they sell out of uncontaminated food to running away from a stray tsunami, if necessary.

And while there are various herbal concoctions and mineral-vitamin melanges on the market offering the promise of stamina in a pill or cup of tea, the only way to access this invaluable resource is from deep within yourself. It begins with a positive thought (or affirmation), such as, 'I am imbued with infinite stamina, with infinite stamina I am imbued!' or something even less poetic. This institutes the right emotional conditions.

Once this choice has been made, you must turn, as it were, to your body, and particularly to the front of your thighs – the quadriceps muscles, to be precise. For it is these, the ancient Taoists discovered, that, when properly exercised, imbue you with said infinite stamina. You may wish to experiment with me while you read, by standing now with feet shoulder-width apart as if standing in parallel skis, arches raised, knees lightly bent over your feet so as not to cave inwards towards each other and pelvis tilted slightly forward. Simultaneously feel as if the top of your head is suspended by an invisible thread to the ceiling. This has the effect of lengthening your spine. Hold this magazine (in both hands) up to to eye level with neck, shoulders and arms relaxed and rounded as if comfortably holding an invisible round pillar to your chest. As you read, gradually let your knees bend more and more deeply, until you look like you're sitting on a low bar-stool with spine vertical.

By now, if you've managed to venture sufficiently groundwards, you will be feeling a pull in the thighs capable of making your entire body tremble like a horse. When this happens, keep breathing freely and simply drop even lower.

Taoist masters (and mistresses) tend to practise this standing posture (without magazine) for approximately 10 full minutes twice a day, with some extreme standers breaking through the 60-minute mark. If continued daily, such practice will, even after only two or three days, increase available accessible stamina by a 'marketable' amount. Be sure to straighten your legs in slow motion when returning to normal standing position.

If you suffer from dodgy knees of any kind or lower back problems, you may find this technique strengthens the appropriate muscles and joints. However, if it's difficult or impossible for you to arrange your limbs comfortably and without pain, great stamina-building benefit can also be gained from simply using your fists to percuss a steady drumroll up and down the length of the front of your thighs while sitting upright in a chair for a few minutes six or seven times a day. There, I bet you never knew there existed such a profound and potentially lifesaving link between the effects of global warming and the front of your thighs, did you?

Walking back to sanity

'Help, help! Where's the off-button?' I heard someone cry. 'There isn't one!' I shouted back. But they didn't hear, so busy were they, they'd already rushed off to the next appointment. And quite understandably so, too. Can you imagine anything much worse than having to miss the next meeting?

The postmodern global beast is galloping faster and faster now, literally postmodern – completely ahead of even its own future – threatening to overtake our collective sanity, not to mention our email in-trays and voicemail boxes. And we just run around bitching about the ridiculous pace, the pressure and of course the weather, as if we're victims of some grandiose alien plot when all along it was us (and is us) who breathe the life into this beast. The beast is us.

But what is it that drives us, the collective beast, to accelerate so uncompromisingly? You could blame it on technology and say it was the fact that we can now access more or less 24/7 global communications and we want instant responses to our messages. Impatient to have what we want and have it now, before all the resources dwindle completely, we run faster and faster – in ever decreasing circles.

But I suspect at a deeper level we are merely witnessing a remarkable global display of our innate lust for life and all its abundant blessings. We're celebrating, that's all. We vigorously lust after every last bit of goodness this earth has to offer. Trouble is, we're wading through the champagne at an alarming rate. And to keep it flowing, we are forced to do more and more, work harder and harder, and rest less and less. So lots of bubbles but not much peace. With increasing frequency you find the in-tray filling faster than you can think, and phones ringing, and more and more relentless demands being made on you, till you want to scream.

Well, firstly, I strongly advise you do, at the earliest opportunity – scream, I mean. If in public or at work, be polite and announce your intention to scream, then take a good lungful of (polluted) air and with throat, chest and belly fully relaxed to avoid strain, scream from the depths of your pelvis till the last drop of sound has been squeezed out from between your lips and then carry on quite naturally as you were. I think we've even got past the point when anyone would think you odd or crazy in any way. Everyone's feeling the stress. They'll understand, and if they don't, subsequent dialogue will enlighten them, I'm sure. You must have an outlet for this inner beast or it will energetically eat away at your vital organs, causing constriction and reduced blood and energy flow, in turn causing extra stress from within. This will result in immune-response drop, bad moods, fits of temper and depression, as well as diminished libido.

A much more well-behaved way of giving the beast a dose of extra freedom is to take it out for a good walk. No little 10-minute shuffle to the shops, mind you, but a full-blown stride for an hour o'er urbanised hill and dale with arms and shoulders swinging freely and hips and thighs engaging, thrusting and stretching like a lion (or lioness). As you do, try the Taoist 'four-stage' breathing technique, useful for keeping lungs and heart under control during any form of exertion. Halfway through the inbreath, pause for a millisecond, then fill up with air to the top. Halfway through the outbreath, do likewise to create a four-beat rhythmic effect along the lines of 'in-in, out-out'. Time each 'beat' to coincide with your footsteps.

I know you'll immediately find 100 schedule-based reasons to reject this advice, but if you were to begin your day one hour earlier to effect the above ambulatory experiment, you would find your overall muscle tone improve within only two days, your breath capacity increase likewise, your mood improve remarkably, any errant flab fall away as if by magic, and your ability to handle stress grow appreciably. Anyone in the unfortunate position of being temporarily or worse, permanently, without use of their legs will tell you it's a crime to waste this near-incredible facility for self-propulsion or in any way to take it for granted.

You can turn off the mobile and fixed landline. You can turn off the computer. You can turn off the digital telly and radio. You can even turn off the fridge if you don't mind your butter going soft. But you can't turn off the ever-growing stream of obligations. And most importantly, you can't turn off your mind and energy. But you can relax, even for a brief moment every now and then, just by using your (own) mind to command your (own) bones, organs, vessels and nerves to let go of all unnecessary tension (because if you can't command it, who can?).

While relaxation is the best approach to whatever confronts you as you undergo your daily paces, doing absolutely nothing whenever at all possible is always of inestimable regenerative benefit. Giving oneself over completely to the doing of absolutely nothing is total anathema to many, I know. Indeed, it requires great yogic training for most to be able to sit or lie still for even five minutes without the body or mind fidgeting. But idling is an ancient art and one that's indispensable if you wish to stay in the game for the duration. Like those legendary cowboys of the Wild West and the ancient Taoists before them, we need to learn to kick back.

Take a walk on the wilder side of life

I just took myself off (by the ear) to a wild and windy mountainside in Wales where, far from 'civilisation', I stayed alone and isolated in an old, unheated, uninsulated, stone barn, miles up a dirt track, for many days, without transport, without even so much as a mobile signal, tapping ferociously on the keys of my laptop until, in spite of the fluctuating voltage from the homespun hydro-electrically generated current, a book came out the other end.

During the first few days, I was almost overcome by waves of self-pity as I suffered cold turkey withdrawal from my addiction to urban comforts, even succumbing to mild despair when the fire I'd lit in the woodstove refused to stay lit. (The wood was damp, as was my towel, as were even the sheets on the bed.)

But I surrendered and hunkered down, and, as soon as I did, I started to love the experience, feeling proud to be able to handle the extreme intensity of cold and solitude, and feeling relieved that I hadn't become too spoilt and mollycoddled by the electric womb of the urban sprawl to be able to hack it in the real world, where just the force of the elements can kill you or at least unhinge you if you don't get a grip.

Now I'm sure all the noble warriors who inhabit those parts, and who I know read this column, will laugh as they read this. 'Urban girl's blouse, making such a fuss!' they will say. Rightly so, too. For they all do it year in year out and look damn well and hardy on it, too.

But it's all relative to what you're used to and, like me, most of us have grown dangerously used to the ease and comfort of urban or suburban life and the convenience it offers. We also deeply dread being alone without stimulation (including TV) for even one night.

But if I could only describe the rush of the boost to my immune system, self-esteem and confidence levels, as well as the profound deepening in my friendship with myself that could only occur as a result of a 'fast' such as this, I would.

Instead (for all fellow urbanites – the rest of you feel free to snigger) let me humbly suggest you likewise take yourself off by the ear for a short break from the things of this world, if only for the blessed silence, and see for yourself.

Moreover, it's good for your heart and I don't mean figuratively. I'll explain. The ability to be alone with yourself, to acknowledge, accept and have the courage to face your feelings and be sufficiently nurtured and fascinated by just your own company is, according to certain Oriental medical beliefs, facilitated by having strong heart energy. It is this energy that supports your sense of self, governs your tone of mind, and therefore colours your entire internal experience of life.

Conversely, when you spend time alone deeply enjoying your own inner dialogue, it makes your heart energy stronger, bringing obvious benefits to overall wellbeing and health.

When your heart chi is weak or scattered through stress, overwork, relationship problems, lack of sleep, or heart disease, for instance, you'll find it nigh on impossible to enjoy your own company – to love yourself in other words. And there isn't a single New Ager in the whole of southern California who wouldn't tell you what damage not loving yourself can do.

But if dragging yourself off for a spell in the bush isn't practical in the foreseeable future, don't despair. You can support your heart chi here and now, and instigate a process of falling deeper in love with yourself and by extension the whole world (if you want) by pressing a point on your wrist known as your 'spirit door'.

Look at your right palm and draw an imaginary line dividing your little finger along its length from tip to base. Continue the line over that side of the palm until it meets the band of faint interwoven lines which form a bracelet effect on the side of your wrist. Use the thumb of your free hand to press in at this intersection with enough gentle force to produce a strong but pleasant ache that radiates along your little finger. Maintain pressure for about 40 seconds and then repeat on the left hand. Then give yourself a big hug and suggest to yourself, 'You're all right, kid!'

By the same token, all you rural guys should take a fast from nature now and then and come for a brief sojourn to the hustle, bustle and filth of the city, if only to reinforce all the reasons you don't choose to live there, but also because it can be a jolly and fun place to be, even if it does make you neurotic hanging out in such close proximity to millions of other people.

But just one thing I don't understand: why, when you left doors open as a child, did people castigate you by demanding to know if you'd been brought up in a barn? Surely those reared in barns would know better than anyone the value of closing every door possible just to keep a bit of heat in?

Don't waste your competitive spirit on macho pursuits

Back in the early days, I was at a gathering of arty, left-wing socialites in Hampstead, where everyone was showing off, and succumbing to the pull, I swung my legs into full lotus position with a flourish. Trouble was, I hadn't warmed up and made the movement too fast. The bang of the ligament snapping in my left knee was so loud everyone jumped. That'll show 'em, I thought as I sat silently handling the searing pain.

And then there was the time the first astanga yoga teacher came to town in the early 80s. Such a god was he, and so striving for nirvanic perfection were his devotees, that I couldn't help but rise to the challenge as I jumped through his series of near-impossible yogic hoops. Well, I wasn't going let anyone think I couldn't keep up, was I? In that session I ripped my right hip joint in such an untoward manner that without constant attention I'm still liable to default to 's' bend mode at any time.

But I'm learning. A few evenings ago, in a bid to exorcise that confounded flu virus which had invaded my defences for the third time in a fortnight, I went to the local gym. Everyone in the pool was racing up and down. I raced with them, maintaining a speed that wouldn't clog the lanes without expending undue energy, and got out when feeling the first wave of tiredness instead of doing my normal superman thing and pushing through it. Then I walked into the steam room, where the usual two suspects had hogged the best seats, arranged myself with a minimum of manly huffing and puffing, and focused my eyes on the floor (as you do).

And that's where it came to me: competitiveness! Even in the steam room we compete to see who's tough enough to sit there longest. Even if it means you have a heart attack. Luckily I didn't. Nor did I stay in the race. As soon as the first tinges of overheated claustrophobia swept over me, I was out of there, to the derisive snorts of the two hard guys in the pool where two lengths of racing were quite enough for me, thank you, and up in the changing rooms where it's all down to who's got the biggest willy. So I was tucked up in bed before the hard men had staggered out of the steam.

I used to imagine I wasn't competitive until one day in a therapy session I realised I was probably the most competitive bastard on the planet, as any trainee analyst could have inferred from reading the above. And I know I'm not alone. Competitiveness is what fuels evolution, let alone a free market economy. And it would be misguided to see it as a Western disease. Having trained for 30-odd years in Chinese martial arts, I can tell you that no one is as competitive as the Orientals. The difference is that they, under the influence of Taoism and Buddhism, learned to use their competitive energy with the things that count. Hence it would be unlikely to find three Triad members seeing who can last the longest in the sauna in Gerrard Street. They'd rather use the energy to see who can win the most money at cards after they've showered off.

Does it really matter who's the most adept at keeping up with an astanga yoga class? Is that what yoga was invented for? I thought it was to find oneself in a state of absolute union with one's inner and outer environment. And yet never has the incidence of yoga injuries been so high (I was just ahead of the fashions when I did my knee in – see, there I am competing again). Because whatever we get hold of in the West, we huff and we puff at it until we blow the wall down. But that's a very hit-and-miss way of doing things. Often we blow down the wrong wall – a supporting wall – and the whole house crumbles.

So as an ex huffer and puffer who at the tender age of 49 with three decades of martial-arts training under his belt is still only just learning to chill in any deep sense, may I pass on the following bit of Taoist advice (I've) verified over the years (the hard way): do not be in denial about your competitiveness. Acknowledge and accept it – this isn't called the human race for nothing. Notice how it makes you huff and puff when you could accomplish more by relaxing and slowing down. Attempt never to strain or use more energy than is required for optimal performance of any action or task. Always move your body (and mind) as a single unit mentally organised around a single point (6cm or so below your navel), keeping muscles soft when not in use. Always keep your breath flowing fluidly in and out, making as much use of your lungs as you can, especially during strenuous movement. Always maintain a cheerful, positive attitude (to prevent unconscious self-sabotage). And don't try sweating out that confounded flu virus in the steam room – it only comes back worse two days later. Pass the echinacea…

Slow and steady wins the race

Do you often find yourself rushing here and there without a moment to stop and notice what's around you? Maybe that's exactly why we rush so much: to avoid looking at the mess we've made of the earth – but without a moment to stop and notice the mess, you don't get to savour the bounty either. Or maybe we rush because we're subconsciously in a race with each other for the perfect rushless life, the best spot on life's beach. Either way, it would seem we were each born with an invisible monkey on our shoulder, whipping us on faster and faster (as we get poorer and poorer).

I realise I'm writing from a skewed perspective, typing as I am on a £2.70 London tube ride, courtesy of one of those palmtops with the silly little key-boards that has all but the most matchstick fingered hitting two keys at once. As it happens, I'm trying to not waste a valuable 30-minute 'window' as I rush from one end of town to the other between engagements, such a busy barefoot am I (I'm not complaining, mind you – I love engagements).

I realise, spending much of my time (rushing) up and down the length of the land, that the rush increases in proportion to population volume and density in your area, but it's all pro rata to your state of mind, and I'm sure if you're in, say, Bristol or Sheffield (not to mention Chipping Sodbury), the rush is reduced to more manageable levels, but a rush it still is.

And what about this absurd business of having to schedule 'appointments' weeks in advance just to see your friends for dinner? Surely it's indicative of an incipient madness grabbing the testicles at the underbelly of our existence and means we've managed to get things well out of balance? Across the Channel, our cousins the continentals seem to have things better balanced. They work fewer hours and more efficiently, earn more money, accumulate more real wealth, their property's cheaper, their cars cost way less, their infrastructure works (far, far) better, they spend more time with family, loved ones and local community, they spend more time in nature, they have more nature to spend it in, they have a lower divorce rate and higher birth rate, women don't despise men as much, men aren't so afraid of women, their food's (way) better (and cheaper), they have far less violence – they don't even have glass windows at the bank, as they still trust each other enough on that basic level to make do with good honest air to separate teller from customer – and by all accounts they have better, more loving sex.

So where have we gone wrong, and is the answer for us all to hightail it off on the next Eurostar once and for all? Being at the 'leading edge' of global culture, we are less conservative and culturally more dynamic than the continentals, but the downside is that we've lost the connection with most of our meaningful traditions (eg, the family and local community) – it's a baby-out-with-the-bathwater scenario. Not that we should be attempting faux traditionalism – heaven forbid – we must stick to our trend-forging strengths and keep moving forward.

But as we do, perhaps it's time to re-create how we do things round here, because as you've probably heard by now from the ever-growing number of amateur new age metaphysicians in our midst, external reality conforms to our beliefs. If collectively we believe we have to rush every minute, working our fingers to the bone just to maintain a second-rate standard of life, then that's what we'll get – at any rate that's what we've got. If, on the other hand, we believe that the more we relax and slow down, the more we'll get done and hence the more money our precious time will be worth, then that's what we'll get.

Obviously big changes like this don't happen overnight – it may even take a year or two before you see proper results, so it's probably best to start the process now by installing the following belief in your hard drive, and if enough of us do it, who knows, we may even beat the continentals at their own game: simply write down on a piece of paper a minimum of six times daily (to give your subconscious enough repetition of data to register it): 'The more I relax, slow down and schedule in time for pure enjoyment, the more I accomplish in every way!' Supplement this by swallowing a few drops of Calm and Clear, the Australian Bush Flower Remedy, each morning. We've got the coffee shops, 'cool' bars, groovy high-street wear and fancy foodstuffs (ciabatta this, ciabatta that; you can't even get an honest sandwich any more) – now all we need is the mindset to enjoy it all.

Right. Now we've got that major issue sorted and dispatched, I'm off for my siesta (yeah, right). Hasta la pasta.

Power to your elbow

Elbow room – that elusive commodity – has definitely been eluding my elbows of late, travelling hither and thither as I have been by train, plane and sometimes crowded automobile, so I thought I'd like to share a little trick I discovered, based on t'ai chi principles and highly effective even with the most avaricious armrest hoggers.

Imagine yourself settling into your seat on the tube, plane or even cinema, and the person next to you has commandeered the entire surface of the armrest between you and has, in fact, even dared breach the invisible dividing line between your bit of space and theirs with knee or thigh.

Selfish sod, you think instinctively, and depending on your particular survival strategies, you either respond by withdrawing your elbow from the disputed territory, thus ceding the game to them altogether (maybe as a ruse to lull them into a false sense of security, ready to slip your elbow in as soon as they inadvertently move theirs later) or you push your elbow into theirs with determined intent to force them off altogether as soon as they show the slightest lack of resolve. Neither of these tends to be satisfactory, especially on a long journey where you have to stick around to soak in the bad energy between you, profile to stony profile, for a few hours subsequently.

Now I tend to err on the overtolerant side – as I see it, everyone's doing the best they can on this planet, each according to his or her own level of individual evolutionary development, even if that level often seems to be extremely low – life's too short and precious to waste a single moment focusing your energy in criticism of others' perceived lack of awareness. But I do find it truly irksome when someone has so little regard for my presence and so little appreciation of what's fair, that they invade my space and cause me discomfort.

That's probably why I was such a fighter as a kid, and my concerned dad got me into aikido when I was but 11, which in turn led me into a lifelong study of, and near obsession with, martial arts: I just didn't want my space invaded. By the same token, I'm always careful not to invade the space of others.

So I started applying martial principles to the armrest scenario – first time was on a plane flying back from New York sitting next to a 'gentleman' of giant proportions and macho demeanour, who, spreading progressively into my space in what felt like quite a purposeful way, supplementing elbow incursion with thigh and knee reinforcement, was beginning to truly piss me off. In response, following the t'ai chi principle of yielding to an opponent's superior force while simultaneously responding by overwhelming them with love, instead of pulling away or pushing back, I simply allowed my own arm and thigh to rest gently alongside his in the softest, most tender way I could manage, as if he was my closest brother. Knowing full well that this level of intimacy would play havoc with his nervous system, I proceeded to transmit as much loving energy through my arm and leg as I could muster, watching to see how it took effect. Within a few seconds he flinched away from me, removed his elbow from the armrest completely, and drew his knees tightly together. Of course, within moments he was encroaching again, but a second application of loving energy had him instantly on the retreat, and I was able to endure the remainder of the flight in relative comfort.

I have subsequently had reason to employ this method on various occasions, and always with the same degree of success. To transmit loving energy in this context or any other through your limbs, a skill which when developed will enable you not just to seize armrests and the like, but to heal others in need, focus your mind in your lower abdomen an inch or two below your navel, and imagining you have an invisible aperture there, feel as if you're breathing in and out through it. On the inbreath, visualise yourself collecting your life force in your belly, and on the outbreath, visualise that force radiating towards and through the relevant limbs like an energetic vapour which penetrates the relevant body parts of the transmittee. At first it feels purely imaginary, but with a bit of practice the sensation and results will be tangible.

I write this in the hope that it will be helpful to you, your elbows and other parts in future, and just think – if it catches on, it'll be so easy to spot the *Observer* readers in your midst. They'll be the ones getting all snugly with irritating, space-invading strangers.

The end isn't nigh

There's been an unusual atmosphere of intensity in the world recently. You could say it's always been intense and you'd be right, but this is different. Maybe it's the effect of springtime and the rising sap – the yang energy in all of us – pushing upwards and outwards to find expression through us with greater intensity. But this feels different to previous springtimes. Perhaps it's astrological, I wouldn't know for sure – you'd have to ask Mr Spencer. It's probably just a combination of 9/11 aftershocks, the Middle East's volatility, and Bush-baby and Blair's bellicosity towards Saddam (the old-school bogeyman) making everyone jittery. Or maybe it's just that every time you flick past the Discovery Channel there's some weirdo telling you an asteroid is about to collide with your head and wipe you out.

Back in the late 70s, I remember the occasional visionary talking about the imminent end of the world, and people thought they were nutters. These days, not a fashionable dinner party goes by without someone casually alluding to the upcoming apocalypse and everyone laughing in knowing agreement as if a great gag's just been cracked. (How can they laugh, I wonder, don't they know an apocalypse can cause incurable migraines or worse?)

One gets the impression that we're (unconsciously?) rushing more – and with greater urgency than ever – to enjoy all the things we want (or are told we should want by the media) before it's too late, while our patience levels seem to be diminishing proportionately. Everyone seems bitten by this bug. So if you're still dawdling along singing a song, snap out of it – you don't want the end of human life as we know it to come to an end before you get rich, famous, laid or whatever it is you want, do you? (Or so you might be forgiven for thinking.)

However, there are times in human history when it's appropriate to go with the crowd, and there are times it's best to go against it. At this particular time, with the crowd seemingly demanding an end to all virtues we originally held dear – good manners, patience, kindness, peacefulness, respect for human life, honesty, honour and other noble sensibilities – it could well be more appropriate to go against it.

You can't force others to act in noble ways, but you can set an example by acting nobly yourself. You can't force the world around you to slow down and relax before it implodes altogether, but by slowing down and relaxing yourself, the improved quality of energy you radiate will gradually infect everyone who chances upon your orbit. So spend a few moments every hour reducing any stress you may have inadvertently accrued, and your true nature will shine more brightly for everyone's benefit. This is based on the premise of: when you're smiling, the whole world smiles with you, hence when you slow down and relax, the whole world will slow down and relax with you, and thus will the intensity of all the pushing and shoving, on both the micro- and macrocosmic scale, be reduced to manageable proportions again.

All mental stress translates itself into physical tension and vice versa, but as it's usually impossible to gain access to the workings of your own mind, it's always more efficient to start by attending to reducing the physical tension and allow the effect of that to trickle back to your mind.

For this purpose there are various trigger (acupressure) points, intelligent stimulation of which will have an instantaneously beneficial effect on your body-mind complex. Start by placing the blunt end of a pencil on a point at the base of your skull in the centre where your spine disappears into your head.

Press in gently but firmly till you feel a pleasant aching sensation radiate across the back of your head. Maintain pressure for half a minute or so and release. You should feel your skull relax a little more and may feel a pleasant sensation in your sinuses.

Next, place the blunt pencil-end on a point in the space between the two vertebrae directly behind the dead centre of your chest and gently apply pressure as before, enjoying the sensation of pleasant ache radiate across your upper back and chest. Finally, place the pencil so it sticks in between the vertebrae level with your waist and (gently) apply pressure as before.

This procedure helps balance the energy in your three main 'psychospiritual' centres, which in turn renders you far more relaxed and wholesome and altogether a pleasure to be around (for yourself as well as others).

Fear of loathing

I just had this moment of weakness. It's the end of an afternoon of meetings and radio in town and I'm on the way to a 'cocktail and canapés' party – also work-related (honestly, where's my social life gone?) – and I'm early by an hour because I wanted to get across town before rush hour. Fine, I think, perfect opportunity to sit in the Italian café and write a piece on my palm (top). I'm in an area replete with clothes shops and my outfit feels distinctly daytime. So perhaps (I also think) I'll pop into a few shops and spruce up the look with a new shirt, maybe a pair of shoes, and hey presto, here I am, credit card swiped twice, a fair few quid lighter. And this on a day when checking my bank balance prompted me to fire off emails in an urgent quest to get some money in.

Schizophrenic or what? Maybe, but at least 'they' won't think me too daytime at the do. And as I sit here peering down at my shiny new shoes, I wonder what this bit of retail anaesthetic is numbing, for to think of it as therapy is self-deluding. My internal turbulence has not been resolved with these purchases.

It started for me on Sunday when, wobbling slowly along on the Intercity (are they still called that?) through a town in the heartlands which shall remain nameless, my gaze was rudely arrested by the sight of a parade. Now I've been on the planet a while and have witnessed parades of all kinds, so it's not that I'm easily shocked by such things. But this one was totally bizarre and sinister looking. What looked like at least 1,000 people – I'm assuming men because of their build and because I find it hard to imagine women engaging in such nonsense (call me sexist), though I couldn't tell on account of their helmets –

were riding slowly, two abreast, through the spectator-lined streets on motor scooters, each bearing aloft the English flag, the cross of St George. I noted that everyone in the enthusiastic crowds was Caucasian, and judging by the riders' hands, necks and other visible body parts, they were, too.

As far as I know, this parade never made the news, so it could have just been the annual Scooter Riders of the English Folk Music Society parade. But seeing as the town in question has a large immigrant population recently swelled by refugees from the Balkan wars, I couldn't help being reminded of both footage of Nazi rallies in pre-war Germany and scenes from *Animal Farm* – it certainly had that vibe about it.

I felt a mixture of fear and shame. Fear, because it looked like a town gone mad, and I never knew so many people were into such parades. And if it was a neo-fascist rally, that means (to sensitive old me) that the 'madness' is spreading fast, and as I'm a diehard liberal, my particular kind of madness doesn't gel well with it. Fear, because I believe that for all the downside of growing pains and adjustment discomfort, it's the wave upon wave of immigrants to these humble shores that has made this culture the most vibrant, sophisticated and exciting of any I've seen (and I've travelled with a big 'T'). Not to mention how lonely it would be not to be topped, tailed and sided by the glorious Celts.

Shame, because though I'm proud to be English, I'm even more proud to be an Earthling, because I don't just love it from Brighton to Carlisle, I love the entire planet, with maybe the possible exception of Lordsburg, Arizona, but that's another story. And I really thought we'd grown past the kind of limiting xenophobia that I felt wafting out from under those helmets.

And so I ask you, in fact beseech you, to resist any urge to narrow your vision – and to prevail on all around you to resist as well. Just before the millennium there was an exhilarating bite in the air. The bite of global consciousness – a burgeoning spiritual awakening. But as soon as the clock struck one, it all seemed to slam into reverse.

It takes but a single candle flame to extinguish the darkness in an entire room. You and I, we are that flame, with a responsibility to shine and to help. The ancient Taoists, no strangers to the wily ways of men in helmets, suggested the following: imagine a breathing aperture in the centre of your chest and breathe in and out purposefully through it. As you do, focus all your awareness on the quality of absolute harmony and feel as if you're breathing that quality in and out until you feel a veritable forcefield of it around you. See this force radiate outwards in ever-increasing circles until it penetrates every mind, and then relax and carry on as you were. Or maybe just go and buy some new jeans as well.

There's only one loser when you harbour negative energy

Most of the trouble on the planet as we look around us is unnecessary. We bring it on ourselves. In this instance I'm not talking about the pollution and destruction of the ecology, because in my naive way I believe we created that in all innocence in a worthy attempt to ameliorate our living conditions.

What concerns me is the suffering inflicted on people by people – the murdering and maiming that goes on by the minute – whether in the name of ideology, land, oil, money or sheer perverted bloody-mindedness. Yet no matter how often well-meaning souls have ranted on about it, it seems that we as a species can't help manifesting stupid, foolish, destructive behaviour. It's the flip side of our immeasurable wisdom and intelligence. And, as we know, you can't have one side without the reverse – that's basic yin and yang stuff.

However, there is in my (again possibly naive) opinion, an entire stratum of this stupidity we could actually tackle effectively – the stratum of revenge. Today, I've been momentarily halted in my tracks through the city by tourists stopping suddenly in front of me for no apparent reason, 'cut up' in my car by a succession of drivers and, walking back from parking the car, the day's pudding was a man bolting out of a shop across my path, stopping dead in front of me and picking his nose – charming.

I could have taken it all personally, even though I'd never come across any of them in the past. I could have shouted 'You stupid bastard!' to each and every one of them. Indeed, some I could have clobbered.

But if my mission, at least in part, is to encourage a general decline in stupidity (dare I be so arrogant), how could I contradict that by adding to it with my own? Instead, I chose to keep letting it go. Feel the anger as it arises as a heat charge in your solar plexus. Feel your body tense up as apeman (or woman) sub-persona comes to the fore, and then mentally release it by exhaling and relaxing.

So stop in front of me, Mr Tourist, it'll remind me to stop and look around more myself. Cut me up Mrs Thoughtless, it'll remind me how unfetching stress looks on someone's face framed in a passing windscreen. Pick your nose in my face Mr Let-it-all-hang-out, it'll remind me to always carry a tissue. Let each go their own way, unhindered by any of my vengeance – I know they didn't mean it personally. I let them all go in peace and let go of any negative energy that would otherwise fester within. Incidentally, venting the anger does not disperse it – it increases it.

All the great metaphysicians from John Donne to Einstein have pointed out, as above so below, as the macrocosm, so the microcosm, and if you want to change something in the world, change it in yourself. So if we want to see peace prevail in the macrocosmic body of humankind, perhaps we can all look inside at that part of us (the microcosm) that wants vengeance on whoever for whatever, however subtly or unconsciously, and heal it so we can forgive, as in let go, instead.

Energetically, anger that festers, fuelling the urge for vengeance, represents a build-up of psychic toxins in your liver. This makes your liver work hard and overheat. This heat then 'stokes the fire' in your heart, the organ said to house your mind – and you start acting crazy. To prevent this, go to a Chinese herbalist or supermarket, buy a bag of dried chrysanthemums, make a strong brew and drink up to five cups a day. That'll keep your liver – and heart – cool enough for your mind to mesh with this sentiment: 'When I forgive myself and the world for everything, it produces a light, a state of heightened consciousness, not peculiar to me as an individual, that pervades everywhere bringing peace to every mind.'

Ready? One, two, three...

Life moves in cosmic cycles

When trying to make some sense of the more bizarre reactionary 'lifestyle' choices of various susceptible sectors of society, here and elsewhere, apropos the spread of incendiary extremist ideologies (specifically neo-fascism and fundamentalism and the unholy alliances being forged between them), it's helpful to adopt a Taoist yin-yang philosophical perspective. For it seems almost incomprehensible that, having generally reached a state of cultural, intellectual and technological sophistication, people would fall prey to regressive doctrines based on fear and hatred. These doctrines are vehicles used to fuel the 'careers' of individuals rather than to further their dubious causes. And the causes are mainly theatrical devices that exploit people's dissatisfaction.

How can you explain the pre-millennial phenomenon of unprecedented economic, social, technological and spiritual growth and expansion being followed by the current tendency towards non-co-operation and siege mentality?

Well, you could put it down to the envious have-nots wanting to spoil the party for the 'haves'. You could say the 'greedy multinationals' are plundering the wealth of nations and must be stopped (though this is belied by the fact that in the developed world, the population has never enjoyed such prosperity levels and that in developing countries things are starting an upturn). You could say it's our punishment for not dropping the Third World debt. You could put it down to people being afraid of change and retrenching reactively to mindsets of bygone centuries. You could even say that, as they have not yet caught on to the 'spiritual path', people's lives have become so devoid of meaning amidst all this prosperity that they'll latch on to anyone with a loud enough voice, even if that voice is shouting for the destruction of everything we hold dear.

All good ponder-fodder and material for endless debate, but if you put the picture in a yin-yang frame, some sense starts to emerge from the conundrum. According to the ancient Chinese Taoists, all phenomena are governed by a cyclical mechanism – light becomes dark as day turns to night and dark becomes light and so on. They called the dark yin and the light yang. By observing the interplay between the two in human affairs, they could to some extent foresee social trends, and thus prepare. This enabled them to maintain a philosophical attitude to the world's madness and so ensure peace of mind.

Yin, the dark force, was attributed the tendency to contract, yang the tendency to expand. They noticed that one followed the other and vice versa – and that the cycle operated at different frequencies simultaneously. So you get infinite cycles of expansion and contraction, the inbreath and outbreath cycles, the hourly, daily, seasonal, three-yearly, 50-yearly, millennial cycles and so on. Nothing goes in a straight line, in other words, but in spirals.

Thus it was inevitable that in line with, say, the three-year cycle, expansionism of the late 90s would be followed by contractionism of the early oos. Just as it's inevitable that the exclusionist, fearful, hateful energy we've seen recently grabbing the fancy of the susceptible will be superseded by another phase of inclusionist, progressive, loving energy that will sweep the world, like the fragrance of a damask rose.

So take courage and shine your love, kindness and inclusive intelligence brighter than ever before. I don't know if that's an answer to the problems facing us, but I'm not sure there was a question in the first place. Perhaps it would be best to sum up with the immortal words of my late, great mate, RD Laing: 'It's a fine life, as long as you don't let the bastards grind you down!'

It's time to let go

Just before leaving for New Mexico in 1979 to live with the Indians (excuse the un-PCness, but even they call themselves Indians), I gave away every possession I loved and sold the others. I sold the record collection that ran almost 20ft along the floor, but gave the stereo and best albums to a friend. There was a remarkable moment on unplugging the stereo – I had to fight back a torrent of tears that nearly knocked me off my haunches as I bent down. My favourite old suede jacket, my Humphrey Bogart mac, my books (other than the *Tao Te Ching* and *I Ching*, which were the only two I allowed myself – what a party animal!) and all the other accoutrements of city living caused nothing more than a flicker, but parting with that stereo – and, a day later, the beautiful old 60s metallic-blue Merc I sold to some crook out in the West Country – cut me to the core. Boys, eh! (And I thought I was 'spiritual'!)

But as each possession left my care and ownership, I was progressively overcome by a lightness of being I hadn't felt since I was in the womb.

Each possession you own requires great amounts of energy from you on the subtle, unconscious plain, to maintain it in place. You actually peg your identity on to each one. As you walk in the living room after a hard day's battle in the urban or rural jungle and sigh with relief as your gaze falls upon familiar objects, you are actually transferring great amounts of subtle life force into those objects. And it weighs you down. Not that you realise it, so deep is the trance of everyday life. But as soon as you let go or are forced to let go, providing you have enough cash in your pocket or faith in the basic benevolence of life that you won't starve, the weight lifts and you're born anew – and that, you do realise.

So when my basement-level London 'crucible' was inundated in the recent floods and almost the entire infrastructure of my working life was destroyed – drowned computer, waterlogged paper files, you name it – all a sodden mush, it elicited nothing more than a simple muttered 'Fuck it!' because of my former training in it all being just 'stuff' (and, of course, there's always the insurance).

You are not your possessions, even though clinging to things (or people) to gauge or reinforce your sense of identity and hence belonging is the norm. We all want that feeling of belonging, and to get it we amass possessions (or people) that we consider belong to us. Ironically, it turns out we belong to them.

According to the Taoist view, all forms arise from nothing, change over time and eventually return to nothing. Wisdom consists of not clinging to anything – simply letting things come and letting them go, you 'sit' serenely watching the play of forms before your eyes.

Feng shui, the Taoist geomantic art, recommends you clear out unnecessary possessions regularly to maintain your life force at optimum levels.

The devastating floods we've witnessed across Europe this summer will no doubt be a regular feature for a while and there's no need to go into the entire litany of awfulness that no doubt awaits us, environmentally and every other way, so it behoves us all to get some practice in now in letting go gracefully of possessions, just in case we're forced to later. In any case, unless you've come across the elixir of physical immortality, a total letting go will be required one day.

To facilitate the most sympathetic energetic state for graceful letting go, there's a profound Taoist meditation. As you inhale, tell yourself you're with-drawing all energy from the world of form and retreating into the undifferentiated absolute state, or Tao, where you own nothing. As you exhale, tell yourself you're breathing life into the world of form to regenerate it in an even better shape than it was. Perform no more than 81 breath cycles like this, then repeat at least six times: 'I am not my possessions!' and go out and buy some good, strong, high-top wellies!

Brave the storm by being sure of your inner core

I woke up this morning... no, this isn't a blues song... contemplating deeply the meaning of endurance.

I was pondering world events and how things are tending to spiral – I hesitate to say out of control because I'm not sure things have ever really been under control – but yes, out of control would be apt. But if you reduce your worldview to its constituent parts, the common denominator is uncertainty and unpredictability. You have no idea how the sinking economy will affect your livelihood, whether terrorism and wars will impinge on your day-to-day reality, whether marriage is the answer to life, or even whether the very land you stand upon will soon be under the sea.

You may not entertain such thoughts consciously, but your instinctive self knows something's up, and inevitably you'll be feeling more insecure than ever before.

So I asked myself what are the qualities that are keeping me on an even keel in the face of all this, and I came up naturally with courage. But then I dug deeper and realised that the essential quality of which courage is merely an effect, when you strip away all the sentiment, is endurance. That no matter what, no matter how altered reality becomes, how painful or, of course, how blissful, you will endure. Like an oak tree in the storm, you will endure.

The ancient Taoist oracle, *I Ching*, says, 'If we meditate on what gives duration to a thing, we can understand the nature of heaven and earth and of all beings.'

So what is it that gives forms, people, institutions, their duration, considering that all forms, people and institutions are in a state of perpetual flux? What is it that remains constant within you (perhaps even after you die) even though in seven years every one of the cells of which your physicality consists will have changed? Well, it's not something you can define in words. You could call it your soul, your immortal spirit, but strip it of hyperbole, and you could simply call it core strength. This applies to all forms, people and institutions. As soon as core strength dissipates, the edifice crumbles. Conversely, as long as core strength is maintained, the edifice will remain standing.

So to endure what looks set to be a well rocky patch of human history with your sanity and hopefully lifestyle intact, it's crucial to begin developing a conscious connection to that unshakeable part within, your core strength, that you may rely on it in times of stress. The way of Taoist warriors of old – for though our wars are remote-control affairs, we must still respond internally as warriors – is to generate core strength in the following manner.

There is a deep energy conduit, known as your thrusting channel, running from your perineum between your legs, up the frontal aspect of your spine all the way into your brain. Inhale and imagine you can feel the breath enter through your perineum and rise up to the level of the nipples. Exhale and feel the breath travel back down into the perineum. Complete nine breath cycles, mentally repeating 'Core strength!' as the breath rises and 'Endurance!' as the breath descends.

The trick is to build a conscious connection to your core – and things don't get much more core than the front of your spine – by practising this exercise on a daily basis during moments of quiet contemplation, say while stuck in traffic jams or lying in bed. Then when stressful situations arise, you default to core-awareness mode, where a few passes of breath up and down the channel will centre you.

It may sound like an inconsequential manoeuvre in the face of momentous global events, but the effects with daily practice are profound. For real, if it works on someone with such a monkey-mind as mine, it can work on anyone.

Where's the party?

I've been examining this push–pull dynamic I have with crowds lately – that flipping between the urge to dive into the throng on the one hand and the mildly agoraphobic urge to retreat on the other, which I know from the steady slew of emails asking for advice on this is not peculiar to me. I'm sure you've experienced it yourself. You're at a party, a wedding, club, festival or any large gathering you happen, by choice or observation of social protocol, to be embroiled in and there's a part of you that wants to leave, a part of you that wants to stay. If you leave you may be missing out on the real fun that would somehow mysteriously start just after you leave (you think). If you stay, you risk bursting from that itch to get on the road or simply go home and put your feet up.

You feel pushed and pulled this way and that. You spend a bit of time flipping in this manner till you finally give in to the dominant urge in your belly and leave – or stay and then leave.

I've often found myself at gatherings of various sorts with my dominant urge being to get away from the crowd as soon as humanly possible. This is not because I wasn't enjoying myself – quite the opposite; I was enjoying myself so much internally, I didn't want to spoil it by being anywhere a moment longer than I felt like.

We need crowds not only to join in with, but to walk away from, too. Fundamentally, if you decide to leave, you can't miss anything because the action, though appearing to be going on around you, is in fact going on inside you – hence wherever you go, whether to nightclub or sleep, is where the action is (for you). However, if you stay when you don't feel like it, you'll just drain yourself, get drunk (or worse) or both.

These musings were all actually sparked up from a moment in France recently, where, having just performed a set at a festival, everyone on the crew wanted me to wait till 3am so we could all go off to the after-show party in the hills. However, being slightly longer in the tooth than all of them and having had my fill of experiences waiting till 3am, which inevitably becomes 5am, to go to a party in the hills, which usually turns out to be a washout on a small mound in the suburbs, I prudently decided to go with my inner urge and leave the heaving throng on a dizzy crescendo to drive like the wind across the border and home to my humble Catalan hillside shack to watch a DVD and drink a nice cup of tea. According to Taoist wisdom, the flip comes from fluctuations in liver energy – your liver is said to provide the force for your personality. When your liver energy, or chi, is weak, you lose your sparkle, your eyes grow dull and making conversation becomes a pain in the ear. Ironically, this is when you're most prone to taking a drink to fire things up a tad, but which will at the same time weaken your liver chi even more.

However, balance the energy in your liver meridian and your drive to mingle will return. While there are many ways to do this, ranging from a few visits to an acupuncturist to a complete detox diet, you can do a quick, on-the-spot job the afternoon before having to go out on the razzle, preferably around 3pm when the liver meridian is more susceptible, which will increase the sparkle factor subtly but significantly by around 9pm.

Lovingly pinch the flesh in the web formed between your big toe and the next on both feet for 33 seconds – this being the 'fire' point on your liver meridian, stimulation of which is the energetic equivalent to a shot of tequila, so don't be afraid to make it sting. As you do, visualise your liver (on the right under the ribs and stretching across all the way over to the left side), softening, relaxing and, yes, smiling. Remind yourself, 'Wherever I am is where the action is!' and carry on as you were.

Get to know your inner child

I've been asked to write about this crazy old life and how you work your fingers to the bone the year long, all but putting yourself and the needs of your inner-most playful child (and possibly your flesh and blood children, too) on hold except for the few precious weeks when you take yourself away from it all to some sunny beach, mountainside, desert or other 'holiday destination' where you spend half the time dealing with breaking the addiction to workaday life and the rest rediscovering the part of you that loves to have fun and be free of responsibility – then just when you've rediscovered it, almost before you've properly had a chance to bond, it's time to fight your way back through crowded roads, aeroplanes, boats, trains, skateboards, or however you travel, and return to the inevitable pile of bills, emails, phone messages, credit-card statements double what you'd reckoned, laundry and, of course, work. Is it any wonder we wonder what it's all about?

So, in case you're suffering from the insidious 'I want to still be on holiday – I don't like being here one jot' syndrome, allow me to present the ancient Taoist take on things and hopefully ameliorate your mood.

We all, whether consciously or not, spend our lives looking for the perfected permanent womblike state (the Tao), where we imagine a life free of responsi-bility, pain or discomfort, where all our needs and desires are fulfilled instantaneously. We search for it when we shop, in property, in a mate, in wealth, in status, alcohol and substances and, of course, going on holiday, but of course we don't find it.

Teased by mere glimpses, we walk around feeling conned of our divine birthright, imagining that if only we could get that £3m or so we've calculated will enable us to sit around by a pool all day till we die, everything would suddenly be OK. But of course it wouldn't. Maybe a little more OK I grant you, but not the real, everlasting deal we're after.

I hate to say it, because getting fooled by the world of externals is such fun (as well as damn painful), but the only way to achieve it – and it is achievable – is to go within.

Consider dispassionately what it was about being on holiday that made you feel so nurtured, and you'll probably be able to break it down to spending a relatively relaxed time daily exercising your body – swimming, walking, dancing – resting, sleeping, contemplating profoundly, reading, engaging in deep dialogues with people you like or love, probably having more sex than usual, and for all of that becoming reacquainted with the playful enthusiastic-for-life spirit at your core – the so-called real you.

Any ancient Taoist will tell you that if you discipline yourself to incorporate even a modicum of those elements into your daily life, you will gradually develop in your relationship with the real you to the point where every day, including even the most responsibility-laden, will be a holiday or literally holy day – sanctified by the conscious presence of the eternal child playing within you as you go about your business.

The name of the alleged founding father of Taoism, Lao Tsu, incidentally, means the eternal child master. Allow yourself to play with this visualisation, for example, guaranteed to induce a warm (inner) glow and reconnect you with the holiday spirit. Close your eyes and see yourself naked, swimming a graceful easy breaststroke alone in a warm natural pool under the stars. Feel the soft water all around you, soothing you, loving you. Feel the life force flow through your body as you imagine your arms and legs stretching and flexing, your chest expanding and relaxing and all the tension in your body melting away. Then shout affirmatively something along the lines, 'Hurray, my life's a holiday!' and carry on as you were.

The Earth

Differentiating night from day

Under cover of darkness (as I'm sure you've found out), many of life's most exciting events occur. Night is a glorious time that is normally, in these frantic, devil-may-care days, associated with naughtiness and pandemonium, when good folks should be asleep.

Indeed, the night has become an institution complete with nightclubs and ladies (as well as, of course, laddies) of the night, which is interesting, because cherishing the night as a concept at all is really a rather childlike idea.

There is, in fact, no night. Not in any a priori sense, anyway. What's happening to create this illusion, as you know, is the earth spinning on its axis at a 1,000mph in an easterly direction in relation to the sun, around which it orbits at 66,000mph every hour of the year. And when the part upon which you situate yourself in the morning has rotated sufficiently, you will find yourself, within approximately eight to 14 hours, depending on current orbital position and respective axial tilt, on the other side of the planet from any available sunlight, other than that possibly reflected by the moon and, to a lesser extent, other planets or various human-made satellites.

But although the night as fact is an illusion (caused by lack of sunlight), the darkness is not. According to the wisdom of the Oriental Taoists, darkness equates to the a priori quality of yin, which represents the passive or static force of nature and light to that of yang, the active or dynamic force. During the sunlight hours, your body soaks up yang energy from the sun, like a solar cell, which it utilises to see you through your waking hours. During the hours of darkness, your body soaks up yin energy from the ground to help it rest.

They, those Taoists of old, were, of course, observing human patterns from the unpolluted vantage point of high mountain caves with no mobile-phone coverage. But electricity and the 24/7 lifestyles it facilitates have confused this natural cycle somewhat and have us now, on the whole, expending inordinate amounts of (yang) energy going out on the razzle and what have you when we would, if following natural laws, be resting.

But following natural laws to the letter, in such a sweetshop as our post-modern, multiple-choice life, makes Jack a dull boy (and, of course, Jacqueline a dull girl). And so together we say 'Bully!' to good old yin and yang and we drink and make merry into the wee, small hours. (And then complain we don't have enough energy, and feel stressed and tired the next day.)

But when after such revelry, or simply after letting yourself be drugged half to death by the gamma rays from your TV set, it finally comes time to touch head to pillow, what can be done to effect the most restorative sleep possible and thus optimise on what the power of nature's yin force has to offer?

Firstly, to induce sleep initially, having applied a drop or two of lavender essential oil to the temples to calm the mind, it is helpful to press the acupressure point known as your 'spirit door' which lies on and has the effect of sedating your heart-energy meridian. According to Oriental medicine, your heart is responsible for your mind and its ability to alter modes, in this case to turn itself off for a few hours, preferably eight.

Locate this point by looking at either palm, running an imaginary line down the middle of your little finger, and over the palm to the wrist-bracelet marking at its base. Press this point bilaterally for a minute or so with pressure firm enough to cause a slight ache. This will help effectively turn your conscious mind off, like a mild sedative, within 10 minutes or so.

In the interim, take this brief opportunity while your mind is at its most susceptible to suggest to yourself both how you'd like to sleep and how (as well as when) you'd like to wake up. For example: 'I will sleep deeply with enjoyable and informative dreams and wake up at seven feeling refreshed, energised, optimistic and ready for the day ahead!'

To help you remain asleep for the duration, it is best to sleep on your right side, both to prevent an overload of venous blood to the heart, which would provoke unpleasant and erratic dreams, and to encourage more blood to circulate through your liver, where it undergoes purification while you sleep.

One of the biggest hindrances to remaining asleep through the night, especially when you are under stress, is the eruption of sudden noise, of say a passing car with throbbing bass bins at four in the morning. These things happen (and mustn't be taken personally, as becoming aggravated when woken makes it much harder to fall asleep again). For this reason, you may wish to avail yourself of earplugs, as a basic precaution.

As for ingesting sleep-enhancing substances, while the allopathic sleeping pills or muscle relaxants favoured by many may be an effective expedient in the short term, they obviously do untold damage if taken habitually. A short course of cranio-sacral therapy is an efficient way to reset your internal clock naturally when disturbed or if you wish to break a sleeping-pill addiction. Bear in mind also that using herbal sleep aids should not be mistakenly considered harmless just because they are 'only herbal'. Habitual use of herbal sedatives can damage your liver and kidneys as much as their chemical cousins.

And so to the almost unmentionable: sex, or more precisely orgasm, as sedative. If you're in a happy relationship, love-making and cuddles often provide all the sedative action you need. If you're alone and know how, you can always meditate, or, excuse me for stating the obvious, even masturbate, which is, as you'd expect, by all accounts one of the most popular drowsiness inducers on the market.

If choosing the former (meditative path), you may find it enjoyable to imagine you are gazing at your boudoir through the middle of your forehead, the so-called third eye, as you drift off, because this encourages conscious dreaming. However, if choosing the latter (hedonistic path)... well, I'm sure you don't need any advice from this barefoot doctor. (Nighty night!)

Combating fear of terrorism

Since the day the 21st century showed us the other, darker side of its face, I've been inundated with emails on how best to deal with the fear and uncertainty we are experiencing in the wake of what has happened and what might happen next. Like someone we've been in love with for years, someone we knew all along wasn't perfect, but who has just shown us an ugliness we didn't want to see, this world has just shocked us with its violence. So how do we deal with it? Do we reject it, tell it we want a divorce and hightail it off to the mountains? Do we go into denial and attempt to carry on as before, as if we didn't really see the ugliness? Do we become scared and panic that all is now ugliness? Or do we say, OK, I can learn to accept the ugliness along with the beauty, the dark along with the light, the yin with the yang, for surely only in a fool's paradise is there only the light and beauty?

According to the Hindu cosmic calendar, this is the Kali Yuga – the age of darkness, when everything speeds up until it spirals right out of control. This goes beyond right and wrong, pleasant or unpleasant. Kali, the goddess of destruction, plays an essential part in 'Shiva's dance' or, in other words, the universe. For, without destruction, there cannot be creation – there'd simply be no room for all the new stuff. Many Hindus and other enlightened souls pray to Kali, not to appease her (we're not dealing on such a primitive level here), but to make friends with her. Just as a t'ai chi boxer embraces the opponent with energy in order to overcome, Kali worshippers embrace the awful destructive qualities of the goddess in order to overcome the fear.

The Hopi have an interesting take on our times. Over 2,000 years ago, they prophesied when we would talk through cobwebs in the air (phone-lines) and build a platform in the sky (sky-lab), the world would be a crazy place in which to live – so much so we'd probably prefer to live on Mars. I actually met the 'keeper of the prophesy', Thomas Benyaka, in the Hopi homeland in Northern Arizona just after the USSR had invaded Afghanistan in 1979 and the West was threatening nuclear strikes. He told me that this war was merely a local enact-ment of a far greater war in the spiritual realms between the forces of destruction and creation and that we had it in our power to help tip the balance one way or the other through our prayers. So as well as visualising peace on earth, remember that this plane of existence only reflects a far greater realm wherein you visualise light gradually overcoming darkness, creativity overcoming destruction.

The Taoist recognises the eternal alternation between yin and yang and says 'out of great darkness will come great light' (as surely as day follows night) and carries on practising being exclusively in the moment, resisting all urges to project into an imaginary future based on information gathered from a past that is no longer. The Taoist would say that in this present moment (and the next one and one after and so on), you are, if internally still enough, able to create reality around you any way you choose. Hence, theoretically with enough focus, intent and chi (energy), a single person – you for instance – is able to actually effect substantial change in external circumstances just by seeing it so. This is also the basis of not only Western magic, but Western religion, too.

But to be in a state capable of manifestations so grandiose and macrocosmic in scope, you have to be relaxed. You can't possibly hope to redress the imbal-ance of dark and light in the heavenly realms or fifth dimension and thus affect healing change out here on this lunatic asylum of a planet when crippled with panic. Firstly, accept these are especially insecure times. There is nothing abnormal in this – human life has always been insecure. Secondly, accept the sensation of insecurity within yourself – there is nothing wrong with insecurity – it's a perfectly respectable state. Thirdly, mentally and manually undo all physical stress accumulated in your body as a result of fighting the insecurity and relax.

Running down either side of your spine is a bank of muscle. Place hands on hips and firmly press with thumbs into the outsides of these muscular ridges until producing a noticeable but strangely pleasant ache. The longer you keep pressing, the longer the muscles have to get the message and relax. Stop before you get thumb-ache, releasing slowly and enjoying fully the sensation of expansiveness that will flood your kidneys (just about now). Then do as the Taoist and proclaim for one and all to hear and be inspired by, 'Out of this darkness will come great light!'

Doing your bit for world peace

It is said – or at least it was many thousand years ago by some ancient Taoist or other – that if just one person in the world can purge their hearts of hatred, violence and destruction, peace will reign throughout the earth. Similar to the doctrine of mea culpa but more upbeat in tone: if you can see the macrocosmos as an outer reflection of the microcosmos, and purify your thoughts sufficiently, the world will respond by becoming peaceful. It's a far-out concept and one that requires a certain willingness to suspend rational judgement in order to experiment with it.

But as I see it, there's nothing much to lose by doing so. It's a tall order, mind you. In fact, purifying your thoughts to the extent that all violence is removed from your heart is probably impossible unless you spend all day, every day, for a decade or so, in a cave, meditating on it. Even then, I bet if some skankster were to come up and pull your hair long and hard enough you'd succumb in the end and would find it hard to tell them to bug off without even so much as a trace of irritation and a desire to give them a slapping. Which is why it is very unlikely that there ever will be 100 per cent peace on earth. There'll always be someone who wants to get the club out and swing it around a bit, no matter how much we all get pure of heart.

Luckily, however, reality is not just about extremes, it's also about balance, and that same ancient Taoist would tell you that if you can tip the scales a minimum of 51 per cent in favour of peace, the world will reflect that by maintaining itself 51 per cent peacefully. Which is great for you, as long as you don't stray into the 49 per cent part (for long). So now, how to purify your heart of violent impulses a minimum of 51 per cent while still going about keeping up with your busy schedule and keeping an eye on the sky for errantly falling objects?

The answer is forgiveness, gratitude and love. Forgiveness means letting go of the need to do violence to self or others on account of some resentment or other, usually unconscious. Gratitude means being in a state of thankfulness to the creative power of the universe (the Tao, or however you wish to think of it) for performing the ineffable miracle of facilitating your unlikely existence on such a fine and particularly exciting planet, as well as gratitude to all life forms for putting on such a splendid show. And love means being open and unblocked to receive as well as give the energy that passes between us freely and with as much kindness as you can muster at all times.

Taking these abstractions as your template for every interaction can provide an exciting strategy for wending your way through the everyday, but may be too vague for some to get their teeth into. Which is why either that same ancient Taoist or some other would gladly tell you that the ability to let go and forgive is governed by your large intestine energy as part of its responsibility for assuring adequate removal of solid waste; the facility to feel grateful for your existence is governed by your spleen energy, just as is your ability to feel satisfied with what you eat; and your capacity for the give and take of love is governed by your heart energy just as is your capacity for processing your arterial and venous blood interchange.

So, jam the thumb of one hand into the side of your other hand at a point at the end of the crack formed when you hold all five digits closed and press till you can't bear the ache a moment longer. Repeat on the other side. This is the 'great eliminator' point on the large intestine meridian. As you do, say, 'I'm willing to let go and forgive myself and everyone else!' Then push the fingers of your right hand gently in and up under your left-hand ribs (your spleen) until the mildly winded sensation disperses and as you do, say, 'I choose to remember to be grateful to be alive!'

Finally, form fists and with the little finger edges percuss a steady, light drumroll on the middle of your breastbone till you get tired of it to stimulate your heart centre energy and, as you do, say, 'I am now willing to give and receive love freely in the appropriate way, all day long for evermore!' Or, just keep repeating the word 'love!' (It's all you need.)

No pain, no gain

Oh, what a perfect day. It starts with me finding a parking space right outside my front door – a rare novelty in London (or any city) these days – 'Ah, perfect!' I exclaim. A little later, driving over the Severn Bridge into Wales, at one in the morning, momentarily glancing up at those awesome columns piercing the dark, again I mutter, 'Perfect!' A fair bit later still, I arrive at the old stone barn on the Pembrokeshire mountainside overlooking the Irish Sea – you may recall me going on about it the last time I came here in the winter. I manoeuvre gingerly up the mile-long, deeply rutted dirt track, delicately uncrumple myself out of my easyCar seat and stare up at a rare alignment of planets in the night sky.

It's 3am, absolutely silent – you can't see another house, there's no mobile signal, no email. I can't help but say it again: 'Damn perfect!'

'Except...' and my mind defaults to its ongoing theme of late, 'What about all the suffering in the world? How can anything be perfect with all this pain and misery around me?'

'Well, I'll tell you...' whispers the old Taoist sage within.

The Tao includes everything that is, was and ever could be. There is nothing that isn't part of the Tao – even nothing is part of the Tao. But the Tao cannot be described or explained – that's its only rule – it's just too big, too all-embracing. So its followers don't even try. Instead, it's just accepted as a premise or a fact.

In *Magic Roundabout* language, suppose the Tao was a huge, limitless being, an intelligent macrocosmos. That being, Big Tao (pronounced dow, by the way), would look about itself, see all the pleasure and all the pain in the entire universe, and being totally enlightened about both the beneficence and cruelty of life, say, 'Perfect. Absolutely damn perfect!' This wouldn't be for any latent sadistic tendencies on its part. When you're big enough to encompass the entirety of all that is, you have the perspective of a span of an infinite number of aeons to see that everything in nature, all its agony and ecstasy, is exactly as it's meant to be and is all perfect. There is no sentimentality at this level.

But 'down here' on the microcosmic human level, pain hurts. Whether suffering yourself or witnessing others doing so, pain is a horrible thing. So as a responsible, feeling human, you do all you can to alleviate this suffering, whether that's giving 20 pounds a month to the Red Cross or organising Live Aid (for instance). The trick is to embrace both levels of awareness, the micro and the macro, simultaneously. Within the physical body, according to the Taoist schema, there exists a finer, more subtle body whose anatomy consists mainly of three so-called inner chambers, together comprising the meta-template of who you are, your innermost being or 'higher self'.

The first chamber is in the centre of your lower abdomen and is responsible for the energy that drives you through life. The second chamber is in the centre of your chest and governs your ability to feel compassion. The third chamber is in the centre of your brain and governs your capacity to witness the effects of the other two and make sense of it all.

Slowing your breath down now and relaxing your body, allow yourself to be aware of the life force in your belly. Softening your chest, allow yourself to compassionately feel your own existential pain and your empathy with others. Relaxing your skull, let yourself witness the absolute perfection of it all.

'Thanks for reminding me,' I whisper back at the old Taoist sage, whipping my bags up the steps and into the barn just in time, as the heavens open up and it starts raining cats and dogs. Inside it's warm and dry. I make a (nice) cup of tea, flip open my laptop, write this piece, flop into bed and fall fast asleep. Perfect, absolutely damn perfect.

Let it bee

I killed a bee today. I know in the annals of crime this doesn't rank highly, but I can't get it out of my mind.

There were no real extenuating circumstances.

True, it was hovering over my son while he slept, but it was a dozy thing and I could have just as easily herded it out the window. Instead, with my bare hand and a piece of kitchen roll, I crushed it, as if it were no more than a piece of fluff, rather than a living creature. Sure, I spoke to its spirit and prayed that by releasing it from its mortal coil it would find rebirth as a higher life form, but still it was murder of a living thing by someone whose identity is based on being a healer.

This destructive act cost me my spiritual equilibrium and I'm finding it hard to connect with all-that-is in a meaningful way.

It makes me wonder how many of us feel cut off from our spiritual source because we feel unworthy, having committed crimes or misdemeanours in the past for which we still feel guilt.

So for the sake of my tortured soul and those of everyone thus afflicted, which I assume is most of us, let's take a moment to consciously feel the connectedness between us and all other living things – and having felt it, humbly surrender to the pain of accepting responsibility for our acts. For only by such acceptance can forgiveness occur, and from that, grace and healing.

In the last hour, 2,000 people have died from starvation, roughly two-thirds of them children, 20,000 acres of rainforest have been destroyed, half a million tons of toxic chemicals have been released into the atmosphere and 50 plant or animal species have been driven into extinction – all by us. And that's not to mention the millions of violent acts or agonising deaths caused by Aids and other diseases.

You may not be a wilful occasional bee-killer like me. You may even let mosquitoes who buzz you at night go in peace. You may feel you have very little direct connection to the mass starvation or destruction of the environment, but collectively we are all responsible. Guilt is a waste of time and only serves to perpetuate denial. Now is the time to heal.

This is achieved initially in small ways – minor acts of generosity and service that trigger a positive emanation. At first, this emanation is relatively local, but if enough of us create these emanations, it sets up a field of resonance that gradually pervades the collective consciousness, all the way to the people who make the big world-changing decisions.

But first must come a moment of feeling connected. The best way to do this is to visualise a tiny being in the centre of your chest. This being represents the perfected version of you. Gently breathing in and out, imagine that with every breath, the being is growing larger and larger, until it overflows the boundaries of your skin, larger and larger, until it outgrows the building you're in, and still larger until it outgrows the town, county, country and planet. Now, mini-you is so huge, the entire planet and all who reside here are contained within you. Now, like a pregnant mother loving the baby in her womb, allow yourself to love each and every creature on this earth as if it were your own child.

Reactions to this may range from thinking it a load of twaddle to bursting into tears of compassion. Either way, be sure to reverse the process and allow your 'perfected self' to shrink back to its original size within your chest again, or you won't be able to fit through the door (metaphysically speaking).

As for me, two big, fat bees just came in to say they understand, and I managed to usher them out of the window just by talking to them nicely. So, I don't know about you, but I'm feeling quite absolved. Thanks for taking part!

Getting in touch with the feminine side

'It's funny, with no women here, I feel it's as if there's no one to show off to!' I said, ever the performing monkey, laughing as I looked out at the sea of a few hundred expectant male faces before me. I had been asked to give the introductory talk to the Brahma Kumaris organisation, which was holding the biggest ever UK event for men to discuss and explore the deeper meaning and relevance of manhood in the 21st century. Then I realised that Dadi Janki, the head of the organisation outside India, whom I regard as my spiritual grandma, was sitting with her female interpreter in the front row, which rendered my opening line a bit lame. But that's showbiz and as she's such an elevated woman and is to all intents and purposes beyond gender, I was able to accommodate the two of them as honorary guys and carry on, sure she was thinking, 'You're such a naughty boy, but I do love you.'

Boys! I see us as kids in the playground, where you learn early on that you have a choice of strategies in terms of getting by in the world of people and in this case, men. You could be a dominator (yang – masculine) or a co-operator (yin – feminine) or often in practical reality, a little of both. Though potentially always a pugnacious little bugger, I usually tended to swerve towards the way of co-operation and teamwork, whether as leader or follower. (I never minded following as long as the leader wasn't a ditherer.) I learnt early that there was little point in expending energy enforcing my will on others as invariably it ended in tears.

Indeed, considering the slight mess us men have got us into on the planet over the past few millennia following the dominator model – domination over each other (men and women), and over nature – it's obvious we need to learn to co-operate more.

Co-operation – a yin, or feminine – principle, is innate in us all. Yin is the source of nurturing, and women are more expert at accessing it. Beyond jumping on one another's backs and messing up their friends' hairstyles after a goal is scored in football, men must develop their latent capacity to nurture each other.

Women are men's mirror image (and vice versa). To be fully rounded is to acknowledge your mirror image and to imbibe the qualities you see there. What men must learn now is the ability to tread softly on the earth and to treat each other with kindness and respect. In short, what men must learn is love. Not just love in an abstract sense, but love in action: in the way we treat each other, men, women, children, and the earth and all her creatures and resources. Because this is all we've got. From co-operation with love comes wisdom. From wisdom comes salvation.

This was the substance of my talk and everyone seemed to agree, at least no one rushed forward to beat me up. I finished, kissed Dadi (meaning 'big sister') Janki's hand, ran up the aisle, down the stairs, out of the doors and into a minicab waiting to whisk me off to Euston to catch the train. I explained to the driver I had 20 minutes to get there. He took up the challenge (like a man) and passed many a long line of traffic at breakneck speed on the wrong side of the road. So fierce was his intent, there were times I actually shielded my eyes and braced myself for the worst.

From the yin of the Brahma Kumaris and Dadi Janki and her wonderful devotees in white, to the yang of the minicab driver's *Italian Job* dash across town, from the sublime to the ridiculous, two faces of man, but I loved that guy with just as much spiritual, brotherly intensity as the calm brothers back at the talk. And he got me to the train on time!

In fact, it's that mix of the yin and the yang – the feminine and the masculine principle within each of us – that provides the key to living a fully balanced life. Too much of the former and you grow soggy inside – too much of the latter and you run away with yourself. And the best way to establish this mix on a moment to moment basis (which, after all, is what ultimately counts) is to concentrate on regulating the inbreath and the outbreath – inhalation being yin, as in drawing life towards you, exhalation being yang, as in sending out life from you. In any case, slowing the breath down – indeed being conscious of it at all – is the number one key to peace of mind.

Getting in touch with the universal

When it comes to shaping your own destiny, there seem to be two levels (at least) operating simultaneously: one is the local mind (the surface you're familiar with, telling you to turn left, turn right, buy this, sell that, etc, according to what feels like whimsy), and the other is the profound universal you (the one you're less familiar with but to whom you may pray from time to time or contact when more meditatively inclined), who holds what looks like a pre-ordained grand plan and knows why it needed you to choose this over that to get you to where you are, who smiles and says, 'That's why you needed to do such and such, it was to get you here now to this moment of perfection, of knowing why.' Or maybe it is just utterly random, and destiny only something you can talk of in retrospect. Perhaps it's just vanity that causes us to believe there's rhyme or reason to the path we choose.

There's an energy centre at the top of your forehead, in the middle just below the front hairline, which is said by Taoists to put you in command of your destiny, to bring those two levels of consciousness together as one, thus making you perfectly aware of why you're doing this or that according to the greater scheme of things, and thus saving you endless hours of worrying whether you've done the right thing or not. Activating it helps you know you're where you're meant to be, doing whatever it is you're doing in the way you're doing it.

To activate it now for experimental purposes, imagine a breathing aperture at the top of your forehead and 'feel' yourself breathing steadily in and out through it until you feel it glow. Augment this by afterwards placing the tip of your forefinger ever so lightly here to produce a subtle tingle. Repeat the procedure every day now for at least 30 days and experience your sense of appropriateness increasing exponentially.

Also, watch out for confirmatory signs, synchronicities occurring like psychic slapbacks – little things like in the cab the other day with my favourite driver negotiating the traffic smoothly as a dolphin, I wanted to ask why he chose manual over automatic but didn't. Coming home later, I had a different cab, with a different driver, who exclaimed, totally unbidden: 'You know the trouble with driving an automatic? It makes your left leg go to sleep from having nothing to do all day!'

It gets more interesting when the choices of an individual or group of individuals seem to affect the destiny of millions of others. I'm not well-informed enough to know the real reasons for a war right now, for instance, but as any martial artist will tell you, the actual use of force indicates a gross error has occurred because everything (if you strip the emotion from the situation) can be negotiated with enough patience, intelligence, wisdom and, of course, when it comes to world affairs, money.

So what I suggest, as insignificant as it may appear, is to invest a bit of time and energy activating the destiny centre as above and, while doing so, visualise a defusing of tensions and a reduction of conflict in general.

I haven't a clue if it'll do any good (or bad) – after all, maybe nature (for we are an expression of nature) deems in her wisdom that a war is necessary on the planet. But maybe she doesn't know either way, and a bit of psychic force in the other direction from a few focused individuals may tip the balance.

I hope so. I truly hate the thought of people killing each other – it's a tragic waste, no matter how much oil's involved.

Never lose sight of the fact that you are one of this planet's 6bn children

The planet, this fine and ultimately mysterious globe you currently find your sit-bones supported by, this stupendous spinning ball careering recklessly around the sun, weighs roughly 6,600,000,000,000,000,000,000 tons. That's the weight required to keep the 6bn or so humans and all life-support systems on its surface merrily dancing along the 'Great Thoroughfare' of life in the quirky, and currently rather dangerous, old way we do. Contemplating that for a moment may help lend perspective when your worldview becomes myopic and you find yourself fretting over details – including your health, relationships, career, finances, social standing and very survival itself. Callous to call these details!? Not a bit of it.

Sometimes you have to take yourself out into (imaginary) space and see your world from a few light-years away to make any sense of it – to be able to stop taking it all so personally – for only then can you relax enough for compassion to arise. So when depression or anxiety sets in as your unconscious mind struggles to assimilate the overload of information assailing it every day, you have the choice to be sucked into the inner maelstrom or view your local earth life with the detached compassion required to generate the energy to carry on.

And this requires relaxation. Relaxation in the face of apparent chaos as one world order, one paradigm, is crunchingly replaced by another. Relaxation even in the face of possible personal dissolution! Relaxation is essential if you're serious about still having some fun on the planet – and if you're not having fun, what's the point?

So rather than tense the soft tissue of your body against impending disaster, thus constricting blood and energy flow, leading to decreased perspective and diminished sense of self, use your commanding mental faculties to relax instead. Simply take a full, slow breath and as you exhale command all the soft tissue in your body to 'Relax!' Repeat this no more than nine times, feeling your body soften more with each exhalation.

Now collect your awareness in the very centre of your brain, so that rather than 'being' in the front of your face, looking out bug-eyed and frantically, you're now 'in' the centre of your brain serenely gazing out through the portholes provided by your two eye sockets. If you shut your eyelids now, you'll notice a deep, dark endless expanse of space between and behind your eyes. In that space, visualise the earth, many light-years distant, picture your local patch as an invisible pinprick – see your affairs and doings, dreams, fears and phobias as nothing more than micro-disturbances on the head of a miniaturised pin, and with your heart full of compassion, let the vision be suffused with softness.

In this extraterrestrially awakened mode, you may experience a slice of awareness of the presence ineffable – the Tao or Great Way – that sense of a benign supraconsciousness connecting and animating all phenomena including those occurring within you. You'll know it if you do – you'll be overtaken by a visceral sensation that everything will turn out fine (in the end). If you don't, then imagine it – it'll make you feel good.

Finally, imagine you can feel the weight of the planet beneath you and feel the speed of its orbit (19mps), and vowing to be a warrior rather than a worrier, open your eyes, take a few moments to re-enter local life, massage the sole of each foot to ground yourself, gently pummel the centre of your chest with fists while chanting 'Aaahhh!' for a few moments to stir the courage in your heart, sensitively massage the kidney region of your lower back for a minute until warm to build your willpower, shake your fingers and toes to get your chi circulating, do a little running on the spot, tell yourself, 'I can do this!', give thanks that your share of the tonnage is holding you up, then go out there, spreading the love for all you're worth, and knock 'em dead!

The Seasons

Spring-cleaning your liver for extra energy

With the daffs in the garden trumpeting in the arrival of spring, it's time to examine the Taoist take on this joyous seasonal transfer. Go 'Brrrr!' and shake off the kidney-crunching cold of winter. Take your fists and use them to massage some warmth into your lower back, then relax while I talk you through the Taoist springtime schema. You have five vital organs: heart, lungs, spleen (including pancreas), kidneys and liver.

During each of the five seasons (summer is split into early and late), a different organ is energetically predominant. Right now we're coming into liver time. It's no accident that your 'liver' is spelt the way it is. It's what gives you the oomph to slough off your inner wallflower, grab your adventure by the ears and live it to the full.

Each of the vital organs is assigned different responsibilities in connection with your self-development. While your kidneys give you willpower, your heart the power to love, your spleen the power to intellectualise and your lungs the power to create, your liver gives you the power to grow and take on new challenges. In this capacity (of self-renewal and, by extension, species renewal), it also gives you the drive to come out of hibernation, both literally and metaphorically, and interact with the external world – socialise, in other words. This is true all year round, but is more pronounced in spring, when nature invites you to partake one way or another in the mating game (and renewal of the species).

However, being the season's predominant organ doesn't come without its drawbacks, vulnerability to climate being one. Spring is traditionally known as the windy season, when the winds of change blow through your system and stir the sap in your sacrum that it might rise through your spinal column to your brain and stimulate you to go out and make a difference to the scheme of things. Which is fine if your energy circuits are clear of blockages. But if – as it is in most cases in this polluted, stressful madhouse of a world we've created – your meridians are somewhat clogged with energetic debris caused by toxic build-up in the system, when the wind blows through it will activate those toxins and place strain on your liver.

This is why it is often recommended to engage in detox activities at this time of year, one of the most effective being a four-day apple and spring-water fast, with honey as an optional add-on to the apples. If you opt for this route, lead into the fast gradually by cutting out alcohol, coffee, stimulants, meats and car-bohydrates a couple of days prior, and do likewise in reverse on the way out, gradually reintroducing all the tasty stuff, rather than launching into a cheese-burger and chips for breakfast on the fifth day. (It has been known!)

You can eat as many apples as you like, including the core, which is perfectly safe if eaten with the rest of the apple. You can choose any brand you like, but Granny Smiths tend to pack the most punch energetically. Be sure to drink ample water. You may experience headaches on the second day as the toxins start surfacing, so it's a good idea to arrange a soothing aromatic massage in the evening. As you may feel rather weak for the first two days, it might be best to begin on the weekend. By day three, your energy will have increased significantly, enabling you to bound into work annoyingly bright-eyed and bushy-tailed, ready to put your sallow-faced colleagues to shame.

Whether you plump for this simple detox suggestion or something more elaborate such as the infamous 10-day brown-rice fast, or skip the whole idea altogether, it will be highly beneficial to invest in an acupuncture or shiatsu session for purposes of seasonal adjustment. More importantly, it is crucial you take up some form of daily, preferably morning, exercise regime.

This is because the liver also governs your tendons and ligaments and therefore the flexibility of your joints and muscles. By upping the exercise ante, not only are you taking advantage of the liver's extra seasonal energy, thus maximising on muscle-toning possibilities, you are also helping to circulate the energy in your meridians and thus clear out the debris. Obviously the efficacy of this depends on both the kind of exercise you do and the way you do it. Huffing, puffing and straining at the weights in a sweaty gym will give you a temporary endorphin high but will not make your energy surge as much as, say, huffing, puffing and releasing your way through a sweaty power-yoga session, and definitely not as much as losing yourself in a concentrated chi-gung or t'ai chi mess-about.

But then again, if you relax and move from your centre, allowing your breath to flow uninterruptedly, smoothly and evenly, with your mind fully engaged in internal body awareness as you would in t'ai chi, for example, any exercise will be of benefit, from cartwheeling to tossing the caber.

If you can warm yourself into it slowly so as not to damage your muscles or joints, it is far more beneficial to do 30 to 60 minutes of exercise, preferably outside or near an open window, in the mornings, when the air is less polluted and the 'yang' daylight energy is most available, than in the evenings when the air is filthy from the day's traffic and your system is clogged by stress.

And contrary to popular belief, it is correct, according to Oriental wisdom, to exercise in a structured way every day, not just three, four or five days a week, as Western exercise specialists often recommend. Exercise is really part of your daily hygiene and to skip a day, except when ill, exhausted or otherwise prevented, is a bit like going out without brushing your teeth: it won't kill you, but it's unpleasant.

Finally, spend a few moments at the end of each day making the Taoist healing sound for the liver. Try it now. Take a deep breath and exhale making the sound, 'SSSHHHHHHHH!', imagining it as a jet of water steam cleaning your liver (under the ribs on your right) from within. Did I hear you say, 'Shush!'? OK, I get the hint. Happy springtime.

Getting to the heart of the matter

According to the ancient tenets of Taoist (Chinese) medical philosophy, every season (they counted five, including late or 'Indian' summer) has a particular effect on the energy balance of your body. Specifically, the general climatic conditions of each season can potentially adversely affect one of your five vital organs. The heat of summertime, albeit often approaching imaginary status in our own sacred island idyl, primarily acts on the heart energy.

'So what!' I can imagine you saying. 'Who cares – it's summer, let's enjoy it.' And it's true – there is nothing more important than the simple enjoyment of being here from moment to moment.

However, if it should so happen that you have a propensity for internally overheating and the oppressive heat of a summer's day manages to breach your body's natural energetic defences and invade your internal meridian system, it will find its way to your heart, and that could be disastrous to the extent that the circulation figures of this very newspaper would be reduced by one.

Taoist physicians consider the heart to be emperor (or empress) of the entire psychophysical and emotional 'multicomplex' that is you. In other words, as well as facilitating your vital life-pulse, it also facilitates your overall sanity and peace of mind. Its innate energy is likened to fire. Without fire, life could not be, but when fire burns uncontrolled, life is extinguished, so it's crucial that your heart's fire remain in a fairly balanced and organised state.

An invasion of summer heat can inflame the intrinsic heart 'fire' to such an extent that you become unsustainably agitated, internally dishevelled and, if you're prone to emotional or mental instability, it can drive you literally round the bend. If, on the other hand, the actual organic mechanics of your heart are not all they should be, such an invasion could even trigger cardiac arrest or heart disease. (So that's what!)

Had I the wry dryness of say, Jack Dee, I would simply say (flatly) that the heat of summer may cause you to become overexcited, overadrenalised and therefore unable to think or operate so effectively, and if suffering from hypertension, insomnia, disturbing dreams, intermittent recall or heart disease – or wishing to prevent same – you should take note of the following.

The heart is a muscle and, like any other muscle, needs to be relaxed to work at optimal efficiency. Indeed, it is actual physical (muscular) strain that causes accumulation of said excess heat or 'fire' around the organ, and which can be largely dispelled by a simple command from the mind.

To demonstrate, tense the muscles of your right forearm and then addressing that forearm as if you were a yoga instructor talking to a class of devotees, say: 'Relax!' and feel the tension release from the muscles. That's how easy and straightforward it is with muscles, and it is no less so if the muscle in question happens to be your body's emperor or empress him (or her) self.

Try it now for a moment, just for a little practice run. Picture – or better still, feel – your heart now. Become aware of its beating. Don't be afraid of it (people often tend to worry that thinking about it may confuse it and cause it to stop). Be the confident yoga teacher instructing the class – or, if you like the traditional emperor or empress model, be that – and give your heart the 'Relax!' command. Then with a long exhalation, consciously allow the entire thoracic region to relax completely.

If fully entered into, this action (or more precisely non-action) will engender an overall sensation of peacefulness and calm. If you concurrently relax your belly and back – and the rest of your body, while you're about it – it will amply demonstrate what those Taoists of old meant when they said the energy of the heart determines the quality of consciousness.

Alternatively, standing comfortably – feet approximately one metre apart, knees slightly bent, pelvis thrust forward a couple of centimetres, and the crown of your head reaching up for the sky so as to elongate your backbone – clasp your hands together in front of your pubis and inhale deeply, thinking of your heart with a smile on its face. Now simultaneously chant an extended 'HAAAH (har)!' sound in the deepest, most resonant note you can manage, while undoing your hands – and with arms relaxed but extended, describe a large 'V' shape in front of you by raising your arms diagonally out to the sides in an upwardly, outwardly trajectory, ending up as if you have just completed a star jump. Feel the vibrations of the sound as it resonates in your chest, micro-massaging your heart. If you've had the patience to follow those instructions, repeat up to eight more times, and rest.

And now, back to imagining that summer.

Banish the blues and have fun in the sun

Summer is the season when the year shakes off its inhibitions, dresses up in its gaudiest, most revealing clothes and comes out dancing in the streets in a vulgar display of lager-fuelled passion. Then there are the seemingly endless sweaty traffic jams, bumping along slowly in the thick pollution to the muffled repetitive thump of Kenwood bass bins – road-rage city – occasionally inter-rupted by afternoons lazing around on lawns eating strawberries and cream to the more discreet repetitive thump of tennis balls. Or barbecues. Or hightailing it out of town, waiting around in airports for the 'delayed' sign to change to 'boarding now', to go and be ripped off in any number of tourist hot spots around the Med.

Yet, like children who know no better, we love the summer. It teases us with nostalgic fantasies of a perfect world where the sky was always blue, the sun warm, not carcinogenic, and the air clean, with few mosquitoes, certainly none bearing Nile Fever. There were no drunken afternoon street brawls, the sea was clean and safe to swim in, and worry over air travel and Sars just a sick idea in some science-fiction writer's head.

The reality, however, is different. For a start, the weather is unreliable even on the Med, where you're just as likely to be inside watching the rain pouring down as you are to be stretched out in the sun lapping up the good life.

Yet still we love the summer because even the slightest rise in temperature causes our kidney and lower abdominal area to relax, and when that happens we stop being so afraid of life and each other. One of the main reasons people in the UK tend towards the repressed and reserved, compared to, say, the southern Italians, is because the cooler temperatures of the other three seasons cause our kidney regions to contract, which, according to the Taoists, engenders an underlying sense of foreboding and existential fear. Which is exactly why we tend to let go during the summer months.

But what about those awful summer blues? You know the feeling: everyone is out in the street laughing, the weather's fine and there's nothing to worry about, at least no more than usual, yet you feel grumpy, down and excluded. And you have no excuse. You can't blame it on the cold or the dark, like you can in winter. You can't blame it on having to stay indoors with nothing to do. So you have to try and work it out for yourself.

Consider this: the organ most affected by the summer climate is your heart. Your heart energy is said to house your spirit, or at least be responsible for keeping it in your body while you're alive. If the excitement of summer overcomes you or passes you by, it can weaken the heart energy, which causes you to become, literally, dispirited.

So if you're beset by an attack of summer blues, start by pummelling gently on the centre of your breastbone while chanting the Taoist heart-healing sound 'Haaaaah' for half a minute or so to wake up the energy. Next, press firmly just below the base of your palm where it meets the wrist on the little finger side. This point is known as the 'spirit door', as it opens the energetic door that allows your spirit back into your body. Then, after eating three radishes (to stimulate heart energy), tell yourself it's OK to feel whatever you're feeling, no matter the season. Keep breathing deeply, smoothly and evenly, and within hours the blues will evaporate and you'll be out there raising hell. Myself, I prefer to hide away in the mountains and wait for the sanity and decorum of winter to return. But then I'm a Virgo.

Don't let an irrational fear of flying stop you spreading your wings

Lately, I've been getting so many requests from people about to fly who want me to write about overcoming the fear of flying, it makes me wonder if airline revenues are really as hard hit as claimed. Indeed, it would seem that all flights are full from now until eternity.

And it's the concept of eternity that's at the root of this problem – that and the awful sensation of sitting scared out of your wits trapped somewhere you really don't want to be and having to deal with it in a cramped-up little seat with stale air that burns your nostrils, screaming kids piercing your eardrums, the danger of bloodclots threatening your equilibrium and every bounce of the wing making your stomach leap up into your throat. And to make matters worse, you've actually had to pay for it.

But the fact is, it's a lot quicker than walking, cycling or taking the bus, train or ship, and unless you've months to spend, the only expedient way of flitting about the planet. You could stay at home for evermore – though sooner or later it's inevitable that, no matter how afraid of flying you are, you'll have to take to the skies one day.

Personally, because of the peripatetic nature of my work, I spend a huge amount of time up in the air – literally, not metaphorically. I overcame my own fear of flying, which began one night in 1980, coming in to land at Miami after a bumpy seven-hour flight from Quito during a violent electrical storm on an old, second-hand Air Equador 707 with rattling seats which, having been struck on the wing by a bolt of lightning, banked sharply and proceeded to fall out of the sky and plummet a few thousand knuckle-blanching feet, complete with the sound effect of women screaming, the smell of urine, faeces, vomit and adrenalin in the air and even the flight attendants looking terrified, before finally stabilising on a cushion of air and eventually landing at Miami in a nothing-special kind of way.

So the next time I got on a plane, this time from New York back to London, hence no short hop, having rubbed a mix of tea tree and lavender oil around the inside of my nostrils to act as an antiseptic filter for the germs – with more of a psychological effect than physical, I'm sure – I practised the following calmative techniques which have worked ever since to the point that I love flying now more than any other form of transport other than water-skiing which I adore but which is useless for long-haul destinations.

First, spend some time on the net researching the facts (various airlines also run courses to help you overcome the fear) and you'll soon realise how safe planes are, even in severe turbulence, for which they are specifically designed.

Second, spend some time meditating, praying or contemplating your own mortality, as well as the concept of destiny, as in: when your number's up it's up. This is crucial at some stage in your personal development, whether you fly in planes or not, as sooner or later you'll have to make peace with the idea of dying.

Third, practise breathing deeply, calmly and slowly, as this keeps the mind from panicking, which is the last thing you need to do on a plane.

Fourth, if given to fantastical visualisations but innately untrusting of technology and machines, picture a being, your guardian angel, as big as a skyscraper, flying along beneath the plane holding it up through any possible turbulence.

Fifth, keep visualising yourself arriving safely at your destination with a smile on your face.

Sixth, gently massage the soft part of each wrist, especially in the area in line with your little fingers, as this stimulates the heart meridian and calms your nerves until before you know it you'll be on the ground again safe and sound as if nothing has happened, already huffing and puffing impatiently while you wait for your luggage.

Taking your child spirit out to play

Remember when you were young? Oh, that inner playful spirit. That indomitable, carefree, innocent spirit for whom there was no question of learning to love the world. You just did. Of course, there were tricky moments when the heavy spirit of adulthood invaded your experience, or when you were caught in a momentary bind with a particularly twisted peer.

Then as you grew (bigger) and the frequency and import of your interactions with the adult (adulterated) world and the effects of its demands on you increased, your sweet, playful spirit went deeper and deeper underground, until nowadays it probably often can't even be accessed at all, save with the help of alcohol or other such social laxatives.

Under our adult disguises we're all still children in the playground of life. (Not children in the postmodern, brand-conscious, little-monster mould of today, but children before artifice, self-consciousness and tendencies to live by the expectations of others have set in.)

According to Taoist philosophy, being 'as a child' is the key to health, enlightenment, longevity and having a damn good time. (So, let's get with our inner children, guys.)

Obviously, along the way, we've learned some pretty useful socialising skills that enable us to get by in the world and have had some useful insights to boot. Repeatedly orbiting the sun will do that for you. But we mustn't be deluded into subscribing to the arrogance of adulthood, because therein lies the fast track to depression – and specifically 'summer depression', seeing as it's that time of year.

Summer depression? Sounds like a contradiction in terms, but that's the point. In summer you're 'meant' to be 'happy'. After all, the birds are singing, the sun is shining, and the foliage is rude in its full bloom. Everyone's out, seemingly having a good time, and the sharp summer light throws any personal existential twists into starker contrast.

Entering into a discussion on depression – summer or otherwise – in any universal sense is naturally futile, as there are as many 'types' of depression as there are people to feel it: from mild, free-floating to the heavy, brick-wall variety. Hence one person's cure is another's poison.

However, there are a few common themes at its root (according to the Taoist healers, both ancient and postmodern). All depression results from an inability to manage one's existential crisis, due to your inner playful spirit (IPS) being weighed (or pressed) down by the (often delusory) concerns of adulthood. This results from a deficiency in that organ or energetic sphere that is said to house your IPS and which makes you do the living of life: namely your liver.

All deficiency of liver energy results from or causes a deficiency of kidney energy at some point in the wash cycle. Ergo, if you want to maintain optimum expression of your IPS, and thus prevent or alleviate summer depression, or if you simply wish to ensure the smoothest inner ride possible for the next few weeks, consider the following.

Both kidneys and liver respond well to gentle exercise, such as walking, swimming, yoga, chi-gung and t'ai chi on a regular daily basis, as well as manipulative therapies like acupuncture and shiatsu. Once kidneys and liver are balanced, the tone of mind associated with depression will shift of itself.

In the Oriental scheme, discovering the personal reason for depression is not prerequisite for alleviating depression. Instead, by altering tone of mind, the reasons will become apparent of themselves over the course of self-healing. The first thing, though, is to shift your tone of mind.

Of course, a by-product of depression is that you're less likely to be willing to motivate yourself to do the things that will help you alleviate it. And, often, great will is required to push yourself enough to make a difference. Moreover, not all forms of depression will respond well to exercise, acupuncture or other manipulative therapies to the exclusion of conventional treatment. Indeed, there are cases of clinical depression where forgoing conventional treatment is highly counterproductive. As I said, it's impossible to universalise about it.

But nothing in life is permanent, from the thickest brick wall to the greatest empire, nor is depression. In fact, as well as exercise and treatment, an enormous amount of positive mind-tone shifting can be achieved by retrieving that IPS and remembering to give it expression as often as possible – even if it requires tricking yourself back into child mode. Try crawling around the house for the next hour or so, pulling yourself up the kitchen drawers to make a cup of tea. Try dancing round the living room with gay abandon for 20 minutes, or talking and singing in gobbledegook.

But most of all, reset your mind to see anew the bewildering glory of the world around you – don't allow your perception of the world to grow tired, in other words. Be a five-year-old, go outside, look up at the sky and, with arms wide open, declare, 'Damn good show!'

From a balanced spleen to unconditional love

Here we are (again) – the end of the summer phase of the annual cycle, always a tricky transition. Having left the vulgar ripeness of high summer behind, we stand at the threshold of our descent through autumn's portal into another tunnel of winter darkness. Move over Wordsworth and Keats! The ancient Taoists linked every phase of the seasonal process with one of the five elements; this 'getting-ready-to-go-back-to-school' time is associated with the earth element, itself represented in the body by your spleen.

On the basis that your entire experience of the world is regulated by the various states of energy flow in your five vital organs (heart, spleen/pancreas, liver, lungs and kidneys), this implies that by attending to the balance of energy in your spleen, you will find yourself in harmony with the process of seasonal transition, and will be thus better poised to thrive through the winter. And it's important to remember that it is still possible to thrive even in hard times. Especially in hard times, in fact. And the key? As any old hippie will tell you, it's love, baby. Not the carnal variety, though that sure is sweet (as we all know), but the unconditional compassion for all humanity.

And why? Because with love between people, no matter how much the madness, violence, disease and mayhem increases, or how much common sense, economic stability and good-times decrease, life will still be livable. Without love, it merely becomes hell on earth. I am not about to preach about love and what it means, save just to say it is expressed through an empathy with the plight of your brothers and sisters (in the larger sense) and a willingness to extend kindness through thought and deed (whenever you can).

But you can't give and receive this higher form of human love effectively unless you yourself are teed up properly to do so. So without further ado, a brief suggestion for self-regulation of spleen energy, and let the teeing up commence. With right palm in front of your belly, raise your right elbow to the side and draw your right palm upwards through your midline until your hand is above your head, palm facing out. Breathe in during the hand's ascent. Breathing out making the sound 'Huuuu! (who!)' as resonantly as you can, draw your hand back down through the same trajectory while twisting at the waist to your left, thus gently compressing the area under your left-hand ribs which houses the spleen and pancreas.

This is the ancient Taoist healing sound and movement for the spleen, and is best repeated six times, preferably in between 9am and 11am (the hours of optimum splenic energy flow) every day for the next three weeks, for most noticeable results. These should include a subtle increase in feelings of being grounded and level-headed, not being thrown off balance by events around you, a healthy appetite without putting on excess weight, an increase in sanguinity (bloodfulness) and vigour, improved muscle tone without exercising more, improved short-term memory and a tendency to worry less. All these are products of balanced spleen energy, but obviously 'huuing' in your armchair isn't the universal panacea for either spleen energy or the woes of the world, so you may wish to supplement the proceedings with a bit of self-massage adapted from the daily regimen of the Yellow Emperor himself, known as 'harmonising spleen and liver'.

Stroke lightly with one palm after another across your upper abdomen from left to right 18 times, and then reverse. The emperor would have this performed on the imperial abdomen 180 times in each direction, four times daily by his personal massage squad, so important did he consider it for maintaining his immune system. But even practising the truncated version will have noticeable effects, especially if done daily for 30 days or so.

It works on the principle that your liver – which provides the impetus to go out into the world and live your story – is by nature a greedy organ, which will, if given half a chance, grab all available energy at upper abdominal level, thus leaving the spleen with a deficit. Stroking from left to right, thus drawing energy from the spleen to the liver, lulls the latter into a false sense of security, by giving it what it wants. Then, a few strokes later, when it has had time to relax and grow careless, you whoosh that chi back into your spleen with a bit extra on top.

Finally, as with undergoing any great transition, it is crucial to not resist, as this only leads to energy wastage which depletes your immune system and animal vigour in a highly counterproductive way. To which end I find repeating to myself, round and round like a simpleton, 'relax, let go, allow!' has a profoundly self-righting effect, especially when listing badly. Relax about everything. Being tense won't help anyone or anything, least of all your state of mind and effectiveness levels. Let go of your fear and consequent desire to control reality. The Tao, the great natural way of things, has an inbuilt wisdom and a penchant for putting on a bit of a show from time to time – this time, for example. Allow the show to develop and flower of itself without interfering (too much). This way all details relevant to your particular part in the drama will resolve with true elegance of a quality only possible with the Tao – nothing less than that. And may it do so most elegantly for you now.

If your conscious self is a coward, fear not

Autumn is the season of change – change of light and temperature, change of atmosphere. Change is inevitable because everything in existence consists of moving parts, and yet accepting that is one of the biggest ongoing personal challenges we face. Why? Because we wish with all our hearts to believe in permanence. We know death awaits at some point down the tracks, but manage to pretend it doesn't. We know the body ages and the last stages of life are a cruel business, but carry on as if that isn't so. But this faculty for denying the perpetual nature of change inevitably causes pain every time the ramifications of change present themselves with enough force not to be denied.

The antidote is to embrace change, and this requires confidence. Eighteen years ago, I was standing on the edge of a cliff in Snowdonia looking down past the protruding jagged rocks at a small pool formed in the river 40ft below. A group of people down there were enthusiastically shouting in unison: 'Jump! Jump! Jump!' 'Impossible,' I thought.

I was trying to organise myself to jump but my legs were rooted to the spot. There was no way in a million years I could do it. Suddenly, without any perceptible sea change of consciousness, I found myself hurtling through the air, and landing with a massive triumphant splash into the ice-cold water.

Foolhardy, perhaps, but I was taking part in a six-day event designed to induce you to overcome fear to help you get on with forging the life you want without being blocked by your own inner resistance, and turning away from the edge, tail between my legs, seemed an even worse option than having bits of me strewn about the rocks. I don't take credit for the jump. My conscious self didn't do it. The spring in my hitherto immobilised legs came from much deeper inside.

And it's the relationship between the waking, conscious self and the deeper self, and how this relationship plays itself out through your physical actions, that forms the basis of true confidence, an attribute we will all undoubtedly be called upon to access in ever greater amounts as events in our world intensify, challenging our inner equilibrium.

Confidence means literally maintaining the faith with yourself and implies a dialogue between your conscious self which does the trusting and your deeper self which has to be trusted if you don't want to lose your bottle. Confidence is not something that can be acquired suddenly; it takes time to develop, and there are many ways to do this, learning a martial art being the most obvious. But anything that affords you regular time developing that dialogue through overcoming your internal obstacles via various challenges will do the trick.

Strengthening your upper body, and specifically the heart region, which in Taoist thought is where your sense of unassailable self originates, has an almost instant beneficial impact on your confidence. If you find push-ups hard, start on all fours, otherwise lie on your front on the floor, palms level with your shoulders and, holding your body in a perfectly straight line, pelvis slightly tucked under and forward, push up slowly and purposefully on an outbreath, inhaling again as you lower yourself back down. Imagine the movement originates deep in your lower belly. Complete nine cycles, gradually building up in multiples of nine (the most force-inducing number in Taoist numerology) until you can do 36 or even 81 (my favourite) without breaking into a sweat. And with every push-up, think: 'I trust myself, I trust myself, I trust myself, I do!'

Then go forth with confidence into this mad, mad world, trusting you'll acquit yourself with utter aplomb no matter what.

Rise to the challenge

With the rustle of dead leaves or the squelch of soggy ones beneath your feet, beyond the usual poetic autumnal symbolism of decline, death (approaching winter) and rebirth in spring, you will probably be aware by now of the physical and emotional challenges presented by seasonal change.

As well as stepping in and out of unnaturally heated buildings, cars, buses or trains – usually swaddled in too many layers while inside and too few while outside – your immune system must contend with rapid variations in temperature caused by the fluctuating changes in wind direction and pressure.

When the wind blows from the west, warmed by the Gulf Stream, the air will be mild, and your energy will tend to be optimistic and abundant. When blowing from the north, the air becomes bone-penetratingly brisk, though usually clean-feeling and invigorating. When the wind blows from the east, however, it carries not only the bitter damp cold of Siberia, but also the pollution of all of Eastern Europe, including its radioactivity, collective frustrations and discontent. The east wind invades your system and blows a host of malevolent viruses through your channels. (The south wind generally takes to hanging around the Med for the autumn and winter months – a wind that knows how to blow in style – but not in our direction.)

Autumn stretches your body's intelligence services to the limit, running first to the eastern rampart of the citadel, then to the north, then to the west, as randomly alternating winds produce sudden unexpected rises and falls in temperature.

Your immune system (the intelligence service's executive arm) works best when you're happy. With less light and shorter days, unless you make a concerted effort to spend time outside, preferably each morning, it's unlikely you'll see much natural light, which can lead to a propensity for depression caused by light deficiency (SAD).

According to Oriental medical philosophy, each of the four seasons (five if you count late summer), gives rise to potential problems in one of the five major organs.

In autumn, it's the turn of the lungs. In practice, this means that when the winds of autumn come whistling through your meridians, the lung meridian is the most vulnerable. The wind stirs up internal dust or respiratory 'impurities', instigating coughs, colds and ear infections that will manifest a short while afterwards during the winter.

Don't let yourself succumb to gloominess, however. Autumn is a time of exquisite beauty, every moment of which must be savoured in the lessening though brilliant silver light that only comes when the planet's tilt is on this particular angle. There is a melancholy grandeur in surrendering with dignity to oncoming winter's dark, cold grip.

Take the challenge on as a warrior. Get up half an hour earlier than you have to. Stretch your body gently and, donning appropriate layers, go outside into the nearest available garden or park. Walk, run, swing your arms about, do t'ai chi if you know some (if not, consider taking lessons), kick up leaves like a child, and embrace the elements. Look at the vastness of the sky and feel grateful for being alive.

Drink mullein tea to open your air passages and prevent respiratory blockages. Take homeopathic aconite if you feel a cold or sore throat threatening. Take tincture of propolis as a daily tonic for the lungs. Visit an acupuncturist for a seasonal immune-system boost.

Finally, using the recently commenced school year as a metaphor for your life, apply yourself to studying or learning something new that will stretch you mentally, physically or both, to give you an alternative focus during the lengthening nights. Additionally, visualise the midday summer sun shining in your solar plexus at all times to increase feelings of positivity. Don't waste a minute feeling sorry for yourself, being blasé or taking things for granted. Appreciate this autumn like never before.

Mastering your impatience

We are coming up to that time of year when we find ourselves delayed at airports, stations and on the roads as the annual wind-up to Christmas comes rolling round again. This stretch of time, anchored in tradition, challenges your patience, tolerance and secretly – come on admit it – confidence in your own sanity. Even the Buddha may have experienced the odd niggle had he been caught in the tussle to get a flight to Thailand. All this is accentuated by that distant memory, triggered now and then by the odd strain of an old American movie wafting from the TV, that this is meant to be the season of 'goodwill to all men'.

Why then did they have to make it in the cold, dark winter when all our true natural self really wants to do is hibernate?

All this – the build-up, the presents, the arrangements, and expectations, the frantic escape plans to fling ourselves far across the face of the earth, the increasing alcohol and calorie levels, the parties, the spending – is possibly just a magnificently constructed foil to distract ourselves from the great void of winter's darkness.

If you find yourself already growing impatient for me to focus my drift, this only serves to illustrate my point. Impatience is perhaps the greatest scourge of our times. Without impatience, there would be none of that involuntary upper abdominal crunching as you huff and puff 10 back in the checkout line as the person paying suddenly can't find their chequebook, then their cheque card, then finally decides to pay by credit card, but the magnetic strip's worn down, and someone's mobile kicks in to the strains of 'William Tell' in Pinky and Perky tones.

That's your liver and spleen contracting. When your liver and spleen contract, it also places a strain on all your other organs, thus restricting blood flow and depleting energy throughout your entire system. And even though you're obviously built to take it, it makes you even more susceptible to impatience.

One could go on indefinitely listing the symptoms arising from the disease of impatience – hypertension, headaches, heart problems and so on, but luckily, according to those Oriental wizards of old, you can develop the treasured and health-enhancing quality of patience for yourself.

First, remind, cajole or even force yourself to see the current cause of impatience, no matter how seemingly great or small, as being a mere blip in the face of eternity.

Second, discipline yourself to consciously release the strain from your musculature, thereby enabling your frame to straighten up and allow your organs their fair share of elbow room, your blood vessels adequate expansion, your nerve pathways clear passages and your bladder and bowels sufficient room to move. This can be best achieved by starting at the back of your neck – often the first place to go rigid (literally stiff-necked) from impatience – and the pleasurable sensation of release once identified. Then allow it to spread to all parts including your belly, chest, face, shoulders and limbs.

To augment this physical release, take Bach Flower remedy 'Impatiens', which really can work wonders. It also helps to instil in yourself an unshakeable trust that whatever occurs – even if it seems to contradict all your carefully conceived plans – is exactly what is meant to happen and will always somehow promote an increase in your general wellbeing and temporal standing.

Yogananda, one of the greatest yogis of the past century, would start his day with the following pronouncement: 'I will go forth in perfect faith in the power of omnipresent good to bring me what I need at the time I need it.'

Or, when confronted by a perceived obstacle to your agenda's speedy passage, survey your surroundings, and however disagreeable, state, 'I am the king (or queen) of no-matter-what.'

On a more ongoing basis, consider taking up a body-centred activity that will provide regular opportunity for your mind to slow down. This could include cycling, running, walking, swimming, weight-training, yoga, t'ai chi or other martial arts, but can be anything that will give the wild animal within you for whom waiting for anything is anathema, a bit of space to let off steam.

Finally, remember not to hold your breath – a common reaction to impatience-triggering situations. Make sure you are breathing slowly and deeply from down in your belly, as this will help your liver and spleen to relax, and before you know it, you'll be sporting that look of unswerving serenity that made saints and Buddhas famous.

Taking long-haul flights in your stride

Sheltering from the storm before the cosy hearth, as the dark nights of fully fledged winter close in on us, we find ourselves again in the season of escaping all this on long-haul flights to far-flung places. Now, you may well be clever enough to have figured a way to afford to turn left when you walk on the plane, but for the shuffling majority turning humbly to the right at the door, stuffed up in the crush of economy, life in the air can present a challenge. It is difficult enough to sit still for hours on end under any circumstances – especially in the air, as your body itches to stretch in order to increase the flow of blood and energy.

The thick, warm, heavy 'air' that gently stings your nostrils as you inhale gets run through the air conditioner but once an hour for a few moments if you're lucky. People who run airlines are no more saintly or altruistic than you or I and, with the increase in fuel prices, are only able to stabilise ticket prices if they save money. The biggest saving to be made is on fuel-driven air conditioning. Observe how everyone falls asleep as the carbon levels rise then wakes up as the hourly dose of freshly conditioned air is circulated.

Cabin pressure, or lack of it, responsible for ear popping on the way up and down, and for that slightly breathless and heavy feeling in the chest, is also kept on the wrong side of comfortable to save fuel. This is known to cause coagulation of the blood, leading to possible clots, which can be fatal. Also potentially fatal are airborne microbes including TB and other respiratory germs running rampant in the cabin.

Additionally, factor in the circadian disorientation associated with crossing time zones on the east–west axis – jet lag, in other words – the inevitable anticlimax on arrival, the difficulty of internal climate adjustment and worst of all the re-entry to our United Kingdom with all its dark angularity in the dread grip of winter.

There are a few simple steps you can take to prevent serious internal malfunction arising from long-haul air travel. Indeed, you can optimise on this most useful facility offered by those magnificent men, and step off a flight spent in economy looking like you were in business (or from business looking like you were in first, or from first looking like you arrived in your own jet, and so on until you're looking like God himself, just blown in by chariot of fire from heaven). Undiluted tea tree oil or lavender rubbed around the nostrils will kill off all airborne germs before they gain entry to your lungs. Half an aspirin each day for a week before flying, including the day of travel, will thin the blood (having first consulted your GP if you feel you must, especially if already on warfarin or other blood thinners). Alternatively, drink nettle tea.

Train yourself to breathe more deeply, for contrary to what you'd think, it's preferable to breathe more deeply when there's less oxygen and more carbon in order to syphon off what oxygen there is. Wriggle your toes constantly while you stretch and flex your feet, bringing your toes toward you and pushing them away throughout the flight to encourage circulation. Stand up and walk around the plane. Don't be shy. Be the odd bod that can't sit still. Stretch discreetly at the back of the plane, especially your hamstrings and shoulders. While sitting, engineer things to enable you to position your legs higher than your hips every now and then, as this helps prevent clots.

Though this may seem sacrilegious, eschew the drinking of alcohol as it will dehydrate you and impinge on the healthy working of your kidneys (even more than it normally does). Instead drink at least one glass of mineral water every hour. Keep eating to a minimum. We tend to eat on flights for comfort rather than to assuage genuine hunger. Eating at such high altitude, however, strains your organs of digestion, especially the spleen and liver. Do try not to mix protein and carbohydrates, as this combo is a real liver strainer at altitude.

Exercise outside in the fresh air before setting off for the airport, preferably with martial arts or some other active meditation movement system, as this will help keep your immune system strong throughout the flight. Additionally, as the immune system responds instantaneously to negative or positive commands (from you), be sure to maintain a positive tone to your thoughts in transit from door to door. Be sure to allow yourself enough time to check in without sweating or becoming anxious. And do your utmost to relax throughout the entire procedure, as this conserves energy and helps support your immune system. To this end, also take tea of astralagus to support your spleen – being associated with the 'earth element', it is, according to Chinese medicine, weakened by leaving the ground, thus impairing your ability to resist those nasty microbes.

As for circadian rhythm displacement (jet lag), set your watch to the time zone of your destination as soon as you take off and hypnotise yourself into believing it's that time from the start, for as any Einstein will tell you, time is pretty arbitrary at the best of times.

Surviving the Christmas party season

The time for officially letting your hair down is here again so it might be timely to examine the procedures involved in deriving optimum enjoyment from the party round. The expression itself implies the loosening of one's bun – or other such constrictions of one's coiffeur – in order to facilitate some sort of catharsis of the wild spirit within. This is usually expressed with the help of alcohol or other mind-bending substances on the dance floor or in broom cupboards at office parties, often followed by bouts of self-recrimination and feigned amnesia the following morning.

It is no coincidence that the expression relates to the head, for according to those old Taoist party animals of bygone eras, the acupuncture points that trigger a release of self-control and inhibition are located at the base of the skull along the gall bladder meridian, that organ being ascribed the function of keeping everything about a person's act in shipshape order. It is interesting also to note that the gall bladder as part of the liver complex is the organ most affected by alcohol and drugs.

So would it follow that by manually unblocking the flow of energy in the meridian through the points at the rear of the skull, you'd be able to slough off your inhibitions and awkwardness and thus have a properly enjoyable knees-up at this season's social gatherings without recourse to hammering yourself with booze or drugs? Yes, partly. But you'll also have to attend to the psycho-emotional mindset, if you wish to party to your full potential with little or no artificial help and thus preclude the possibility of saying or doing things you may regret in the sober light of day.

The kind of excessive self-control causing inhibition, often appropriate for the working environment, is patently inappropriate for party time. It makes you appear wooden, wood being the element associated with the gall bladder, by the way, and as you know, it's not easy to let go and have a good time when you feel like a plank.

If you're interested in attempting a substance-lite bun release, begin immediately, as the effects take some days to build up in the system. Place your thumbs at the points at the base of the skull where the trapezius muscles meet the bone in two ridges, one either side of the spine. Keeping your arms and shoulders relaxed, gently press in, under and upwards towards the centre of the brain, until you feel the muscle tissues soften and give a little. Now whatever position you find yourself in, try and hold yourself completely rigid, making no movement whatsoever. You will quickly notice that this is all but impossible and that from somewhere deep inside comes an urge to make movement. Now, instead of succumbing to that urge, maintain stillness of the outer shell while allowing movement to be instigated within the skin – micro-movement, in other words.

To explore this fully requires a time and place where you won't be disturbed and a willingness to bypass habitual internal chatter to enable your awareness to focus within. Once you have located and followed it for a moment or two, this micro-movement becomes amplified until it feels like a full-blown belly dance occurring within your skin. At the point when the dance feels too vibrant to contain, allow it to take over your physical form altogether until you find yourself dancing round the room with gay abandon. Not only will regular practice of this derigidifying technique benefit your circulation, calm your mind, engender cheerfulness and positivity and make you more supple, but it will also help you enjoy yourself far more when you actually do go out dancing, an activity which must come near the top of the list for helping maintain elasticity and youthfulness of mind, body and spirit.

To lock the benefits of this exercise into real-time party situations, some psycho-emotional reframing is also necessary. As with all healings – for freeing one's inhibitions surely constitutes a healing – there are two primary tools which must always be utilised: breathing and self-acceptance. So when you walk into the party feeling awkward and shy, pay attention to not holding your breath, enabling it to flow in and out freely, and rather than fighting off or denying the shyness, accept it. Simply remind yourself over and over, 'It's perfectly natural and OK for me to feel shy and awkward.' Because it is. In fact, shyness and awkwardness, when one is open and accepting about it, can be quite fetching. Thom York, for example, has made a career from it. So be shy, but be proud to be shy. Don't be ashamed of it or yourself. If you find it hard to make conversation without being drunk and filled with false bonhomie, try asking people about themselves and their lives – they'll always be glad of the opportunity to talk about themselves.

Finally, try a little auto-suggestion by telling yourself enough times for it to penetrate your unconscious, 'When I display my vulnerability with dignity, people find me irresistible, which makes it a doddle for me to let my hair down every time!'

If you find that all falls short of the season's mark, remember to take milk thistle complex before and after the party to help support the liver, and drink a glass of mineral water with half a freshly squeezed lemon to cool down your gall bladder.

Season of misgiving

So the season of giving is upon us again, prompting questions of what it means to be generous, often to the point of boosting credit-card company profits to your own detriment, causing enough stress – along with the stress of shopping in the seasonal crush – to overshadow any joy in the actual act of giving.

When the – mostly pointless – gifts are finally unwrapped, the overwhelming emotion is one of relief at having discharged that duty for the year and at having not put yourself in the unthinkable position of 'humbug' (surely a propaganda device employed by the advertising industry).

In fact, the whole ritual must by now be seen in its proper light as the fulfilment of a collective duty on the part of every citizen to do their bit to keep the economy afloat via the high street and out-of-town shopping-mall tills. It is increasingly difficult to find the faintest shred of spiritual or religious significance in the festival these days. Originally, in pre-Christian times, the five-day 'festival of lights' was linked to the winter solstice and signified rebirth of the light and hope at the darkest time of year. Later, when the Romans adopted Christianity, they grafted the Christmas myth on to their existing pagan calendar, as a celebration of the birth of Jesus, or if you like, a chance to ignite the rebirth of the 'godhead' within. And now, in the post-Christian era, it's become a celebration complete with huge offerings (and sacrifices) to Mammon, the god of gold and silver, sterling, dollars, even euros. Not that there's anything intrinsically unspiritual about Mammon, other than it being a bit of a silly-sounding name – money is only a symbol of energy in disguise and the divine runs through all our transactions, no matter what face or name you give it, after all.

And a festival is a festival, no matter what the prevailing rationale behind it, and we do need such events on a cyclical basis, lest the passage of time becomes just so much temporal sludge.

But behind all this insane and frenzied activity, the burnt offerings at the nation's cash (and plastic) registers, Freudian revelations unwrapped beneath the tree, gastric assault, square eyes from watching *The Sound of Music* and James Bond films (yet again), and interpersonal tensions surfacing as subtexts come to light (yet again), there appears to be an innate imbalance. For how can there be true giving if there is not true receiving?

I don't mean receiving as in unwrapping the socks you don't need, the jumpers that don't fit or suit, or the powertools you'll never use, and feigning pleasure while inwardly grimacing. I mean truly receiving the love that, along with the sense of duty and unthinkable fear of being seen as a humbug, informed those purchases.

The Sufis (the lighthearted, mystical Muslim sect which includes the whirling dervishes) say it is easy to give with an open heart, but to reach enlightenment you have to learn to receive with an open heart, which is far more difficult.

Kabbalah (the lighthearted mystical 'yoga' of Judaism, involving among other practices, meditation on the 'tree of life') literally means 'to receive'.

In Taoist thought, to give is a function of yang energy, while to receive is a function of yin. Any preponderance of one over the other will eventually cause an imbalance affecting all aspects of your life, including your health, wealth and happiness.

So while casting the odd thought over what it means to give during the silly season, cast a couple more over what it means to receive.

Still with the Taoist scheme of things, the organ in the body responsible for enabling you to receive is your spleen. The spleen governs your ability to take in energy in any format the material plane has to offer, whether that be food, money, knowledge, recognition or even love. Your splenic energy, in short, is responsible for your being fed each and every moment you're alive.

So while reminding yourself, 'the more I am willing to receive, the more I am able to give', place a warm palm over your solar plexus (upper abdomen), slightly more towards the left side than the right, so you feel the warmth penetrate and hold it there for a good six minutes or so.

At the same time, think of relaxing your entire chest and upper abdominal area in order to reduce frontal muscular armouring levels, and visualise a stream of positive seasonal energy entering your personal field, just about... now (get it?). Happy Christmas.

If you're feeling the strain, a detox will get you back in the race

Following on from the probable random excesses of your Christmas and New Year celebrations, it's likely by now you'll be beating yourself up more or less gently and wondering how to make amends to your body and mind. We talk a lot about how drugs, alcohol, antidepressants and even natural remedies change our moods and physical states, but rarely do we mention the most widely used mood and body transformer of all (after sleep, that is): food.

Now I'm no food expert – far from it – I leave that to the esteemed colleagues who, loosely speaking, flank me: Nigel and Dr John. My speciality is more states of mind, and it's in that light I divulge the following, taught to me originally by my Chinese-American Taoist hippie Oriental medicine master as a method for settling the mood, clearing the mind of its habitual clutter and making quantum leaps in meditation practice, and which happens, as a side effect, also to cleanse the liver, flush bowel and bladder, clear up all manner of blemishes from the skin, cause all excess fat to fall off and make your eyes sparkle like a saint, to boot.

I'm sure I've mentioned it before, but such a winning method is it that I feel perfectly justified in giving it another airing. All it involves is the willingness to temporarily stop changing your mood and internal environment for just four days, relinquishing drugs, alcohol and stimulants during that time and eating only one locally occurring fruit – in our case apples are best and the peptic acid coincidentally helps flush the liver. You can eat as many apples as you like each day, munching flesh and core alike and drink as much water as thirst dictates.

Usually you'll find that after day one, three apples are more than ample.

Leading into it, wean yourself off meats and cooked foods a couple of days prior, going raw but varied and tasty. During day one proper, the challenge to your will is enough to distract you from the gnawing hunger. During day two, your stomach will have shrunk slightly and it'll be easier to enjoy and give humble thanks for your apples. If by this time you're getting constipated, craving sweets so badly you're getting jumpy, or indeed are starting to feel like Mr Ed, the talking horse, take your fruit with honey. It's also possible towards the end of day two that the toxins being flushed from your system but not yet released give you headaches, for which two or three cups of extra-strong peppermint tea will usually suffice to alleviate most of the discomfort.

As day three wears on, you're starting to feel like a bird in flight as you go through your day. Your mind feels sharp as a diamond, your skin is glowing, muscle tone improving and people are telling you how great you look. But day four is the big pay-off – you are like a hawk on the wing, swooping through your everyday world feeling invulnerable and impervious to stress and looking beautiful and radiant into the bargain. Obviously initially you may feel weak, so perhaps plan things so day one falls on, say, a Friday night, giving you Saturday and Sunday to take it easy, then by the time Monday morning comes around, you're so high on fruit that nothing can intervene to spoil your fun – not even the rush-hour ride into work after the weekend.

Generally, it's best to keep taking prescribed medication when necessary, so do consult your GP or someone conversant with such things before getting fruity as above. Same applies if pregnant or suffering from any serious condition.

Coming out of it, reverse the process, where it's all but possible to orally orgasm at the taste of a radish or quiver with delight on biting into a pepper or become a drooling fool for a raw onion for instance, working your way back to cheeseburgers, or whatever your mood-altering device or culinary vice of choice may be, gradually over a few days.

Never mind an apple a day keeps the doctor away, one thing's for sure, after this you'll never look at an apple in the eye and feel the same way again. Quick, dammit, pass me that raw onion!

Finding your way around

January is in the 'dark' time of year, when according to the Native Americans and other pre-consumerist cultures, the Earth Mother sleeps in order to regenerate herself in readiness for pushing through the new life of spring. And we, 'her children', would, if following our natural seasonal rhythms (and presumably if living as Native Americans in, say, pre-30s Arizona or New Mexico), retire to our adobe dens for a few weeks and not make too much noise or fuss lest we wake her and in her wrath she blights next season's crops – doesn't bring us breakfast, in other words.

It is worth, then, discussing the phenomenon of momentary or semi-permanent disorientation, because we don't, on the whole, follow our natural rhythms, live for the most part in adobe houses, or know anything whatsoever about being quiet.

Nestled instead in our ubiquitous electric womb, we seem only to know how to make a great noise and bruhaha – phones beeping, TV sets blaring, pile-drivers (to lay more TV cable) pile-driving, engines revving and digitally generated tribal music mimicking the sound of all of the above, in an intensified and amplified sonic melange for us to celebrate as we dance.

Our homes, vehicles and to a lesser extent our clothing and footwear are all designed not only to shield us from the sensation of interacting with the elements, but to skew the experience till we all but forget there actually are any elements – until we experience the extremes of flooding and hurricanes. Even then it's mostly a TV experience. And if we don't like the weather here, we're never more than a few hours' worth of congested flight path from a heatwave happening somewhere on the planet. The whiff of anything remotely biological has been all but masked by scent, and short of a solar storm or worse knocking out the grid, we never have to worry about being in the dark again. This is all fine and dandy for those who are whole or part robots, but for the rest of us, whose ancestors so recently evolved from the running-semi-wild-in-front-of-the-cave state, this masking of the natural is obviously disorienting at a fundamental, existential level.

As well as being one or more steps removed from our natural rhythms and rhymes, we have even managed to deconstruct our weather patterns and render the integrity of our land masses questionable as the pace of everyday life surges forth in an orgy of unbridled microprocessed acceleration. Indeed, the rules of the game of human existence are changing so rapidly it is redundant to talk of the everyday. That we will soon allegedly be witnessing the creation of animal-human hybrids might suggest that we are completing the creation circle and returning to the days of pure myth where centaurs roamed the land and nests of vipers in one's coiffeur would raise no eyebrows.

It is only to be expected, then, that during this upcoming partial crack in the schedule between TV programmes, you ponder your place in the grand scheme of things and may well experience moments of fundamentally unsettling, existential disorientation. Disorientation means literally a moving away from the east – away, in other words, from the direction of the earth's spin, which is not unlike sitting with your back to the direction of the train (not that you'd notice at the speed they're running).

So the first step in reorienting yourself and aligning yourself to some degree with the natural order and beginning to regain equipoise on every level, is to face east. Next, become aware of being on a planet in space rotating on its own axis at 1,000mph in the direction of your gaze, while simultaneously travelling in orbit around the sun at 66,000mph or 19mps. Once this meta-realisation of physical context has penetrated for even one micro-instant, you could find your sense of wonder and adventure return and with it perhaps the perspective of being on a long space voyage, during which you make as many friends as possible and amuse yourself and them as best you can for the duration. For when you finally disembark a few trillion miles down the line, it may appear somewhat of a waste to have spent precious chunks of the journey at odds with yourself and your environment.

In other words, don't let disorientation upset you or resort to habitually numbing yourself to it through shopping, sex or substance abuse. Instead use it as an automatic reminder to reorient yourself to what's actually going on here – a megasonic ride through space on an organically produced mother ship, supported by a crumbling biosphere with the most bizarre assortment of sideshows from all the best and worst sci-fi movies ever made, to stop us, the natives, getting too restless and trying to jump off.

The world is going through a rocky patch, but peace will come

Many years ago, one New Year's Eve in the Catalan interior, I was at a party with a whole bunch of Catalans, one of whom, Carlos, misheard my happy new year greeting thinking I'd said 'Happy new you!' Once his faux pas was pointed out (not by me), so chuffed was he with the philosophical implications, he spent the next hour singing 'Happy new you' to anyone who'd listen, and it inspired me to pick up a guitar. Strumming a haunting yet bouncy groove, he and I composed a song with 'Happy new you' as its rousing chorus. Before long, all assembled guests were singing along in full voice. So profoundly did the concept affect us that we continued in this ebullient way for over two hours and finished in giggling heaps on the floor.

The first Gulf War was either raging or just had been at the time and the atmosphere abroad was not dissimilar to the present one, but the idea that happiness was derived from within by accessing a fresh part of the self, as if tearing off another wet-wipe from the packet, and that it depended on nothing but being present in the moment without thought of projected time spans, fuelled us into a state of pure revelry and celebration in spite of external conditions.

Generation after generation have been convinced the world would end during their lifetime. We are no different. But I have this innate sense that the world, including the world of people, will continue at least a while longer – that because, for every warmongering outlaw (heads of states included), there are a million kindly souls. And though we don't have our fingers on the 'don't touch that' button, we do have power en masse to significantly alter the global view – by accessing the kindness in our souls and causing that to emanate from us, suffusing our immediate atmospheres with the nurturing essence of human warmth and decency. Gradually, as more and more of us so emanate, our combined loving atmospheres will eventually overwhelm the unloving atmospheres of the other guys, until the air feels so sweet no one would even think of lifting a finger to harm another, even if the other has oil or a differing ideology.

But to access that kindness within, we have to divest ourselves of any old traces of us-and-them small-heartedness. We have instead to be subtly reborn to that part of us that naturally radiates the true currency of this universe, love.

Things will change in the end – make no mistake, as George W and his mates would say. In time will come an era of peace, when wisdom rules the world instead of ignorance, fear and greed. It will happen. It's been predicted in every prophesy, from the biblical to the Hopi, for thousands of years now. This was always going to be a rocky patch. But, next, ladies and gentlemen, comes the age of enlightenment.

So do whatever you can to strengthen body and mind that you may endure till then, but remember true strength comes from the love you feel for yourself, life and others, and the love you allow to reach your heart from others.

Love everything and everyone. Make it tangible now by pressing the centre of your breastbone with your finger and rubbing the flesh over the bone rapidly up and down like a human vibrator until you feel your entire chest warm up and relax. Then simply allow that warmth to flow from you all the time.

Happy New YOU!